Grade Aid

for

Boyd and Bee

Lifespan Development

Fifth Edition

prepared by

Karen P. Saenz
Houston Community College—Southeast College

Boston   New York   San Francisco
Mexico City   Montreal   Toronto   London   Madrid   Munich   Paris
Hong Kong   Singapore   Tokyo   Cape Town   Sydney

ISBN-13: 978-0-205-64339-4
ISBN-10:   0-205-643339-6

Printed in the United States of America

10 9 8 7 6 5 4 3 2 1   12 11 10 09 08

GRADE AID CONTENTS

HELEN BEE'S STUDENT PROJECTS

Chapter 1
- Research Project 1: A First Observation of a Child: An Example of a Narrative Report
- Research Project 2: Naturalistic Observation of a Nursing Home Resident
- At-Home Project 3: Analysis of Research Presented in Popular Sources

Chapter 3
- Investigative Project 4: Available Prenatal Services
- Investigative Project 5: Investigation of Birth Options

Chapter 4
- Research Project 6: Observation in a Newborn Nursery

Chapter 5
- Research Project 7: Development of the Object Concept

Chapter 6
- Research Project 8: Observation of Turn Taking
- Research Project 9: Assessment of Day-Care Centers
- Investigative Project 10: Investigation of Day-Care Options

Chapter 7
- Research Project 11: Assessing the Child's Theory of Mind
- Research Project 12: Beginning Two-Word Sentences
- Research Project 13: Conversation between Mother and Child

Chapter 8
- Research Project 14: Observation of Altruistic Behavior

Chapter 9
- Research Project 15: The Game of Twenty Questions
- Research Project 16: Conservation of Mass, Number, and Weight
- Investigative Project 17: Investigation of IQ Testing in Local Schools

Chapter 10
- Research Project 18: Understanding of Friendship
- At-Home Project 19: Television Aggression
- At-Home Project 20: Sex Roles on TV

Chapter 11
- Research Project 21: The Pendulum
- At-Home Project 22: Plotting Your Own Growth

Chapter 12
- Research Project 23: Who Am I?

Chapter 13
- At-Home Project 24: Estimating Your Own Longevity

Chapter 14
- Research Project 25: Social Networks among Young Adults

Chapter 15
- At-Home Project 26: Assessing Your Own Diet

Chapter 16
- Research Project 27: Social Networks among Middle-Aged Adults

Chapter 17
- Research Project 28: Facts on Aging Quiz
- Research Project 29: Definitions of Wisdom

Chapter 18
- Research Project 30: Visiting and Assessing a Nursing Home

PREFACE

The goal of this *Grade Aid* is to provide a user-friendly guide to the fourth edition of the *Lifespan Development* text. It is designed to help you focus your reading and study of the key elements of each chapter with the ultimate goal of helping you learn the material and apply the concepts to your life as well as to your career.

Each chapter begins with a Chapter Summary, Learning Objectives, and Term Identification. Make flashcards using the terms as you go, using the definitions in the margin of the text for help. If you write the definitions in your own words, though, you will remember them better! The Guided Study Questions include the Learning Objective for each section, as well as specific questions about the material in the text. There is a Practice Test at the end of each section. Check your answers at the end of each chapter. The Critical Reflection Exercises provide you with an opportunity to apply what you have learned to real-life examples. The Comprehensive Practice Test at the end of the chapter serves as a preview of exam questions. A crossword puzzle gives you another opportunity to use the key terms. Most chapters include one or more Student Projects that your instructor may assign as part of a written assignment or even as extra credit. The chapter concludes with the answers to the Practice Tests and the puzzle.

Following the Preface are two sections for making the most of your psychology course. The first, *What to Know about Studying Psychology*, offers study suggestions to maximize your study time. The second, *A Model for Critical Thinking*, provides hints to help you apply the material in the course.

Lifespan Development may be one of the most useful courses you will ever take. It provides explanations and resources for your personal and workplace relationships, hints for rearing your children, and insight into the joys and concerns of your parents and grandparents. It may even help you learn more about yourself. Enjoy!

ACKNOWLEDGEMENTS

Unending thanks go to my family—both immediate and extended—for providing me with the lifespan perspective. In the time since I prepared the third edition, our son and his wife gave birth to our two grandchildren (currently ages eight weeks and three-and-a-half years), our daughter married and was widowed 16 months later, my husband and I celebrated 37 years of marriage, and my father-in-law died leaving my mother-in-law (age 90) alone. Among us, we've got the chapters covered! Each has patiently "rearranged the world" to allow me time to write. Thank you!

Karen P. Saenz
Houston Community College System—Southeast College
Houston, Texas

WHAT TO KNOW ABUT STUDYING PSYCHOLOGY

CLASS PREPARATION AND STUDY GUIDELINES

The study of psychology is not hard, but there is a lot of material to learn. Students are expected to keep up with all of the assigned reading. You should understand the material and be able to relate it to real human behavior. The information presented below is designed to help you learn the subject by providing the kinds of study hints you can employ successfully in any college class you take.

HOW MUCH TIME SHOULD I SPEND STUDYING PSYCHOLOGY?

To be successful, a good guideline for any college class of the amount of time you need to invest outside of class is two hours for each hour you spend in class. If you can make this commitment, you should encounter no serious problems in completing all assignments and preparing comfortably for tests. You should spend your time doing the following:

Read Ahead

The best starting place is the Course Schedule in your Syllabus. It will specify the material that needs to be covered in the sequence deemed most appropriate by your instructor. You should always maintain a disciplined reading schedule so that you can stay current with assigned readings; falling behind in your reading can be disastrous. You should read ahead all the material that will be covered in the next class. This reading will acquaint you with the Learning Objectives that will be covered in class. With this knowledge, you will be prepared to ask questions and discuss relevant topics.

Read Effectively

Create a comfortable reading environment for yourself. Avoid distractions and interruptions. Be alert and attentive. Don't rush yourself. These "little things" will increase your comprehension of the subject. Use your *Study Guide* as a guide for your reading. Keep a dictionary by your side to look up any unfamiliar words. From time to time, you may need to look back at a previous chapter to refresh your memory of the concepts. Remember, as in sports, music, dance, or other arts, learning takes time and effort; the more you put in, the more you will get out of the learning process.

SHOULD I ATTEND CLASS?

Studies indicate that students who attend their classes do better than students who do not attend. In class, you will not only cover important course-related information, but, additionally, announcements will be made, due dates assigned, and study suggestions offered. In college, you are largely responsible for your own learning. Your instructor is a facilitator. Use class time to ask questions, seek clarification, and participate in discussions. The more involved you are in your own learning, the more fruitful the activity will be, and the more you will learn.

WHAT SHOULD I DO DURING CLASS TIME?

There are several things you can do to improve your chances of being successful in your class. You are in control of all of them, so do the following things to maximize the benefits of being in class.

Be On Time

The start of class is an important time. Be prepared to take notes, participate, or take a test. Tardiness is disruptive to you and your classmates.

Take Good Notes

Good note taking keeps your mind focused on the subject being discussed. Attentiveness should lead to better comprehension. Note taking provides you with documentation about what the instructor feels is the most relevant, important, difficult, or interesting information about a subject. You should couple your notes with related text material for a comprehensive understanding of the subject. Use your notes to prepare for assignments and tests. Make sure your notes are legible, thorough, and organized.

Participate in Class Discussions

Whenever you have the opportunity to participate, do so! Show off what you have learned, but do it in a way that contributes to a positive learning environment for you and your classmates. Be involved in the learning process. Ask relevant questions. Offer insights. Give examples. Participation should be constructive and fun.

Get to Know Your Classmates

Together you can do several things that enhance learning. Every time you explain a concept to someone else, you increase your understanding of the material. You can share ideas and information. You can check each other to make sure you are learning the material. You can "bounce" ideas around. You can study together in advance of tests. If you miss a class, you'll know someone who will share notes with you or who can tell you about up-coming assignments or tests.

These suggestions are offered to assist you in making the most of your study of psychology, and indeed, of your college experience. You are exceptional because you chose to pursue higher learning. *Invest in yourself and you should be successful.*

A MODEL FOR CRITICAL THINKING

Several good resources exist on how to develop and practice critical thinking skills, so that critical thinking can be applied to specific issues and problems. Randolph Smith (1995) suggests the following seven characteristics of critical thinkers:

1. Critical thinkers are flexible—they can tolerate ambiguity and uncertainty.
2. Critical thinkers identify inherent biases and assumptions.
3. Critical thinkers maintain an air of skepticism.
4. Critical thinkers separate facts from opinions.
5. Critical thinkers don't oversimplify.
6. Critical thinkers use logical inference processes.
7. Critical thinkers examine available evidence before drawing conclusions.

Thinking and critical thinking differ in at least three important ways.

- Thinking involves basic information processing; critical thinking involves understanding that information in such a way that the information is useful and usable.
- Thinking is often based on emotion and supposition; critical thinking sets emotions aside and addresses a problem from the position of facts.
- Thinking is based on the information that is known; critical thinking requires more than what is already known because it may reveal that not enough is known. This revelation, of course, then requires that more facts be gathered.

Most individuals take their ability to think for granted. In this fashion, the development of critical thinking ability requires that the individual be taught to take a more controlled and systematic approach to one's thinking. Benjamin Bloom (1956) suggested that critical thinking requires going beyond a simple recitation of facts that most testing situations require. From this, Bloom suggested a progression of cognitive levels that individuals can be taught to use in their thinking. Bloom's taxonomy suggests that thinking and understanding are only truly accomplished when an individual takes information through six levels.

BLOOM'S COGNITIVE OBJECTIVES

Level	Skill	Description
1	Knowledge	Specific, isolate, factual information
2	Comprehension	Understanding of those facts
3	Application	Can generalize those facts to current and/or other situations
4	Analysis	Can break the problem down, recognize connections between sub-parts, analyze whether each sub-part is meaningful, and discard those that are deemed meaningless
5	Synthesis	Can reassemble meaningful parts into a more meaningful whole
6	Evaluation	Can look at the end product and critically evaluate and use that information to begin a continuous reassessment

A specific example may demonstrate how our thinking becomes more complex as we progress through the cognitive levels of Bloom's theory. A friend of yours states that someone you are about to meet is pretty aggressive. When you ask your friend how she knows this, she reports that she saw him yell at someone in the hall for absolutely no reason. Your job as a critical thinker is to take this piece of information and determine what to do with it. In order to accomplish this, you must take the information that you know and take it through the cognitive levels of Bloom's theory.

1. **KNOWLEDGE**: At this level, we have the statement by our friend that the individual is aggressive. We may also have some information about our friend including the following:
   - how accurate she has been about others in the past
   - whether "aggressive" is a label she uses a lot
   - whether it is unusual for her to categorize someone

2. **COMPREHENSION**: At this level, we utilize the facts that we have to try and understand the implications of our knowledge. In this case, the only concrete facts we have is that the friend has labeled the other person as "aggressive." From this, we determine what we understand "aggressive" to mean.

3. **APPLICATION**: At the application level, we try to apply information to the current situation. In this case, our friend has suggested that the person we are about to meet is aggressive and she is using his "yelling at someone" as evidence for that label.

4. **ANALYSIS**: From the application of facts to the current situation, we break the information down into meaningful units. In this scenario, we have a label of "aggressive" being placed on someone because he yelled at someone else. There are several questions that a critical thinker would ask him or herself in this situation. These questions include:
   - Is there a definite connection between "yelling" and being "aggressive"?
   - Are there any other possible explanations for why the individual yelled at someone else?
   - Does yelling at someone in one situation predict that the individual will behave "aggressively" in other situations?
   To the extent that I cannot answer these questions affirmatively, I should discard any assumptions based upon them.

5. **SYNTHESIS**: Now that I have discarded any meaningless information, I put the meaningful pieces back together to draw my conclusions. In this case, I cannot critically utilize any of the information that I have been given. Thus, the only usable information I have going into the situation is that I am about to meet someone.

6. **EVALUATION**: Once I have discarded meaningless information (or information that is based on opinion rather than fact), I am better suited to approach the situation in an unbiased fashion. I can objectively evaluate the person that I am meeting, make unbiased observations about his behavior, decide whether his behaviors are average given the situation in which I am observing him, and reach my own conclusions about his relative degree of aggressiveness.

What are the implications in this case if I had not done critical thinking before I approached the situation and met this new person? It is highly probable that I would have approached the individual assuming that he was going to be aggressive. From this, a few simple questions and their answers can reveal the potential impact of not engaging in critical thinking. These questions and answers are:

Q: How do we act toward individuals whom we assume are going to be aggressive?
A: We behave cold or even aggressive.

Q: How do others act toward us when we act cold or aggressive to them?
A: They tend to act aggressive or hostile.

Q: What do we, then, assume about that individual?
A: That he or she is aggressive.

In this cycle, the expectations we had about the person caused us to behave in ways that elicited, in return, behaviors from the other person that verified our original assumptions. It is just as likely, however, that he would not have behaved aggressively if we had not precipitated those behaviors through our own actions. The cycle that results because of the bias introduced into our behaviors due to our expectations is called a self-fulfilling prophecy. It is defined as a tendency for our expectations about others to be confirmed because we engage in behaviors that elicit from others the very behaviors that we expected. Our lack of critical thinking might have caused an unpleasant encounter that could have been prevented.

BASIC CONCEPTS AND METHODS

BEFORE YOU READ . . . CHAPTER SUMMARY

The goal of scientists who study human development is to produce observations and explanations that can be applied to as wide an age range of human beings and contexts as possible. To accomplish this goal, they study both change and stability. Additionally, they study cultural expectations; make predictions about development and use scientific methods to test them; and hope their findings can be used to positively influence development in individuals.

An Introduction to Human Development

- The philosophical concepts of original sin, innate goodness, and the blank slate have influenced Western ideas about development. The concept of developmental stages comes, in part, from Darwin's evolutionary theory. G. Stanley Hall identified norms at which developmental milestones happen. Gesell focused on genetically programmed sequential patterns of change.
- Important changes occur during every period of development across the lifespan, and these changes must be understood in the cultures and contexts in which they occur.
- There are three broad categories, called domains of development, to classify the changes—physical, cognitive, and social. In addition to domains, developmentalists use a system of age-related categories known as periods of development.

Key Issues in the Study of Human Development

- Historically, developmentalists have looked at nature and nurture as an either-or debate. Modern developmentalists understand that developmental change is a product of both genetics and the environment.
- A key issue in the study of human development is the continuity-discontinuity issue. The question is whether age-related change is primarily a matter of amount or degree (continuity) or it involves changes in type or kind (discontinuity).
- Normative age-graded changes are universal; normative history-graded changes affect each generation differently; and Nonnormative changes result from unique, unshared events.
- The context in which the child is growing is impacted by the factors such as the family, the neighborhood, and the larger society.

Research Methods and Designs

- Developmental psychology uses the scientific method to achieve its goals: to describe, explain, predict, and influence human development from conception to death.
- Descriptive research methods are used to study the relationship between variables. Case studies are in-depth examinations of single individuals. The laboratory observation method attempts to exert some degree of control over the environment. Surveys collect data about attitudes, interests, values, and various kinds of behavior. Correlational studies measure the relationship between variables.
- To test causal hypotheses, experimental designs in which subjects are assigned randomly to experimental or control groups are necessary.

- There are three choices for studying age-related change: a cross-sectional design to study different groups of people of different ages; a longitudinal design to study the same people over a period of time; and a sequential design to combine cross-sectional and longitudinal designs in some fashion.
- Cross-cultural research helps developmentalists identify specific variables that explain cultural differences.
- Ethical principles in human developmental research include the following: protection from harm, informed consent, confidentiality, knowledge of results, and protection from deception.

AS YOU READ . . . LEARNING OBJECTIVES

After completing Chapter 1, you should be able to:

1.1   What ideas about development were proposed by early philosophers and scientists?
1.2   What is the lifespan perspective?
1.3   What major domains and periods do developmental scientists use to organize their discussions of the human lifespan?
1.4   How do developmentalists view the two sides of the nature-nurture debate?
1.5   What is the continuity-discontinuity debate?
1.6   How do the three kinds of age-related change differ?
1.7   How does consideration of the contexts in which change occurs improve scientists understanding of human development?
1.8   What are the goals of scientists who study human development?
1.9   What descriptive methods are used by developmental scientists?
1.10   What is the primary advantage of the experimental method?
1.11   What are the pros and cons of cross-sectional, longitudinal, and sequential research designs?
1.12   Why is cross-cultural research important to the study of human development?
1.13   What are the ethical standards that developmental researchers must follow?

AS YOU READ . . . TERM IDENTIFICATION

Ageism (p. 8)
Atypical development (p. 9)
Case study (p. 12)
Cognitive domain (p. 8)
Cohort effects (p. 15)
Control group (p. 14)
Correlation (p. 13)
Critical period (p. 9)
Cross-sectional design (p. 14)
Dependent variable (p. 14)
Ethnography (p. 17)

Experiment (p. 13)
Experimental group (p. 14)

Human development (p. 2)
Independent variable (p. 14)
Laboratory observation (p. 12)
Lifespan perspective (p. 4)
Longitudinal design (p. 14)
Maturation (p. 4)
Naturalistic observation (p. 12)
Nature-nurture debate (p. 6)
Nonnormative changes (p. 9)
Normative age-related changes (p. 7)
Normative history-graded changes (p. 8)
Norms (p. 4)
Physical domain (p. 5)

Population (p. 13)
Qualitative change (p. 7)
Quantitative change (p. 7)
Research ethics (p. 18)
Sample (p. 13)
Sensitive period (p. 9)
Sequential design (p. 14)
Social clock (p. 8)
Social domain (p. 5)
Stages (p. 7)
Survey (p. 12)

AS YOU READ . . . GUIDED STUDY QUESTIONS

AN INTRODUCTION TO HUMAN DEVELOPMENT

Philosophical and Scientific Roots (pp. 3-4)

1.1   *What ideas about development were proposed by early philosophers and scientists?*

1.   Define human development (p. 2).

2.   Compare how the philosophies of original sin, the blank slate, and innate goodness, explain development.

Philosophy	*Explanation of Development*
Original Sin	
Blank Slate	
Innate Goodness	

3.   Define the following terms:
      a.   norms (p. 4)

      b.   maturation (p. 4)

4.   State the major contributions to developmental psychology by each of the following theorists:
      a.   Charles Darwin

      b.   G. Stanley Hall

      c.   Arnold Gesell

The Lifespan Perspective (pp. 4-5)

1.2   *What is the lifespan perspective?*

5.   Define the lifespan perspective (p. 4).

6.   List two reasons why psychologists' views of adulthood have changed recently.
▪

▪

7.   List the three key elements in the lifespan perspective.
    ▪

    ▪

    ▪

Domains and Periods of Development (pp. 5-6)

1.3   What major domains and periods do developmental scientists use to organize their discussions of the human lifespan?

8.   Define the following terms:
    a.   physical domain (p. 5)

    b.   cognitive domain (p. 5)

    c.   social domain (p. 5)

9.   Give an example of how the domains are interrelated.

10.   List and describe the eight periods of development in the lifespan:

Periods	Description of Periods
1.	
2.	
3.	
4.	
5.	
6.	

Periods	Description of Periods
7.	
8.	

AFTER YOU READ . . . PRACTICE TEST #1
THE SCIENTIFIC STUDY OF HUMAN DEVELOPMENT

_____ 1.	The gradual unfolding of genetically programmed sequential patterns of change.	a. Blank slate
_____ 2.	Domain that focuses on the size, shape, and characteristics of the body.	b. Cognitive
		c. Charles Darwin
_____ 3.	View that asserts that all human beings are naturally good and seek experiences that help them grow.	d. G. Stanley Hall
		e Arnold Gessell
_____ 4.	The scientific study of age-related changes in behaviorism thinking, emotion, and personality.	f. Human development
		g. Innate goodness
_____ 5.	Average ages at which developmental milestones are reached.	h. Lifespan perspective
		i. Maturation
_____ 6.	The view that maintains that important changes occur during every period of development.	j. Norms
		k. Original sin
_____ 7.	Used "baby biographies" in the hope of finding evidence to support the theory of evolution.	l. Physical
		m. Plasticity
_____ 8.	The capacity for positive change in response to environmental demands.	n. Social
_____ 9.	Domain that emphasizes changes in thinking, memory, problem-solving, and other intellectual skills.	
_____ 10.	His research suggested the existence of a genetically programmed sequential pattern of change.	

KEY ISSUES IN THE STUDY OF HUMAN DEVELOPMENT

Nature versus Nurture (pp. 6-7)

1.4   How do developmentalists view the two sides of the nature-nurture debate?

11.   Define nature-nurture debate (p. 6).

12.   Give examples of each of the following:
   a.   inborn biases shared by virtually all children.

   b.   inborn biases that vary from one individual to another.

13.   What is the key element of the concept of internal models of experience?

14.   How do vulnerabilities and resiliences (protective factors) interact with a child's environment?

Continuity versus Discontinuity (p. 7)

1.5 ***What is the continuity-discontinuity debate?***

15.   Define the following terms:
    a.   quantitative change (p. 7)

    b.   qualitative change (p. 7)

16.   Give examples to distinguish between continuity and discontinuity.

Three Kinds of Change (pp. 7-8)

1.6 ***How do the three kinds of age-related change differ?***

17.   Define the following terms:
    a.   normative age-graded changes (p. 8)

    b.   social clock (p. 8)

    c.   ageism (p. 8)

    d.   normative history-graded changes (p. 8)

    e.   nonnormative changes (p. 9)

    f.   critical period (p. 9)

    g.   sensitive period (p. 9)

    h.   atypical development (p. 9)

18. Distinguish among the three kinds of age-related changes by giving an example of each.

Kind of Change	Example
Normative Age-Graded Changes	
Normative History-Graded Changes	
Nonnormative Changes	

Research Report: Children and Adolescents in the Great Depression: An Example of a Cohort Effect (pp. xx-xx)

19. Give examples of cohort effects.

Contexts of Development (pp. 9-10)

1.7 How does consideration of the contexts in which change occurs improve scientists understanding of human development?

20. Give an example of each of the following concepts to distinguish them.

Concept	Example
Vulnerability	
Resilience	

21. How does gender affect a person's experiences?

AFTER YOU READ . . . PRACTICE TEST #2
KEY ISSUES IN THE STUDY OF HUMAN DEVELOPMENT

1. The relative contribution of biological processes and experiential factors is known as _____.
    a.   the continuity verses discontinuity issue
    b.   the nature-nurture debate
    c.   atypical development
    d.   nonnormative change

2. The basic notion that children are born with tendencies to respond in certain ways is called _____.
    a.   nurture
    b.   age norms
    c.   inborn biases
    d.   atypical development

3. If you regularly hear criticism in other people's comments, we might infer that you will develop an internal model of experience. To which of the following basic assumptions is it most similar?
    a.   "I usually do things wrong, and that is why others criticize me."
    b.   "I usually do things wrong, and people are cruel."
    c.   "Apparently others do not see things in the same way that I do."
    d.   "When I do things wrong, I can depend on others to help me."

4. The _____ issue concerns whether age-related changes are a matter of degree or changes in type or kind.
    a.   nature-nurture
    b.   continuity-discontinuity
    c.   universal-specific
    d.   individual differences

5. A change in amount is called _____ change.
    a.   a specific
    b.   atypical
    c.   a qualitative
    d.   a quantitative

6. The social clock, or a set of _____, defines a sequence of normal life experiences.
    a.   vulnerabilities
    b.   inborn biases
    c.   age norms
    d.   internal models

7. The idea that there may be specific periods in development when an organism is especially sensitive to the presence (or absence) of some particular kind of experience is called _____.
    a.   individual differences
    b.   a cohort
    c.   atypical development
    d.   the critical period

8.   **Atypical development is also known as each of the following EXCEPT _____.**
        a.   maladaptive behavior
        b.   normal development
        c.   psychopathology
        d.   abnormal behavior

9.   **Each of the following is an example of a context of development EXCEPT _____.**
        a.   the school
        b.   the occupation of the parents
        c.   the neighborhood
        d.   the child's genotype

10.   **By far the most negative outcomes for a child are the result of a _____.**
        a.   highly vulnerable child
        b.   poor or unsupportive environment
        c.   combination of high vulnerability and poor environment
        d.   combination of low vulnerability and unsupportive environment

RESEARCH METHODS AND DESIGNS

The Goals of Developmental Science (p. 11))

1.8   What are the goals of scientists who study human development?

22.   List and define the four goals of human development.

Goal	Definition
1.	
2.	
3.	
4.	

Descriptive Methods (pp. 11-13)

1.9   What descriptive methods are used by developmental scientists?

23.   Define the following terms:
        a.   naturalistic observation method (p. 12)

        b.   case studies (p. 12)

        c.   laboratory observation (p. 12)

    d.   survey (p. 12)

    e.   population (p. 13)

    f.   sample (p. 13)

    g.   correlation (p. 13)

24.   State the advantages and disadvantages of each of the following research methods:

Method	Advantages	Disadvantages
Naturalistic Observation		
Case Study		
Laboratory Observation		
Survey		
Correlation		

25.   How do researchers prevent possible observer bias?

26.   What does each of the following correlations indicate?
    a.   +1.00

    b.   -1.00

    c.   0.00

27.   Give an example of a relationship (such as the example of temperature and air conditioner use in the text) of each of the following:
    a.   positive correlation

    b.   negative correlation

The Experimental Method (pp. 13-14)

1.10   What is the primary advantage of the experimental method?
28.   Define each of the following terms
      a.   experiment (p. 13)

      b.   experimental group (p. 14)

      c   control group (p. 14)

      d.   independent variable (p. 14)

      e.   dependent variable (p. 14)

29.   Suppose you want to see if children who watch violence on television are more aggressive than children who do not watch violent television. Identify the following parts of the experiment for this research:
      a.   Independent Variable

      b.   Dependent Variable

      c.   Experimental Group

      d.   Control Group

Designs for Studying Age-Related Changes (pp. 14-15)

1.11   What are the pros and cons of cross-sectional, longitudinal, and sequential research designs?
30.   Define the following terms:
      a.   cross-sectional design (p. 14)

      b.   longitudinal design (p. 14)

      c.   sequential design (p. 14)

31.   Identify the advantages and disadvantages of each of the following designs:

Design	Advantages	Disadvantages
Cross-Sectional		
Longitudinal		
Sequential		

No Easy Answers: It Depends . . . (p. 15))

32.   Why are there few clear-cut answers to hard questions?

Cross-Cultural Research (pp. 17-18)

1.12   Why is cross-cultural research important to the study of human development?

33.   Define ethnography. (p. 17).

34.   Describe two ways investigators may conduct cross-cultural research.
    ▪

    ▪

35.   List two reasons why cross-cultural research is important to developmental psychology.
    ▪

    ▪

Research Ethics (pp. 18-19)

1.13   What are the ethical standards that developmental researchers must follow?

36.   Define research ethics (p. 18).

37.   Describe each of the following ethical standards:
    a.   Protection from Harm

b.   Informed Consent

    c.   Confidentiality

    d.   Knowledge of Results

    e.   Deception

The Real World: Thinking Critically about Research (p. 19)

38.   Give examples of ways you can use your knowledge of research to become a "critical consumer" of research.

AFTER YOU READ . . . PRACTICE TEST #3
RESEARCH METHODS AND DESIGNS

_____ 1.   A detailed description of a single culture or context.

_____ 2.   A research design in which groups of different ages are compared.

_____ 3.   Guidelines researchers follow to protect the rights of animals and humans who participate in studies..

_____ 4.   The goal of human development that involves telling why a particular event occurs.

_____ 5.   A research design in which people in a single group are studied at different times in their lives.

_____ 6.   The process of studying people in their normal environments.

_____ 7.   A study that tests a causal hypothesis.

_____ 8.   A relationship between two variables that can be expressed as a number ranging form +1.00 to –1.00.

_____ 9.   In depth examination of a single individual.

_____ 10.   The goal of human development that simple state what happens.

a. Case studies
b. Correlation
c. Cross-sectional
d. Describe
e. Ethnography
f. Experiment
g. Explain
h. Longitudinal
i. Naturalistic observation
j. Predict
k. Sequential
l. Research ethics

AFTER YOU READ . . .CRITICAL REFLECTION EXERCISE

Critical Evaluation of Research

1.   You are reading the newspaper, and you read a story about a product called Melatonic. It is described as a derivative of a natural brain chemical and is touted to "make you feel better, help you sleep, and increase your sex drive." The article goes on to cite the research evidence supporting these claims. According to the article:
   - white mice given 500 mg doses, slept 40% longer than mice not given the tonic.
   - subjects given a free 30 day trial sample of the tonic reported "feeling invigorated, having fewer troubles falling asleep, and having sex once each week during the trial period."

Write out answers to the following questions and cite the reasons you have for each of your answers:

a.   What are the facts as they are presented?

b.   What are the implications if these facts are true?

c.   How have those facts been applied to the current research?

d.   When you analyze the information to determine what is verifiable, and discard what is meaningless, what facts are left?

e.   What questions do you have about the information that would need to be answered to make the original information more meaningful? (For example, "Is a 500 mg dosage a lot for a white mouse?").

f.   Now that you have only the meaningful pieces, what conclusions can you draw about the effects of Melatonic?

g.   What kind of a study could you develop to test the claims made in the article about Melatonic? Make sure that your study includes methods for testing (rather than assuming) that the claims are accurate.

2.   You are a teacher, and a colleague of yours tells you that Rachel (a second grader) is a victim of child abuse. When you ask how she has reached this conclusion about Rachel she states, "She has all of the classic symptoms:
- she can't sit still,
- she is performing below her ability,
- she has trouble making friends,
- she has difficulty concentrating, and
- she only partially completes her assignments."

Write out answers to the following questions and cite the reasons you have for each of your answers.

a.   What evidence is the teacher citing for her conclusion that Rachel is an abuse victim?

b.   Can you verify that this evidence is accurate? How might you verify this?

c.   What other information would you need to gather (or what other questions do you think would need to be answered) in order for you to determine if this teacher's conclusion is accurate?

d.   Describe how this teacher's conclusion, if invalid, could actually lead to a self-fulfilling prophecy as outlined earlier in this chapter.

e.   Based on the facts that you have, what conclusions can be drawn about Rachel?

f.   What other alternative explanations can you think of (besides abuse) that might explain Rachel's behaviors?

g.   How could you attempt to test your alternative explanations from question number 6?

AFTER YOU READ . . .COMPREHENSIVE PRACTICE TEST
MULTIPLE CHOICE QUESTIONS

1. The scientific study of age-related changes in behavior, thinking, emotion, and personality is termed _____.
    a. ageism
    b. maturation
    c. cohort effect
    d. human development

2. The philosophy which proposes that adults can mold children into whatever they want them to be is called _____.
    a. morality
    b. The blank slate
    c. original sin
    d. innate goodness

3. The term used to describe the average age at which milestones happen is _____.
    a. norms
    b. baby biographies
    c. case studies
    d. cohort effect

4. Genetically programmed sequential patterns of change are termed _____.
    a. growth
    b. maturation
    c. learning
    d. development

5. Each of the following is one of the domains of development EXCEPT _____.
    a. social
    b. cohort
    c. physical
    d. cognitive

6. The behavior of an individual _____.
    a. is completely fixed by his or her genetic inheritance
    b. will be entirely consistent over a person's lifespan
    c. will always be a joint product of the genetic pattern and the environment
    d. is based on his or her socioeconomic status

7. Qualitatively distinct periods of development are called _____.
    a. stages
    b. cohort effects
    c. case studies
    d. norms

8. **Thomas is forced to retire at age 70, even though he is physically and mentally healthy and does his job well. This is an example of _____.**
   a. age norms
   b. ageism
   c. the social clock
   d. culture

9. **Unique, unshared events are called _____.**
   a. nonnormative changes
   b. normative age-graded changes
   c. quantitative changes
   d. qualitative changes

10. **The idea that experiences occurring at the expected times for an individual's culture or cohort will pose fewer difficulties for an individual than experiences occurring at unexpected times is called _____.**
    a. the critical period
    b. the historical period
    c. the sensitive period
    d. on-time and off-time events

11. **Nicole studies parents and their children by watching them interact at the zoo. This is an example of the _____.**
    a. naturalistic observation method
    b. case study method
    c. experimental method
    d. correlational method

12. **As the temperature climbs, so does the number of air conditioners in use. This is an example of _____.**
    a. a positive correlation
    b. a negative correlation
    c. no correlation
    d. a hypothesis

13. **An experiment is testing the effects of observed violence on children's behavior. One group of children views a violent cartoon. A second group views a humorous non-violent cartoon. A third group is not exposed to any cartoon. The first group is the _____.**
    a. experimental group
    b. control group
    c. comparison group
    d. observational group

14. **In the cross-sectional method, _____.**
    a. the same group of subjects is repeatedly given the same test over a twenty-year period
    b. surveys are administered to samples of people from around the country
    c. groups of subjects of different ages are observed
    d. the behaviors of subjects in a laboratory environment is compared with their behaviors in their natural setting

15. **Which of the following ethical standards for research involves the right to a written summary of a study's results?**
   a. knowledge of results
   b. deception
   c. informed consent
   d. confidentiality

TRUE-FALSE QUESTIONS

1. _____ The doctrine of original sin teaches that all human beings are naturally good and seek out experiences that help them grow.

2. _____ The lifespan perspective maintains that important changes occur during every period of development.

3. _____ The social domain includes variables that are associated with the relationship of an individual to others.

4. _____ A qualitative change involves the continuity side of the continuity-discontinuity debate.

5. _____ In each culture, the social clock defines a sequence of normal life experiences.

6. _____ The four goals of research into human development are to describe, to explain, to predict, and to influence.

7. _____ The independent variable in an experiment is the presumed causal element.

8. _____ Cross-cultural research is important in identifying universal changes.

ESSAY QUESTIONS

1. Choose a typical event from human development, and give examples of how the three domains interact. Events could include starting school, going to college, getting married, having a baby, experiencing menopause, retiring, etc.

2. Describe how inborn biases, internal models of experience, and the ecological approach are aspects of the nature-nurture controversy.

3. Describe how cross-cultural research is important to the study of human development.

WHEN YOU HAVE FINISHED . . . PUZZLE IT OUT

Across

3. A single group of people are studied at different times
7. Individuals who share the same historical experiences
10. Average ages at which developmental milestones are reached
11. Debate about relative contributions of heredity and environment
12. A prejudicial view of older adults
13. Some system of meanings and customs
15. Important changes occur in every period of development
17. A study that tests a causal hypothesis
18. Combines cross-sectional and longitudinal

Down

1. Genetically programmed sequential patterns of change.
2. Researchers must not reveal the identities of participants
4. A detailed description of a single culture or context
5. Change in amount
6. Changes in the size, shape, and characteristics of the body
8. Relationship between two variables expressed as +1.00 to -1.00
9. Groups of different ages are compared
14. Changes in thinking, memory, problem-solving
16. Changes in variables associated with the relationship to others

Created by Puzzlemaker at DiscoverySchool.com

WHEN YOU HAVE FINISHED . . . RESEARCH PROJECT

Student Project 1: A First Observation of a Child: An Example of a Narrative Report

There are several purposes in suggesting this project. First, if you have had relatively little contact with young children, you may need to spend some time simply observing a child to make other sections of the book more meaningful. Second, it is important for you to begin to get some sense of the difficulties involved in observing and studying children. Later projects involve other types of observation, but it is helpful to start with the least structured (but perhaps the most difficult) form, namely a narrative report in which the observer attempts to write down everything a child does or says for about one hour.

Step 1: Locate a child between 18 months and 6 years of age; age 2, 3, or 4 would be best.

Step 2: Obtain permission from the child's parents for observation, using whatever form and procedure are specified by your instructor. When you speak to the parents, be sure to tell them that the purpose of your observation is for a course assignment, and that you will not be testing the child in any way but merely want to observe a normal child in his or her normal situation.

Step 3: Arrange a time when you can observe the child in his or her "natural habitat" for about one hour. If the child is in a nursery school, it is acceptable to observe him or her there as long as you get permission from the teachers. If not, the observation should be done in the home or in some situation familiar to the child. You must not baby-sit during the observation. You must be free to be in the background and cannot be responsible for the child during the observation.

Step 4: When the time for the observation arrives, place yourself in as unobtrusive a place as possible. Take a small stool with you if you can, so that you can move around as the child moves. If you are in the child's home, he or she will probably ask what you are doing. Say that you are doing something for school and that you will be writing things down for a while. Do not invite any kind of contact with the child; do not meet the child's eye; do not smile; and do not talk except when the child talks directly, in which case you should say that you are busy and will play a little later.

Step 5: For one hour, try to write down everything the child does. Write down the child's speech word-for-word. If the child is talking to someone else, write down the other person's replies, too, if you can. Describe the child's movements. Throughout, keep your description as free of evaluation and words of intent as you can. Do not write "Sarah went into the kitchen to get a cookie." You don't know why she went. What you saw was that she stopped what she had been doing, got up, and walked into the kitchen. There you see her getting a cookie. Describe the behavior that way, rather than making assumptions about what is happening in the child's head. Avoid words like "tries," "angrily," "pleaded," "wanted," and the like. Describe only what you see and hear.

Step 6: When you have completed the observation, reread what you wrote and consider the following questions:
- Did you manage to keep all description of intent out of your record?
- Were you able to remain objective?
- Since you obviously could not write down everything that the child did, think about what you left out.
- Did you find that you paid more attention to some aspects of behavior than others, such as listening to language rather than noting physical movements?
- What would such a bias do to the kind of information you could obtain from your narrative?

- Would it be possible for you or some other person doing the rating to obtain systematic information about the child from your record, such as a measure of the child's level of activity or a score reflecting the number of times the child asked for attention?
- What changes in this method of observation would you have to introduce to obtain other sorts of information?
- What do you think were the effects of your presence on the child?

WHEN YOU HAVE FINISHED . . . RESEARCH PROJECT

Student Project 2: Naturalistic Observation of a Nursing Home Resident

Follow the same procedure as in Project 1, except instead of observing a young child, observe an elderly adult in a nursing home. Permission will be required from the nursing home, and from the individual to be observed, following whatever procedure your instructor specifies.

Arrange to spend at least an hour in the nursing home. Inquire about the daily schedule and choose a time when the residents are likely to be together in some kind of recreational activity, or at least when not isolated in their individual rooms. Place yourself as inconspicuously as possible by the side of the room, and observe your selected subject for one hour. As with the observation of the child, attempt to write down everything your subject does for that hour. When you are finished, ask yourself the same questions as in Project 1.

WHEN YOU HAVE FINISHED . . . AT HOME PROJECT

Student Project 3: Analysis of Research Presented in Popular Sources

Find at least eight separate mentions of research on children, adolescents, or adults in newspapers and magazines, and analyze each one. For each item, describe the research design that appears to have been used.

- Is that design appropriate for the question being asked?
- Are there any flaws you can detect?
- Does the report in the magazine or newspaper give you enough detail to decide whether the research was any good?
- What other information would you want to have to decide on the quality of the research?

Some sources you might try for suitable articles are as follows:

1. The *New York Times* has a section on science every Tuesday which includes articles about behavior and development fairly regularly. The *Times* also has a column on personal health every Wednesday that often covers relevant material, as well as a column on children's behavior or on parenting every Thursday.

2. *Time* and *Newsweek* have sections on behavior that may be relevant.

3. Most so-called "women's magazines" (*Ladies Home Journal*, *Redbook*, *Family Circle*, etc.) have columns on child-rearing or children's development.

CHAPTER 1 ANSWER KEY

Practice Test #1 The Scientific Study of Human Development

1. i   2. l   3. g   4. f   5. j   6. h   7. c   8. m   9. b   10. e

Practice Test #2 Key Issues in the Study of Human Development

1. b   2. c   3. a   4. b   5. d   6. c   7. d   8. b   9. d   10. c

Practice Test #3 Research Methods and Designs

1. e   2. c   3. l   4. g   5. h   6. i   7. f   8. b   9. a   10. d

Comprehensive Practice Test

Multiple Choice Questions

1. d   2. b   3. a   4. b   5. b   6. c   7. a   8. b   9. a   10. d
11. d   12. a   13. a   14. c   15. a

True-False Questions

1. F   2. T   3. T   4. F   5. T   6. T   7. T   8. T

Essay Questions

1.   ▪ Answers should include aspects of all three domains for the event.

2.   ▪ Answers should include how each of the three (inborn biases, internal models of experience, and the ecological approach) relate to nature versus nurture.

3.   ▪ Cross-cultural research is helpful in identifying universal changes and in producing findings that can be used to improve people's lives. Answers should include reference to both functions.

Puzzle It Out

Across

3. Longitudinal
7. Cohort
10. Norms
11. NatureNurture
12. Ageism
13. Culture
15. Lifespan
17. Experiment
18. Sequential

Down

1. Maturation
2. Confidentiality
4. Ethnography
5. Quantitative
6. Physical
8. Correlation
9. CrossSectional
14. Cognitive
16. Social

CHAPTER 2

THEORIES OF DEVELOPMENT

BEFORE YOU READ . . . CHAPTER SUMMARY

Three "families" of theories have significantly influenced the study of development. Some biological and ecological theories focus on individual differences, while others deal with universal aspects of development. The comparison of theories is based on three assumptions about theories and evaluated by criteria for usefulness.

Psychoanalytic Theories

- Freud's emphasis is on the importance of both conscious and unconscious processes. The personality is composed of the id, the ego, and the superego that influence our motives. He proposed five psychosexual stages, and he believed that each of the first three stages potentially impact our development.
- Erikson's theory stated that social forces are more important than unconscious drives as motives for development. He proposes eight stages of personality development across the lifespan, each of which involves resolving a crisis.
- Psychoanalytic theories provide useful concepts, such as the unconscious, that contribute to our understanding of development. They are, however, difficult to test.

Learning Theories

- Classical conditioning is learning through the association of unrelated stimuli such that a formerly meaningless stimulus now elicits a response. It helps explain the acquisition of emotional responses, such as fear.
- Skinner's operant conditioning involves learning based on the consequences of our actions. Reinforcement is a consequence of a behavior that increase the chances of that behavior being repeated. Punishment is a consequence of a behavior that decreases the chances of that behavior being repeated.
- Bandura's social-cognitive theory focuses more on the cognitive elements of learning, such as modeling.
- Learning theories provide useful explanations of how behaviors are acquired, but they fall short of a truly comprehensive picture of human development.

Cognitive Theories

- Piaget's focus is on the development of logical thinking across four stages in childhood and adolescence.
- Vygotsky's sociocultural theory is important in developmentalists' attempts to explain how culture impacts development.
- Information-processing theory uses the computer as a model to explain intellectual processes such as memory and problem-solving.
- Research confirms the sequence of skill development that Piaget proposed, but it suggests that young children are more capable than he believed. Information-processing theory helps to clarify some of the cognitive processes underlying Piaget's findings as well as our understanding of memory.

Biological and Ecological Theories

- Behavior geneticists study the influence of heredity on individual differences and the ways in which individuals' genes influence their environments.
- Ethologists study genetically determined traits and behaviors that help animals adapt to their environments. Sociobiologists emphasize the genetic basis of behaviors that promote the development and maintenance of social organizations in both animals and humans.
- Bronfenbrenner's bioecological theory helps developmentalists categorize environmental factors and their impact on individuals.

Comparing Theories

- Theories vary on three basic assumptions: Are individuals active or passive in their own development? How do nature and nurture interact to produce development? Does development happen continuously or in stages?
- Useful theories provide hypotheses to test their validity, are heuristically valuable, provide practical solutions to problems, and explain the facts of development.
- Eclecticism is the use of multiple theoretical perspectives to explain and study human development.

AS YOU READ . . . LEARNING OBJECTIVES

After reading Chapter 2, you should be able to answer the following questions:

2.1   What are the main ideas of Freud's theory?
2.2   What is the conflict associated with each of Erikson's psychological stages?
2.3   What are the strengths and weaknesses of psychoanalytic theory?
2.4   How did Watson condition Little Albert to fear white, furry objects?
2.5   How does operant conditioning occur?
2.6   In what ways does social-cognitive theory differ from other learning theories?
2.7   How well do the learning theories explain development?
2.8   How does cognitive development progress, according to Piaget?
2.9   How did Vygotsky use the concepts of scaffolding and the zone of proximal development o explain cognitive development?
2.10 How does information-processing theory explain the findings of developmental psychologists such as Piaget and Vygotsky?
2.11 What are some of the important contributions and criticisms of the cognitive theories?
2.12 How do behavior geneticists explain individual differences?
2.13 What kinds of behaviors are of interest to ethologists and sociobiologists?
2.14 What is the main idea of Bronfenbrenner's Bioecological theory?
2.15 What assumptions do the three families of theories make about development?
2.16 On what criteria do developmentalists compare the usefulness of theories?
2.17 What is eclecticism?

AS YOU READ . . . TERM IDENTIFICATION

Make flashcards using the following terms as you go. Use the definitions in the margin of this chapter for help. If you write the definitions in your own words, though, you will remember them better!

Accommodation (p. 37)
Assimilation (p. 36)
Behavior genetics (p. 41)
Behaviorism (p. 32)
Bioecological theory (p. 43)
Classical conditioning (p. 32)
Cognitive theories (p. 36)
Eclecticism (p. 47)
Ego (p. 27)
Equilibration (p. 37)
Ethology (p. 42)
Extinction (p. 27)
Id (p. 27)
Information-processing theory (p. 39)

Learning theories (p. 32)
Neo-Piagetian theory (p. 39)
Observational learning, modeling (p. 34)
Operant conditioning (p. 33)
Psychoanalytic theories (p. 27)
Psychosexual stages (p. 28)
Psychosocial stages (p. 29)
Punishment (p. 33)
Reinforcement (p. 33)
Scheme (p. 36)
Sociobiology (p. 43)
Sociocultural theory (p. 38)
Superego (p. 27)

AS YOU READ . . . GUIDED STUDY QUESTIONS

PSYCHOANALYTIC THEORIES

Freud's Psychosexual Theory (pp. 27-28)

2.1   What are the main ideas of Freud's theory?
1.   Define the following terms:
        a.   psychoanalytic theory (p. 27)

        b.   id (p. 27)

        c.   ego (p. 27)

        d.   superego (p. 27)

        e.   psychosexual stages (p. 28)

2.   Describe the function of each part of the personality.

Structure	Function
Id	

Structure	Function
Ego	
Superego	

3.   What would the three parts of Freud's theory "say" to you about your desire for your favorite cheesecake? Choose one of the following for each of the examples listed:

id   ego   superego

a.   _____ "Don't even think about eating cheesecake. You know it has too much fat, too much sugar, and too much cholesterol. Besides, if you eat it all you'll get sick to your stomach. Forget it and go get a carrot stick!"

b.   _____ "Go for it—and put whipped cream and a cherry on top! Just bring me the whole thing."

c.   _____ "How about a small piece?" "If I eat some now, then I will just have a small salad for supper and I'll do extra exercises tomorrow."

4.   List, in order, Freud's five psychosexual stages, and summarize each by completing the following table.

Name of Stage	Age	Focus of Libido	Developmental Task	Characteristics of Adult Fixation
1.				
2.				
3.				
4.				
5.				

5.   Describe the Oedipus Complex for boys and the Electra Complex for girls.

6.   Explain the process of identification.

No Easy Answers: The Repressed Memory Controversy (p. 29)

7.   Explain how the defense mechanisms of repression and denial may cause distress in the
        personality.

8.   Write a support statement for each side of the controversy surrounding repressed memories.
        ▪   Therapists should try to uncover repressed memories.

        ▪   Therapists should not try to uncover repressed memories.

Erikson's Psychosocial Theory (pp. 28-31)

2.2   What is the conflict associated with each of Erikson's psychosocial stages?
9.   Define psychosocial stages (p. 28).

10.   According to Erikson, how does a person develop a healthy personality?

11. List, in order, Erikson's eight psychosocial stages, and complete the following table.

Stage	Age	Positive Characteristics Gained and Typical Activities
1.		
2.		
3.		
4.		
5.		
6.		
7.		
8.		

12. Describe the parents' behavior that might result in an infant learning trust, and describe the parents' behavior that might result in an infant learning mistrust.

13. What must an adolescent do to achieve identity?

14. Why did Erikson believe that identity must be established before intimacy?

15. List several ways a middle-aged adult could achieve generativity.

Evaluation of Psychoanalytic Theories (p. 31)

2.3 What are the strengths and weaknesses of psychoanalytic theory?

16. List five strengths of psychoanalytic theory.
   1.

   2.

   3.

4.

5.

17.   What is the greatest weakness of psychoanalytic theory?

AFTER YOU READ . . . PRACTICE TEST #1
PSYCHOANALYTIC THEORIES

1.   The _____ is the instinctual drive for physical pleasure.
   a.   libido
   b.   conscious
   c.   ego
   d.   superego

2.   The _____ is responsible for keeping the three components of personality in balance.
   a.   libido
   b.   id
   c.   superego
   d.   ego

3.   In Freud's view, the ego generates a way of thinking about a situation that reduces anxiety that is called _____.
   a.   the structure of personality
   b.   a defense mechanism
   c.   a psychosexual stage
   d.   suppression

4.   The psychosexual stage in which a girl experiences the Electra complex is _____ .
   a.   oral
   b.   anal
   c.   phallic
   d.   genital

5.   According to Erikson's theory, a healthy personality is built on the formation of _____.
   a.   self-awareness
   b.   autonomy
   c.   initiative
   d.   trust

6.   According to Erikson's theory, if an individual does not make a successful transition through adolescence, he or she develops _____.
   a.   an inferiority complex
   b.   role confusion
   c.   a sense of isolation
   d.   a sense of personal guilt

7.   In order for the young adult to realize a successful outcome in Erikson's sixth stage, she or he must learn to establish a sense of _____.
   a.   identity
   b.   intimacy
   c.   initiative
   d.   industry

8.   **Psychoanalytic theories highlight the importance of _____.**
   a.   genetically determined survival behaviors
   b.   mental aspects of development such as logic and memory
   c.   the child's earliest relationship with caregivers, and suggest that the child needs change with age
   d.   development in terms of behavior changes caused by environmental influences

LEARNING THEORIES

Classical Conditioning (p. 32)

2.4   *How did Watson condition Little Albert to fear white, furry objects?*

18.   Define the following terms:
    a.   behaviorism (p. 32)
    b..   learning theories (p. 32)

    c.   classical conditioning (p. 32)

19.   In classical conditioning, the conditioned response is always very similar to the unconditined response. Why?

20.   A child learns to associate a teddy bear with a loud noise that scares him. Match the classical conditioning term to its appropriate action.

a. _____ fear (of teddy bear)	1. unconditional stimulus
b. _____ fear (of loud noise)	2. unconditional response
c. _____ loud noise	3. conditional stimulus
d. _____ teddy bear	4. conditional response

21.   How is classical conditioning relevant to the study of development?

Skinner's Operant Conditioning (p. 33)

2.5   *How does operant conditioning occur?*

22.   Define the following terms:
    a.   operant conditioning (p. 333)

    b.   reinforcement (p. 33)

    c.   punishment (p. 33)

    d.   extinction (p. 33)

23.   You want your daughter to clean her room. Label the following operant conditioning term that matches the action:

positive reinforcement   **negative reinforcement**   **punishment**

a.   _____ If she cleans her room, she doesn't have to do the dishes.

b.   _____ If she cleans her room, she can go to the movies.

c.   _____ If she does not clean her room, she cannot watch TV.

24.   Describe how you can use extinction to stop your son's whining.

The Real World: Learning Principles in Everyday Life (p. 34)

25.   You're at the cereal aisle of the grocery store. At the same aisle is a mom with a preschool child in the shopping cart. The child wants an expensive, sugary cereal, and the mom says no. The child has a temper tantrum, and everyone in the aisle turns to see what happened. The mom gives in and puts the cereal in the basket, and the child stops screaming.
a.   Who received positive reinforcement? How?

b.   Who received negative reinforcement? How?

c.   How could extinction be used in this scenario?

Bandura's Social-Cognitive Theory (pp. 33-35)

2.6   In what ways does social-cognitive theory differ from other learning theories?
26.   Define observational learning, or modeling (p. 34).

27.   List two factors that determine whether or not an observer will learn from watching someone else.
1.

2.

Evaluation of Learning Theories (pp. 35-36)

2.7 ***How well do the learning theories explain development?***

28.   Give an example of each of the following implications of the learning theories:
   a.   Learning theories can explain both consistency and change in behavior.

   b.   Learning theories tend to be optimistic about the possibility of change.

   c.   Learning theories give an accurate picture of the way many behaviors are learned.

29.   Why are learning theories not considered to be developmental theories?

AFTER YOU READ . . . PRACTICE TEST #2
LEARNING THEORIES

1. **Conditioned response is to unconditioned response as _____.**
   a.   unlearned is to learned
   b.   nature is to nurture
   c.   learned is to unlearned
   d.   learned is to forgotten

2. **All of the following are examples of an unconditioned response EXCEPT _____.**
   a.   Tony's eyes tear up when he is peeling an onion.
   b.   John's pupils dilate in response to a bright light.
   c.   Rich wipes his dirty hands off on his pants before he grabs the mail off the table.
   d.   Mike pulls his hand back quickly after touching a hot stove.

3. **In operant conditioning, the response comes _____.**
   a.   before the consequence
   b.   after the consequence
   c.   during the consequence
   d.   between the consequence and the unconditioned stimulus

4. **You take aspirin for your headache. This is an example of which of the following?**
   a.   positive reinforcement
   b.   negative reinforcement
   c.   punishment
   d.   extinction

5. **The gradual elimination of a behavior through repeated nonreinforcement is called _____.**
   a.   shaping
   b.   punishment
   c.   reinforcement
   d.   extinction

6. **All of the following are factors that determines whether or not an observer will learn from watching someone else EXCEPT _____.**
   a.   what she pays attention to
   b.   what she is physically able to do
   c.   what she read in her textbook
   d.   what she is able to remember

7. **Bandura's notion that we acquire expectations about what we can and cannot do is called**
   _____.
   a.   self-efficacy
   b.   modeling
   c.   conditioning
   d.   shaping

8. **Which of the following is a weakness of learning theories?**
   a. They give an accurate picture of the way many behaviors are learned.
   b. They are not really developmental theories.
   c. They tend to be optimistic about the possibility of changing behavior.
   d. They can explain both consistence and change in behavior.

COGNITIVE THEORIES

Piaget's Cognitive-Developmental Theory (pp. 36-38)

2.8   How does cognitive development progress, according to Piaget?

30.   Define the following terms:
   a.   cognitive theories (p. 36)

   b.   scheme (p. 36)

   c.   assimilation (p. 36)

   d.   accommodation (p. 37)

   e.   equilibration (p. 37)

31.   Your present scheme for drive-in windows at fast-food restaurants includes the following:
   - Order from a menu at the speaker box.
   - Drive to the first window and pay.
   - Drive to another window and pick up your food.

   You stop at the drive-in window of a new fast-food restaurant and discover that the window to pay and pick up your food is on the passenger side of the car, not the driver's side. According to Piaget, what process is involved in changing the scheme based on the new information?

32.   List, in order, the four stages of Piaget's theory, and complete the following table.

Stage	Age	Description
1.		
2.		

Stage	Age	Description
3.		
4.		

Vygotsky's Sociocultural Theory (p. 38)

2.9   How did Vygotsky use the concepts of scaffolding and the zone of proximal development to explain cognitive development?

33.   Define sociocultural theory (p. 38).

34.   How does the role of the teacher differ in the Vygotskian classroom from the Piagetian classroom?

Information-Processing Theory (pp. 38-39)

2.10   How does information processing theory explain the findings of developmental psychologists such as Piaget and Vygotsky?

35.   Define the following terms:
        a.   information-processing theory (p. 38)

        b.   neo-Piagetian theory (p. 39)

36.   Did you listen to music on the radio this morning while you were getting ready for school or work? If so, do you remember all the songs you heard? Probably not, even though you might have sung along with several of them. Which ones do you remember? Why don't we remember everything that enters our sensory memory?

Evaluation of Cognitive Theories (pp. 39-40)

2.11   What are some of the important contributions and criticisms of the cognitive theories?

37.   List three contributions of Piaget's theory.
1.

2.
3.

38.   In what area was Piaget sometimes wrong?

39.   List two areas of Vygotsky's ideas that are supported by research.
1.

2.

40.   How has information-processing theory helped clarify some of the cognitive processes underlying Piaget's findings?

41.   What are the criticisms of information-processing theory?

Research Report: Piaget's Clever Research (p. 41)

42.   Give examples of how Piaget's method of study tested children's understanding of the concepts of conservation and multiple categories.

AFTER YOU READ . . . PRACTICE TEST #3
COGNITIVE THEORIES

1. The group of theories known as _____ emphasizes mental aspects of development such as logic and memory.
   a. learning theories
   b. cognitive theories
   c. biological theories
   d. useful theories

2. A _____ is an internal and cognitive structure that provides an individual with a process to follow in a specific circumstance.
   a. model
   b. stage
   c. reflex
   d. scheme

3. _____ is the process of balancing assimilation and accommodation to create schemes that fit the environment.
   a. Behavior
   b. Equilibration
   c. Cognition
   d. Learning

4. In the _____ stage, children acquire symbolic schemes, such as language and fantasy.
   a. sensorimotor
   b. preoperational
   c. concrete operational
   d. formal operational

5. In the _____ stage, Proposed that adolescents learn to think logically about abstract ideas and hypothetical situations.
   a. sensorimotor
   b. preoperational
   c. concrete operational
   d. formal operational

6. According to Vygotsky, children's learning of new cognitive skills is guided by an adult, who structures the child's learning experience, a process he called _____.
   a. scaffolding
   b. cognition
   c. equilibrium
   d. assimilation

7. Another name for short-term memory is _____.
   a. sensory memory
   b. episodic memory
   c. long-term memory
   d. working memory

8.   _____ is unlimited in capacity.
    a.   short-term memory
    b.   long-term memory
    c.   working memory
    d.   sensory memory

BIOLOGICAL AND ECOLOGICAL THEORIES

Behavior Genetics (p. 41)

2.12   *How do behavior geneticists explain individual differences?*
43.   Define behavior genetics (p. 41).

44.   Describe how genetics and the environment interact to influence a person's behavior.

Ethology and Sociobiology (p. 42)

2.13   *What kinds of behaviors are of interest to ethologists and sociobiologists?*
45.   Define the following terms:
a.   ethology (p. 42)

b.   sociobiology (p. 42)

46.   What are the criticisms of each theory?

Theory	*Criticisms*
Ethology	
Sociobiology	

Bronfenbrenner's Ecological Theory (pp. 43-33)

2.14   *What is the main idea of Bronfenbrenner's bioecological theory?*
47.   Define bioecological theory (p. 43).

48.   Give examples of each of the contexts in Bronfenbrenner's theory.

System	Context	Example
Macrosystem		
Exosystem		
Mesosystem		
Microsystem		
Person		

AFTER YOU READ . . . PRACTICE TEST #4
BIOLOGICAL AND ECOLOGICAL THEORIES

Match the term in the second column with its definition in the first column.

_____ 1. The study of society that emphasizes genes that aid group survival.

_____ 2. The socioeconomic context that includes the institutions of the culture that affect children's development indirectly.

_____ 3. The child's genetic make-up and developmental range that affect development.

_____ 4. The study of the role of heredity in individual differences.

_____ 5. The theory that explains development in terms of relationship between individuals and their environments.

a. Behavioral Genetics
b. Biological Context
c. Bioecological
d. Ethology
e. Exosystem
f. Macrosystem
g. Mesosystem
h. Microsystem
i. Sociobiology

COMPARING THEORIES

Assumptions About Development (p. 45)

2.15   What assumptions do the three families of theories make about development?

49.   State at least one theory that views development as each of the following:

Active	
Passive	
Nature	
Nurture	
Continuity	
Discontinuity	

Usefulness (pp. 45-46)

2.16 **On what criteria do developmentalists compare the usefulness of theories?**

50.   State at least one theory that fits each criteria of usefulness.

Criteria	Theory that Fits the Criteria
Testability of Theory	
Criteria	Theory that Fits the Criteria
Heuristic Value	
Practical Value	
Explains Facts	

Eclecticism (p. 47)

2.17 **What is eclecticism?**

51.   Define eclecticism (p. 47)

52.   Give examples of how the interdisciplinary nature of today's developmental science may contribute to eclecticism.

AFTER YOU READ . . . PRACTICE TEST #5
COMPARING THEORIES

Indicate whether each of the following statements is True or False.

_____
1.   Passive theories maintain that development results from the environment acting on the individual

_____
2.   Theories claiming that biology contributes more to development than does environment are on the nurture side of the nature-nurture debate.

_____
3.   Theories that refer to stages assert that development is a stable, continuous process.

_____
4.   The point of comparing theories is not to conclude which one is true.

_____
5.   The interdisciplinary nature of today's developmental science contributes to eclecticism.

AFTER YOU READ . . . CRITICAL REFLECTION EXERCISE

Match the theoretical perspective to the statement describing it.

_____ 1. Behavior is associated with the consequences of our actions.

_____ 2. Uses multiple theoretical perspectives to explain and study human development.

_____ 3. Development occurs in a series of stages, based on the libido, through which the child moves in a fixed sequence.

_____ 4. This theory explains the relationship between people and their environment, or contexts.

_____ 5. Emotional responses, such as fear, are developed by associations.

_____ 6. Complex forms of thinking have their origins in social interactions rather than in the child's private explorations.

_____ 7. This theory focuses on the affect of heredity on individual differences.

_____ 8. The goal of the theory is to explain how the mind manages information.

_____ 9. Focus of the theory is on the development of logical thinking.

_____ 10. Learning can occur by watching others

a. Psychoanalytic (Freud)
b. Psychoanalytic (Erikson)
c. Classical Conditioning
d. Operant Conditioning
e. Bandura's Social-Cognitive
f. Piaget's Cognitive-Developmental
g. Information-Processing
h. Behavior Genetics
i. Vygotsky's Socio-Cultural
j. Bronfenbrenner's Bioecological
k. Eclecticism

AFTER YOU READ . . . COMPREHENSIVE PRACTICE TEST
MULTIPLE CHOICE QUESTIONS

1. **Which term best describes Freud's theory of development?**
   a. psychosocial stages
   b. ego development
   c. id integrity
   d. psychosexual stages

2. **Erikson's theory differed from Freud's in that Erikson _____.**
   a. emphasized instincts more heavily than Freud
   b. believed that our urges are primarily destructive
   c. believed that development continued throughout the lifespan
   d. is considered more pessimistic than Freud

3. **Which of the following is a weakness of the psychoanalytic theories?**
   a. They are hard to test and measure.
   b. They provide helpful concepts, such as the unconscious, that are part of everyday language.
   c. They invented psychotherapy.
   d. They focus on the emotional quality of the child's earliest relationship with caregivers.

4. **Whenever the eye doctor puffs air in your eye, you blink. Now, before she puffs the air, she says "ready," puffs the air, and you blink. After doing this several times, you begin to blink as soon as she says "ready." In this example, what kind of learning has taken place?**
   a. classical conditioning
   b. sensitization
   c. operant conditioning
   d. habituation

5. **What is the unconditioned stimulus in the previous question?**
   a. blinking of the eye
   b. saying the word "ready"
   c. the puff of air
   d. fear of the puff of air

6. **Which of the following is an example of positive reinforcement?**
   a. Grounding your daughter for missing her curfew.
   b. Placing your daughter in "time out."
   c. Praising your son for his good grades.
   d. Withholding allowance from your son when he talks back.

7. **Bandura suggests that learning can take place without direct reinforcement. What is this type of learning called?**
   a. positive reinforcement
   b. modeling
   c. instrumental conditioning
   d. classical conditioning

8.   You learn how to drive a car with an automatic transmission, then you try to drive a car with standard transmission. The adjustment you make is an example of the process of:
      a.   equilibration.
      b.   assimilation.
      c.   accommodation.
      d.   hierarchical categorizing.

9.   Chris is in elementary school and has learned to solve problems logically. Which of Piaget's stages best describes her level of cognitive development?
      a.   concrete operational
      b.   sensorimotor
      c.   preoperational
      d.   formal operational

10.   Which of the following is the goal of information-processing theory?
      a.   to distinguish the relative impact of nature and nurture
      b.   to trace the stages of how thinking develops
      c.   to uncover the hidden meaning of dreams
      d.   to explain how the mind manages information

11.   Which of these theories focuses on genetically determined survival behaviors that are assumed to have evolved through natural selection?
      a.   ecological
      b.   learning
      c.   psychoanalytic
      d.   sociobiology

12.   Arrange the following contexts of Bronfenbrenner's Ecological Theory in the proper order, from the largest circle to the smallest.
      a.   macrosystem, exosystem, microsystem, biological context
      b.   microsystem, biological context, macrosystem, exosystem
      c.   biological context, exosystem, microsystem, macrosystem
      d.   macrosystem, biological context, microsystem, exosystem

13.   Which of the following theories is most likely to be influenced by nature rather than nurture?
      a.   Freud's Psychosexual Theory
      b.   Classical Conditioning
      c.   Operant Conditioning
      d.   Piaget's Cognitive Developmental Theory

14.   In which of the following theories is a person most likely to be an active participant in her own environment?
      a.   Freud's Psychosexual Theory
      b.   Classical Conditioning
      c.   Operant Conditioning
      d.   Piaget's Cognitive-Developmental Theory

15. **Which of the following is NOT one of the criteria of usefulness listed in the text?**
    a. Does it stimulate thinking and research?
    b. Does it explain the basic facts of development?
    c. Does it explain a person's motivation for their behavior?
    d. Does it generate predictions that can be tested with scientific methods?

TRUE-FALSE QUESTIONS

_____ 1. Defense mechanisms lessen the pain of anxiety, but they do not cure the problem.

_____ 2. Erikson believed that the young adult builds on the identity established in adolescence to confront the crisis of intimacy versus isolation.

_____ 3. In classical conditioning, the conditioned response is seldom similar to the unconditioned response.

_____ 4. Positive reinforcement strengthens behavior, negative reinforcement weakens behavior, and punishment eliminates behavior altogether.

_____ 5. Assimilation is the process of using schemes to make sense of experiences.

_____ 6. In Vygotsky's theory, scaffolding mean developing a firm sense of self-identity.

_____ 7. According to Bronfenbrenner, the contexts of development are like circles within circles.

_____ 8. By adopting an eclectic approach, developmentalists' theories and studies may more closely match the behavior of real people in real situations.

ESSAY QUESTIONS

1. Describe each of Freud's five stages of development, giving the ages, sources of conflict and possible solutions, with their accompanying impact on adult behavior.

2. Explain the major differences between classic conditioning and operant conditioning.

3. Provide an example of each of the following as they apply to Piaget's theory of cognitive development: schemes, assimilation, and accommodation.

WHEN YOU HAVE FINISHED . . . PUZZLE IT OUT

Across
1. Causes behavior to stop
2. Gradual elimination through repeated nonreinforcement
4. A procedure to use in a specific circumstance
5. Part of the personality that is the moral judge
9. The thinking element of the personality
10. Using a scheme to make sense of an event
12. Focuses on the study of animals in their natural environments
14. Learning because of their consequences

Down
1. Erkison's stages
2. Change a scheme as a result of new information
6. Freud's stages
7. Emphasizes genes that aid group survival
8. Causes behavior to be repeated
11. Motivates the person to seek pleasure and avoid pain

Created by Puzzlemaker at DiscoverySchool.com

CHAPTER 2 ANSWER KEY

Practice Test #1 Psychoanalytic Theories

1. a   2.   3. c   4. b   5. d   6. b   7. b   8. c

Practice Test #2 Learning Theories

1. c   2. c   3. a   4. b   5. d   6. c   7. a   8. b

Practice Test #3 Cognitive Theories

1. b   2. d   3. b   4. c   5. d   6. a   7. d   8. b

Practice Test #4 Biological and Ecological Theories

1. i   2. e   3. b   4. a   5. c

Practice Test #5 Current Trends

1. T   2. F   3. F   4. T   5. T

Critical Reflection Exercise

1. d   2. k   3. a   4. j   5. c   6. i   7. h   8. g   9. f   10. e

Comprehensive Practice Test
Multiple Choice Questions

1. d   2. c   3. a   4. a   5. c   6. c   7. b   8. c   9. a   10. d
11. a   12. a   13. a   14. d   15. c

True-False Questions

1. T   2. T   3. F   4. F   5. T   6. F   7. T   8. T

Essay Questions

1.
- Stage 1, Oral Stage, birth to about 12 months. Conflict is weaning: too little or too much gratification. As an adult, may be either dependent , gullible, and overly optimistic or extremely pessimistic, sarcastic, hostile, and aggressive. Also tend to eat, drink, smoke, and talk too much.
- Stage 2, Anal Stage, 1-3 years. Conflict is toilet training: If too harsh or too lenient the child will become fixated. As an adult, if anal retentive, they will be overly clean, neat, stingy, precise, and may become hoarders. If anal expulsive as an adult, will be sloppy, rebellious, hostile, and destructive.
- Stage 3, Phallic Stage, 3-6 years. Conflict is resolving Oedipus or Electra complex. Child develops a conscience and imprints on the same-sex parent so that they may achieve a healthy heterosexual relationship as an adult. As an adult, they will be vain, reckless, sexually dysfunctional, or sexually deviant.
- Stage 4, Latency, 6-12 years. No conflict.
- Stage 4, Genital, 12+ years. No conflict. Adults who have successfully integrated earlier stages should emerge with sincere interest in others and mature sexually.

2. ▪ In classical conditioning an association is formed between two stimuli; in operant conditioning the association is established between a response and its consequences.
   ▪ In classical conditioning the subject is generally passive and reacts to the environment; in operant conditioning, the subject is active and operates on some aspect of the environment.
   ▪ The range of responses in classical conditioning is relative simple; responses involved in operant conditioning are simple to highly complex.
   ▪ The types of conditioned responses in classical conditioning are generally associated with emotions; operant responses are goal-oriented.
   ▪ Classically conditioned responses are reflexive; operant responses are voluntary.

3. ▪ Schemes: When you pick up a ball, you use your picking-up scheme. When you throw it to someone, you use your looking scheme, your aiming scheme, and your throwing scheme.
   ▪ Assimilation: When a baby grasps a toy, she is assimilating it to her grasping scheme.
   ▪ Accommodation: When a baby grasps a square toy for the first time, he will accommodate his grasping scheme; the next time he reaches for a square object, his hand will be more appropriately bent to grasp it.

Puzzle It Out

Across
1. Punishment
3. Extinction
4. Scheme
5. Superego
9. Ego
10. Assimilation
12. Ethology
13. Modeling
14. Operant conditioning

Down
1. Psychosocial
2. Accommodation
6. Psychosexual
7. Sociobiology
8. Reinforcement
11. Id

CHAPTER 3

PRENATAL DEVELOPMENT AND BIRTH

BEFORE YOU READ . . . CHAPTER SUMMARY

Human development begins with the genes and chromosomes passed on to the new individual at the moment of conception and is impacted by the prenatal environment. From conception to birth, prenatal development follows a truly amazing course that begins with a single cell and ends with a crying, but curious, newborn making his or her debut in the outside world.

Conception and Genetics

- The first step in the development of an individual human being happens at conception when a sperm fertilizes an ovum (egg cell). Fraternal twins come from two eggs that are fertilized by two separate sperm; identical twins result when a single fertilized ovum separates into two parts and each develops into a separate individual. Assisted reproductive techniques are available to couples who have trouble conceiving.
- At conception, the combination of genes from the father in the sperm and the mother in the ovum creates a unique genetic blueprint, the genotype, that characterizes the individual. The phenotype is comprised of an individual's expressed characteristics. The simplest set of genetic rules is the dominant-recessive pattern in which a single dominant gene strongly influences phenotype.

Genetic and Chromosomal Disorders

- Many disorders appear to be transmitted through the operation of dominant and recessive genes. Autosomal disorders are caused by genes located on the autosomes (chromosomes other than sex chromosomes); the genes that cause sex-linked disorders are found on the X chromosome.
- A variety of problems can be caused when a child has too many or too few chromosomes, a conditional referred to as chromosomal error or chromosomal anomaly.

Pregnancy and Prenatal Development

- Pregnancy is a physical condition in which a woman's body is nurturing a developing embryo or fetus. Pregnancy is usually divided into trimesters, three periods of three months each.
- Prenatal development, or gestation, is the process that transforms a zygote into a newborn. The three stages of prenatal development are defined by specific developmental milestones and are not of equal length.
- Because prenatal development is strongly influenced by maturational codes that are the same for both males and females, there are only a few sex differences in prenatal development.
- Prenatal behavior includes fetal responses to music and other stimuli. Fetal learning is the subject of research to determine what fetuses can learn and how the learning may affect later development.

Problems in Prenatal Development

- Deviations in prenatal development can result from exposure to teratogens, substances that cause damage to an embryo or fetus. The general rule is that each organ system is most vulnerable to harm at the time when it is developing most rapidly.

- Prescription drugs, over-the-counter drugs, illegal drugs, tobacco, and alcohol can negatively influence the developing child. Such substances that cause damage to an embryo or fetus are known as teratogens.
- Teratogens include maternal diseases, such as rubella and HIV, and radiation.
- The mother's diet, her age, and her mental and physical health can also adversely affect prenatal development.
- Medical tests, such as ultrasonography, chorionic villus sampling and amniocentesis, are used to identify problems prenatally.

Birth and the Neonate

- Once gestation is complete, the fetus must be born into the world. In industrialized countries, especially in the United States, parents have several choices including the location of the birth, birth attendants, and whether or not to use drugs during delivery.
- Labor is typically divided into three stages. Stage 1 covers dilation and effacement, stage 2 is the delivery of the baby, and stage 3 is the delivery of the placenta and other material from the uterus.
- A baby is referred to as a neonate for the first month following birth. The health of the neonate is assessed with the Apgar scale at one minute and five minutes after birth. The Brazelton Neonatal Behavioral Assessment Scale is used to track a newborn's development over the first two weeks or so following birth.
- Classification of a neonate's weight is another important factor in assessment. All neonates below 2500 grams, about 5.5 pounds, are classified as low birth weight (LBW). Most LBW infants are preterm, born before the 38th week of gestation; infants that are small-for-date have completed 38 weeks or more of gestation but are still LBW.

AS YOU READ . . . LEARNING OBJECTIVES

After completing Chapter 3, you should be able to answer the following questions:

3.1   What are the characteristics of the zygote?
3.2   In what ways do genes influence development?
3.3   What are the effects of the major dominant, recessive, and sex-linked diseases?
3.4   How do trisomies and other disorders of the autosomes and sex chromosomes affect development?
3.5   What are the characteristics of each of the trimesters of pregnancy?
3.6   What happens in each of the stages of prenatal development?
3.7   How do male and female fetuses differ?
3.8   What behaviors have scientists observed in fetuses?
3.9   How do teratogens affect prenatal development?
3.10   What are the potential adverse effects of tobacco, alcohol, and other drugs on prenatal development?
3.11   What are the risks associated with teratogenic maternal diseases?
3.12   What other maternal factors influence prenatal development?
3.13   How do physicians assess and manage fetal health?
3.14   What kinds of birth choices are available to expectant mothers?
3.15   What happens in each of the three stages of labor?
3.16   What do physicians learn about a newborn from the Apgar and Braselton scales?
3.17   Which infants are categorized as low birth weight and what risks are associated with this?

AS YOU READ . . . TERM IDENTIFICATION

Amnion (p. 66)
Anoxia (p. 84)
Axon (p. 68)
Cell body (p. 67)
Cephalocaudal pattern (p. 64)
Cesarean section (c-section) (p. 82)
Chromosomes (p. 55)
Dendrites (p. 68)
Deoxyribonucleic acid (DNA) (p. 55)
Dominant-recessive pattern (p. 57)
Embryonic stage (p. 66)
Fetal stage (p. 67)
Gametes (p. 55)
Genes (p. 55)
Genotype (p. 57)
Germinal stage (p. 66)
Glial cells (p. 69)

Gonads (p. 55)
Implantation (p. 66)
Low birth weight (LBW) (p. 85)
Multi-factorial inheritance (p. 59)
Neonate (p. 84)
Neurons (p. 66)
Organogenesis (p. 66)
Phenotype (p. 57)
Placenta (p. 66)
Polygenic inheritance (p. 58)
Proximodistal pattern (p. 66)
Synapses (p. 67)
Teratogens (p. 70)
Umbilical cord (p. 66)
Viability (p. 67)
Zygote (p. 55)

AS YOU READ . . . GUIDED STUDY QUESTIONS

CONCEPTION AND GENETICS

The Process of Conception (pp. 55-57)

3.1: What are the characteristics of the zygote?

1.　　Define the following terms:
　　a.　chromosomes (p. 55)

　　b.　gametes (p. 55)

　　c.　zygote (p. 55)

　　d.　deoxyribonucleic acid (DNA) (p. 55)

　　e.　gene (p.)

　　f.　gonads (p. 55)

2.　　Trace the paths of the ovum and the sperm in the process of fertilization.

3. Explain why gametes only have 23 chromosomes.

4. Explain how the sex of a zygote is determined.

5. Distinguish between dizygotic and monozygotic twins.

Fraternal Twins (Dizygotic)	Identical Twins (Monozygotic)

6. Identical twins are always the same sex. Why?

7. List two factors that underlie the association between multiple birth rate and maternal age.

Research Report: Twins in Genetic Research (p. 56)

8. What do twin studies tell us about the impact of environment on development?

How Genes Influence Development (pp. 57-60)

3.2   In what ways do genes influence development?

9. Define the following terms:
    a.   genotype (p. 57)

    b.   phenotype (p. 57)

    c.   dominant-recessive pattern of inheritance (p. 57)

    d.   polygenetic inheritance (p. 58)

    e.   multi-factorial inheritance (p. 59)

10. Distinguish between genotype and phenotype.

Genotype	Phenotype

11.   Distinguish between homozygous and heterozygous.

Homozygous	Heterozygous

12.   Explain how a child's phenotype is influenced by the inheritance of a dominant gene. How does that differ from the inheritance of a recessive gene? Give examples.

13.   Explain the impact of expressivity on phenotypes. Give examples.

14.   Give examples of polygenic traits in which the dominant-recessive pattern is at work.

15.   What is genomic imprinting?

16.   How does mitochondrial inheritance differ from other types of inheritance patterns?

17.   Give an example of multi-factorial inheritance.

18.   List five general principles proposed by Rutter that help explain how genes and the environment work together to produce variations in traits.
    ▪

    ▪

    ▪

    ▪

    ▪

AFTER YOU READ . . . PRACTICE TEST #1
CONCEPTION AND GENETICS

1. Conception typically takes place in the _____.
   a. uterus
   b. womb
   c. fallopian tube
   d. ovary

2. Zygotes containing _____ develop into females.
   a. DNA
   b. one X and one Y chromosome
   c. two X chromosomes
   d. 23 single chromosomes

3. All of the following statements about multiple births are true EXCEPT:
   a. Women who use fertility-enhancing drugs are more likely to have multiple births than a single birth.
   b. Over 75% of twins are monozygotic twins.
   c. Women over age 35 are more likely to conceive twins and other multiples.
   d. The annual number of multiple births has increased in the United States in the past 25 years.

4. People who carry one dominant and one recessive gene are said to be _____.
   a. homozygous
   b. dizygotic
   c. monozygotic
   d. heterozygous

5. The degree to which any gene influences phenotypes varies from person to person. This is called _____.
   a. expressivity
   b. dominance
   c. recessiveness
   d. co-dominant

6. _____ is the pattern of inheritance in which many genes influence a trait.
   a. mitochondrial inheritance
   b. co-dominance
   c. expressivity
   d. polygenic inheritance

7. In _____, children inherit genes that are passed only from the mother to the child.
   a. polygenetic inheritance
   b. mitochondrial inheritance
   c. co-dominance
   d. multi-factorial inheritance

Genetic and Chromosomal Disorders

Genetic Disorders (pp. 60-61)

3.3   What are the effects of the major dominant, recessive, and sex-linked diseases?

19.   Indicate whether each of the following disorders that is caused by the dominant-recessive pattern of inheritance is autosomal or sex-linked, and list the symptoms for the disorder:

Disease	Autosomal or Sex-Linked	Symptoms
Phenylketonuria (PKU)		
Sickle-Cell Disease		
Sickle-Cell Trait		
Tay-Sachs Disease		
Huntington's Disease		
Red-Green Color Blindness		
Hemophilia		
Fragile-X Syndrome		

Chromosomal Error (pp. 61-62)

3.4   How do trisomies and other disorders of the autosomes and sex chromosomes affect development?

20.   Explain how trisomy 21, or Down syndrome, affects development.

21.   Indicate whether the likelihood of each of the following disorders is influenced by the mother's age, and list the symptoms for the disorder:

Disease	Influenced by Mother's Age	Symptoms
Klinefelter's Syndrome (XXY)		
Turner's Syndrome (XO)		
Extra X Chromosome (XXY)		
Extra Y Chromosome (XYY)		

AFTER YOU READ . . . PRACTICE TEST #2
GENETIC AND CHROMOSOMAL DISRODERS

Match the genetic disorder in the right hand column with the examples of disorders in the left column. Some answers will be used more than once.

_____ 1.	Fragile-X syndrome	a. autosomal disorders
_____ 2.	Hemophilia	b. sex-linked disorders
_____ 3.	Huntington's disease	c. trisomies
_____ 4.	Klinefelter's syndrome	d. sex-chromosome anomalies
_____ 5.	Phenylketonuria (PKU)	
_____ 6.	Red-green color blindness	
_____ 7.	Sickle-cell disease	
_____ 8.	Tay-Sachs disease	
_____ 9.	Turner's syndrome	
_____ 10.	XXX pattern	

PREGNANCY AND PRENATAL DEVELOPMENT

The Mother's Experience (pp. 63-64)

3.5   What are the characteristics of each of the trimesters of pregnancy?

22.   Distinguish between pregnancy and prenatal development.

23.   Summarize the events, discomforts, prenatal care needed, and serious problems frequently associated with each trimester of pregnancy.

Trimester Begins/Ends	Events	Discomforts	Prenatal Care	Serious Problems
First				

Trimester Begins/Ends	Events	Discomforts	Prenatal Care	Serious Problems
Second				
Third				

24.   Prenatal care during the first trimester is critical to the prevention of birth defects because _____

_____ .

Prenatal Development (pp. 64-68)

3.6   What happens in each of the stages of pre natal development?

25.   Define the following terms:
   a.   cephalocaudal principle (p. 64)

   b.   proximodistal principle (p. 66)

   c.   germinal stage (p. 66)

   d.   implantation (p. 66)

   e.   placenta (p. 66)

   f.   umbilical cord (p. 66)

   g.   amnion (p. 66)

   h.   embryonic stage (p. 66)

   i.   neurons (p. 66)

   j.   organogenesis (p. 66)

k.   fetal stage (p.)

l.   viability (p. 67)

m.   cell bodies (p. 67)

n.   synapses (p. 67)

o.   axons (p. 68)

p.   dendrites (p. 68)

q.   glial cells (p. 68)

26.   Summarize the major events in each prenatal stage, and indicate when they occur.

Prenatal Stage Begins/Ends	Major Events
Germinal	
Embryonic	
Fetal	

Sex Differences (pp. 68-69)

3.7   *How do male and female fetuses differ?*

27.   Why are there only a few sex differences in prenatal development?

28.   List some of the documented sex differences in prenatal development.

Prenatal Behavior (pp. 69-70)

3.8   *What behaviors have scientists observed in fetuses?*

29.   List some of the documented behaviors of fetuses.

AFTER YOU READ . . . PRACTICE TEST #3
PREGNANCY AND PRENATAL DEVELOPMENT

1. If a zygote implants in the fallopian tubes instead of the uterus, the condition is called _____.
    a. a spontaneous abortion
    b. a miscarriage
    c. morning sickness
    d. an ectopic pregnancy

2. A type of diabetes that happens only during pregnancy is called _____ diabetes.
    a. gestational
    b. vaginal
    c. temporary
    d. pregnancy

3. A sudden increase in blood pressure that can cause a pregnant woman to have a stroke is called _____.
    a. spontaneous abortion
    b. toxemia of pregnancy
    c. morning sickness
    d. ectopic pregnancy

4. _____ is the term for the pattern of growth that proceeds from the head downward.
    a. amniotic pattern
    b. blastocyst pattern
    c. proximodistal pattern
    d. cephalocaudal pattern

5. The brain and the spinal cord develop from the _____.
    a. gonads
    b. glial cells
    c. yolk sac
    d. neural tube

6. The ability of the fetus to live outside the womb is called _____.
    a. organogenesis
    b. viability
    c. engagement
    d. the cephalocaudal pattern

7. Which statement is TRUE about the behavior of fetuses?
    a. Newborns do not remember stimuli to which they were exposed prenatally.
    b. Fetuses can distinguish between familiar and novel stimuli as early as the 20th week.
    c. Prenatal behavior is stable in male fetuses but not in female fetuses.
    d. Fetuses can distinguish between familiar and novel stimuli by the 32nd or 33rd week.

PROBLEMS IN PRENATAL DEVELOPMENT

How Teratogens Influence Development (pp. 70-72)

3.9   *How do teratogens affect prenatal development?*

30.   Define teratogen (p. 70).

31.   Explain why the embryonic and fetal stages are critical periods of development.

Drugs (pp. 72-74)

3.10   *What are the potential adverse effects of tobacco, alcohol, and other drugs on prenatal development?*

32.   List some health conditions of a woman for which she might have to take prescription drugs during her pregnancy.

33.   List symptoms of exposure to each of the following teratogens:

Teratogen	Symptoms
Tobacco	
Drinking Alcohol	

Teratogen	Symptoms
Marijuana	
Heroin	
Cocaine	

Maternal Diseases (pp. 74-75)

3.11 What are the risks associated with teratogenic maternal diseases?

34.   Complete the following table:

Teratogen	When Most Vulnerable?	Symptoms
Rubella		
HIV		
Syphilis		
Genital Herpes		
Gonorrhea		
Cytomegalovirus		

Other Maternal Influences on Prenatal Development (pp. 75-77)

3.12 What other maternal factors influence prenatal development?

35.   Summarize the potential problems to the developing fetus if the mother's diet is inadequate in specific nutrients.

36.   Describe the problems if the mother has insufficient overall calories and protein.

37.   Why is the impact of maternal malnutrition greatest on the developing nervous system? (Hint: consider the principles of development.)

38.   List several problems of the fetus which are associated with the mother's age (over 30 and young teens).

39.   List several problems that are associated with the mother's chronic illness (emotional and physical).

40.   List and describe six environmental hazards to prenatal development.

Environmental Hazard	Description
1.	
2.	
3.	
4.	
5.	
6.	

41.   How are a pregnant woman's hormones related to her psychological state?

Fetal Assessment and Treatment (pp. 77-79)

3.15   How do physicians assess and manage fetal health?

42.   List the assessment tests that can indicate chromosomal errors and many genetic disorders before birth.

Assessment	When Used?	Purpose
Ultrasonography		
Chorionic Villus Sampling (CVS)		
Amniocentesis		
Alpha-Fetoprotein Test		
Fetoscopy		

AFTER YOU READ . . .PRACTICE TEST #4
PROBLEMS IN PRENATAL DEVELOPMENT

1. **All of the following statement about smoking during pregnancy are true EXCEPT:**
   a. Prenatal exposure to tobacco may have long-term effects on children's development.
   b. There may be higher rates of learning problems and anti-social behavior among children whose mothers smoked during pregnancy.
   c. Children of mothers who smoked during pregnancy are more likely than their schoolmates to be diagnosed with attention deficit hyperactivity disorder (ADHD).
   d Infants of mothers who smoke are on average half a pound heavier at birth than infants of nonsmoking mothers.

2. **The most frequently used illegal drug the world over is _____.**
   a. cocaine
   b. heroin
   c. marijuana
   d "crack" cocaine

3. **Which of the following is NOT a sexually transmitted disease that may cause birth defects?**
   a. rubella
   b. syphilis
   c. cytomegalovirus
   d genital herpes

4. **_____ is caused by inadequate amounts of folic acid during prenatal development.**
   a. Brain stunting
   b. Turner's syndrome
   c. Spina bifida
   d Cytomegalovirus

5. **Each of the following may be an environmental hazard on prenatal development EXCEPT:**
   a. mercury
   b. lead
   c. epilepsy
   d parasite-bearing substances

9. **_____ can be used to identify chromosomal errors and many genetic disorders prior to birth.**
   a. Fetoscopy and amniocentesis
   b. Chorionic villus sampling (CVS) and ultrasonography
   c. Ultrasonography and fetoscopy
   d Chorionic villus sampling (CVS) and amniocentesis

BIRTH AND THE NEONATE

Birth Choices (pp. 79-80)

3.14 What kinds of birth choices are available to expectant parents?

43.   Describe four available options for the location of the birth.

Birth Option	Description

44.   Distinguish between certified nurse-midwives and certified midwives.

Certified Nurse Midwife	Certified Midwife

45.   Distinguish among the following drugs that may be used during delivery:

Analgesics	Sedatives or Tranquilizers	Anesthesia

46.   Describe how natural childbirth, such as the Lamaze method, helps women avoid drugs during delivery.

The Physical Process of Birth (pp. 80-84)

3.15   What happens in each of the three stages of labor?

47.   Define the following terms:
   a.   cesarean section (c-section) (p. 82)

   b.   anoxia (p. 84)

48.   List the length of each of the phases of stage 1 of labor, and the major events occurring in that phase.

Phase	Approximate Length	Major Events
Early		
Active		
Transition		

49.   Describe what happens in stage 2 and stage 3 of labor.

Stage	Description
Stage 2	
Stage 3	

50.   List several situations that justify the use of a cesarean section.

51.   List some complications of the process of birth.

Assessing the Neonate (pp. 84-85)

3.16   What do physicians learn about a newborn from the Apgar and Brazelton scales?

52.   Define neonate (p. 84)

53.   Distinguish between the following scales of assessment of the neonate:

Apgar Scale	*Brazelton Neonatal Behavioral Assessment Scale*

The Real World: Parenting: Singing to Your Newborn (p. 83)

54.   List the two categories of infant-directed singing, and give examples of each.
        1.

        2.

55.   List the important contributions of infant-directed singing to babies' development in each of the following areas:
        a.   preterm infants

        b.   language development

        c.   attachment

Low Birth Weight and Preterm Birth (pp. 85-86)

3.17   Which infants are categorized as low birth weight and what risks are associated with this?

56.   Define low birth weight (LBW) (p. 85).

57.   Distinguish between preterm neonates and small-for-date neonates.

Preterm Neonate	*Small-for-Date Neonate*

58.   What are some factors that may impact a low-birth-weight neonate's chances of catching up to his normal peers within the first few years of life?

No Easy Answers: When Do Preterm Infants Catch Up With Full-Term Infants? (p. 85)

59.   Give an example of "corrected age."

60.   List four factors that predict development in preterm infants for many years following birth.
   ▪

   ▪

   ▪

   ▪

61.   How do the parents' responses to the child contribute to how rapidly she develops?

AFTER YOU READ . . . PRACTICE TEST #5
BIRTH AND THE NEONATE

_____ 1.   Often called the Lamaze method.

_____ 2.   Another name for hyaline membrane disease.

_____ 3.   An infant's feet or bottom are delivered first.

_____ 4.   The delivery of the placenta.

_____ 5.   Neonates born before the 38th week of gestation.

_____ 6.   The flattening out of the cervix.

_____ 7.   When given later in labor to block pain.

_____ 8.   The phase of labor during which the last two centimeters of the cervix are dilated.

_____ 9.   Tracks a newborn's development over about the first two weeks following birth.

_____ 10. Oxygen deprivation to the fetus during delivery that can result in death or brain damage.

a. Active phase
b. Afterbirth
c. Analgesics
d. Anesthesia
e. Anoxia
f. Apgar Scale
g. Brazelton Neonatal Behavioral Assessment
h. Breech presentation
i. Dilation
j. Early phase
k. Effacement
l. Low birth weight
m. Natural childbirth
n. Preterm
o. Respiratory distress syndrome
p. Sedatives
q. Small-for-date neonates
r. Transition phase

AFTER YOU READ . . .CRITICAL REFLECTION EXERCISES

Healthy Pregnancies

Imagine you have a friend who has just discovered that she is pregnant. She is taking a lifespan development course, and they are discussing all of the things that can "go wrong" during prenatal development. She is worried that the chances of her baby being born healthy are very slim. Utilizing information from this chapter, answer the following questions from your friend:

1. What things can I do to minimize the risks to my developing baby? (Provide at least four examples for your friend.)

2. What if my baby is born "low birth weight?" Is there anything I can do to minimize the long-term effects of this? (Provide at least three examples for your friend.)

3. How much smoking or drinking can I do while pregnant? Is there a "critical period" during which the effects of these would be most harmful?

Genotype Versus Phenotype

Utilizing the information from the text, match the appropriate statements as to whether they illustrate "Genotype," "Phenotype," or the "Interaction" between genotype and the environment. You may use each answer more than once.

_____   1.   The observed characteristics of the person.

_____   2.   The genetic material received from the mother and father.

_____   3.   Observable sexual characteristics.

_____   4.   Developmental limits.

_____   5.   Developmental patterns within developmental limits.

_____   6.   Eye color.

_____   7.   Measured intelligence.

AFTER YOU READ . . . COMPREHENSIVE PRACTICE TEST
MULTIPLE CHOICE QUESTIONS

1. **Conception occurs when _____.**
    a.   the zygote implants in the uterine wall
    b.   a sperm penetrates an ovum
    c.   an ovum is released from the ovary
    d.   gametes are produced

2. **The unique genetic blueprint from the mother and the father that characterizes a specific individual is called a_____.**
    a.   phenotype
    b.   chromosome
    c.   gamete
    d.   genotype

3. **Which statement is true about recessive genes?**
    a.   They are not a part of one's genotype.
    b.   They can be passed on genetically.
    c.   They are related only to physical characteristics.
    d.   They are related to inherited diseases.

4. **Which of the following is NOT one of the general principles proposed by Rutter about multi-factorial inheritance?**
    a.   People act on their environment so as to shape and select their experience.
    b.   The interplay between persons and their environments needs to be considered within an ecological framework.
    c.   People are passive recipients of environmental forces.
    d.   Individuals differ in their reactivity to the environment.

5. **_____ is a serious sex-linked recessive disorder.**
    a.   Hemophilia
    b.   Klinefelter's syndrome
    c.   Trisomy-21
    d.   Huntington's disease

6. **An anomaly in which a girl receives only one X chromosome and no Y chromosome is called _____.**
    a.   Klinefelter's syndrome
    b.   Turner's syndrome
    c.   fragile-X syndrome
    d.   Tay-Sachs disease

7. **Which of the following statements about pregnancy is true?**
    a.   Pregnancy is a physical condition in which a woman's body is nurturing a developing embryo or fetus.
    b.   Pregnancy is the process that transforms a zygote into a newborn.
    c.   Pregnancy is divided into three stages that are defined by specific developmental milestones.
    d.   Pregnancy begins when ovulation occurs.

8.   **The three stages of prenatal development, in order, are _____.**
    a.   germinal, embryonic, fetal
    b.   viability, organogenesis, germinal
    c.   embryonic, fetal, viability
    d.   embryonic, germinal, fetal

9.   **Which statement most accurately represents the sex differences in prenatal development?**
    a.   There are numerous sex differences in prenatal development.
    b.   Female fetuses are more active than male fetuses.
    c.   There are only a few sex differences in prenatal development.
    d.   Male fetuses are more sensitive to external stimuli than female fetuses.

10.   **Which of the following diseases is most likely to cause damage to the embryo or fetus early in prenatal development?**
    a.   syphilis
    b.   gonorrhea
    c.   rubella
    d.   cytomegalovirus

11.   **At what age does the risk for complications in pregnancy increase significantly?**
    a.   25
    b.   30
    c.   35
    d.   40

12.   **Which of the following medication is sometimes used during the transition period or the second stage of labor to block pain?**
    a.   analgesic
    b.   sedative
    c.   anesthesia
    d.   tranquilizer

13.   **During which stage of labor will the actual delivery take place?**
    a.   second
    b.   transition
    c.   third
    d.   first

14.   **Which of the following is used immediately after birth to assess the neonate's health?**
    a.   Brazelton Neonatal Behavioral Assessment Scale
    b.   chorionic villus sampling
    c.   Apgar scale
    d.   alpha-fetoprotein sampling

15.   **Which statement is true about low-birth-weight babies?**
    a.   Low-birth-weight girls are more likely to show long-term effects than boys.
    b.   Low-birth-weight infants show markedly lower levels of responsiveness.
    c.   Most low-birth-weight babies never catch up to their normal peers.
    d.   Low-birth-weight is not related to the neonate's health.

TRUE-FALSE QUESTIONS

_____ 1. Monozygotic twins will always be the same sex.

_____ 2. The implications of genomic imprinting will be different if the defective gene is from the father or from the mother.

_____ 3. The most common trisomy is trisomy 21, or Down syndrome.

_____ 4. Problems resulting from fetal alcohol syndrome seldom persist past infancy.

_____ 5. The technical term for organ development is organogenesis.

_____ 6. Most experts accept 23 weeks as the average age of viability.

_____ 7. Anoxia can result in death or brain damage.

_____ 8. It is impossible for an infant to have completed 38 weeks or more of gestation and still be a low-birth-weight baby.

ESSAY QUESTIONS

1. Explain why it is important for women to begin receiving prenatal care during the first trimester.

2. List at least four different kinds of teratogens and describe the effect they may have on prenatal development.

3. Describe and give examples of the problems caused when an infant is a low-birth-weight baby.

WHEN YOU HAVE FINISHED . . . PUZZLE IT OUT

Across

6. Strings of genetic material
7. Cells that unite at conception
8. Process of organ development
11. Second stage of prenatal development
13. Third stage of prenatal development
15. First stage of prenatal development
16. Single cell created when sperm and ovum unite
17. The unique genetic blueprint of each individual

Down

1. Fluid-filled sac in which the fetus floats
2. Growth from the head downward
3. Term for a baby between birth and one month of age
4. Growth from the middle of the body outward
5. Pieces of genetic material that influence traits
9. Oxygen deprivation experienced by a fetus
10. Ability of the fetus to survive outside the womb
12. Substances that can cause birth defects
14. Observed characteristics of an individual

Created by Puzzlemaker at DiscoverySchool.com

WHEN YOU HAVE FINISHED . . . INVESTIGATIVE PROJECT

Student Project 4: Available Prenatal Services

Basic Questions to Answer

The purpose of the project is to discover what kinds of prenatal services are available to poor mothers in your area.

- What programs are available through the public health service, local hospitals, or other clinics?

- What funds are available to support those services from local, state, and federal sources?

- How many women take advantage of such services? Is there a waiting list? Is there any information available about the percentage of local women who receive no prenatal care at all, or receive such care only in the final trimester?

- Has there been any change in the availability of such services in your area in the past decade or two? (This may be difficult to determine, but it is worth a try.)

- What is the infant mortality rate for your state, and for your community? How does this compare to national statistics?

Sources

Some of the statistics may be available through the federal document center at the library. The annual volume, *Statistical Abstract of the United States*, normally has state-by-state figures on infant mortality; more detail may be available through data from the Centers for Disease Control. The December issue of the journal *Pediatrics* also has a summary paper each year. Most states have departments of vital statistics that may be helpful.

For local information, try the city, county, or state public health departments. The Yellow Pages of your local phone book is a good place to start. A visit to the offices of the local public health department is likely to be fruitful. You should of course explain that this is part of a class project, and that you wish to be able to report back to your class.

WHEN YOU HAVE FINISHED . . . INVESTIGATIVE PROJECT

Student Project 5: Investigation of Birth Options

Basic Questions to Answer

- How many of the four main choices of birth options (regular hospital, hospital-based birth center or birthing room, free-standing birthing center, or home delivery) are available in your area? When did non-hospital delivery become available in your area?

- How are the local births distributed among the options?

- What is the relative cost of each option?

- Who sponsors or runs each program? Are the deliveries in the birth center or at home done by midwives? Do midwives deliver babies at hospitals as well?

Sources of Information

The Yellow Pages may be your best first source. If that does not yield information, you might make inquiries of several local obstetricians' offices. You will then need to call hospitals, birthing centers, and midwives for further information, or visit each site to get a firsthand look, and to obtain brochures, etc. At all times you should represent yourself accurately as a student working on a project for a class on human development. Do not present yourself as a pregnant woman looking for a place to deliver. Remember always that your questions may be seen as an intrusion on the busy work days of your respondents, so be sensitive to the demands you are placing on them.

Reporting

Your instructor may want you to report back to the class on your findings, either orally or in writing. In any case, you should prepare a written report of what you did, to whom you talked, and what you found out.

CHAPTER 3 ANSWER KEY

Practice Test #1 Conception and Genetics

1. c   2. c   3. b   4. d   5. a   6. d   7. b

Practice Test #2 Genetic and Chromosomal Disorders

1. b   2. b   3. a   4. d   5. a   6. b   7. a   8. a   9. d   10. d

Practice Test #3 Pregnancy and Prenatal Development

1. d   2. a   3. b   4. d   5. d   6. b   7. d

Practice Test #4 Problems in Prenatal Development

1. d   2. c   3. a   4. c   5. c   6. d

Practice Test #5 Birth and the Neonate

1. m   2. o   3. h   4. b   5. n   6. k   7. d   8. r   9. g   10. e

Critical Reflection Exercise: Genotype Versus Phenotype

1. Phenotype   2. Genotype   3. Phenotype   4. Genotype   5. Interaction
6. Genotype   7. Interaction

Comprehensive Practice Test

Multiple Choice Questions

1. b   2. d   3. b   4. c   5. b   6. b   7. a   8. a   9. c   10. c
11. c   12. c   13. a   14. c b   15. b

True-False Questions

1. T   2. T   3. T   4. F   5. T   6. F   7. T   8. F

Essay Questions

1.
   - Identification of maternal conditions that may prevent birth defects.
   - Encouragement by doctors and nurses to abstain from drugs and alcohol early in prenatal development, when such behavior may prevent birth defects.
   - Protection of the woman's health by identification of potential problems, such as ectopic pregnancy.

2.
   - Autosomal disorders: phenylketonuria (PKU), sickle-cell disease, sickle-cell trait, Tay-Sachs disease, Huntington's disease.
   - Sex-linked disorders: red-green color blindness, hemophilia, fragile-X syndrome.
   - Trimosies: trisomy 21 (Down syndrome).
   - Sex-chromosome anomalies: Klinefelter's syndrome, Turner's syndrome, XXX pattern, XYY pattern.
   - Maternal Disease: rubella, HIV/AIDS, syphilis, genital herpes, gonorrhea, cytomegalovirus.
   - Drugs: smoking tobacco, drinking alcohol (including fetal alcohol syndrome), marijuana, heroin, cocaine.
   - Other Maternal Influences: diet, age, chronic illness, environmental hazards, maternal emotions.

3.
- Retarded fetal growth.
- Lower levels of responsiveness at birth and in the early months of life.
- Respiratory distress syndrome (or hyaline membrane disease) and other breathing problems.

Puzzle It Out

Across
6. Chromosome
7. Gametes
8. Organogenesis
11. Embryonic
13. Fetal
15. Germinal
16. Zygote
17. Genotype

Down
1. Amnion
2. Cephalocaudal
3. Neonate
4. Proximodistal
5. Genes
9. Anoxia
10. Viability
12. Teratogens
14. Phenotype

SHOULD PREGNANT WOMEN WHO USE ILLICIT DRUGS BE PROSECUTED?

Learning Objective: Summarize the issues about prosecuting pregnant women who use drugs (pp. 82-83).

1. Define the following terms:
   a. delivering drugs to a minor
   b. injury to a child

2. Specify the issues involved in determining whether a fetus can be considered legally equivalent to a child.

3. What fairness issues are involved in the controversy?

4. What are the questions involved with determining the kind of evidence that is required?

5. What problems are incurred if doctors are required to report drug use by their pregnant patients?

6. Describe three alternatives to prosecution.

7. Policies addressing drug use during pregnancy are different in every state. What are the relevant government and institutional policies in your area? Research could include answering the following questions:
   a. Do hospitals in your area routinely test newborns for drug exposure? If so, how?

   b. What do doctors in your area do when they suspect a baby's problems are caused by prenatal drug exposure?

   c. Does your state require doctors to report pregnant women who use drugs to the police or state agency?

   d. Are there drug rehabilitation programs specifically for pregnant women in your area?

   e. Has your state prosecuted any women for using drugs while pregnant? What were the details of the case(s)?

   f. Do you agree or disagree with the way this issue is addressed in your state and city? Why?

CHAPTER 4

PHYSICAL, SENSORY, AND PERCEPTUAL DEVELOPMENT IN INFANCY

BEFORE YOU READ . . . CHAPTER SUMMARY

During the first two years after birth, infants go from being relatively unskilled newborns to toddlers who can move about efficiently, formulate goals and plans, and use words. There are also many important developmental variations across individuals and groups.

Physical Changes

- At birth, the midbrain and the medulla are the most fully developed structures of the brain. Changes in the nervous system in the first two years include dendrite and synaptic development, the "pruning" of synapses, and myelinization of the nerve fibers.
- Adaptive reflexes, such as sucking, help infants survive; primitive reflexes, such as the Moro or startle reflex and the Babinski reflex, disappear in about six months. Neonates move through five states of consciousness in a cycle that lasts about two hours.
- The acquisition of motor skills depends on brain development as well as substantial changes in other body systems, such as the bones, the muscles, the lungs, and the heart.

Health and Wellness

- Babies depend on the adults in their environments to help them stay healthy. They need the right foods in the right amounts.
- Malnutrition in infancy can seriously impair a baby's brain because the nervous system is the most rapidly developing body system during the first two years.
- Infants need medical care and immunizations to protect them from a variety of diseases.

Infant Mortality

- Death within the first year after birth is defined as infant mortality. Sudden infant death syndrome (SIDS) is the most common cause of death in the first year.
- The infant mortality rate in the United States is highest for African-American and Native-American babies. The relationship between poverty and infant mortality is complex.

Sensory Skills

- Visual acuity and visual tracking skills are relatively poor at birth, but develop rapidly in the first few months.
- Hearing skills, smell, taste, and touch are well-developed at birth.

Perceptual Skills

- The preference technique, habituation, and dishabituation are used to study perceptual development.

- Depth perception is present in at least rudimentary form by three months. The "looking" strategies of newborns seem to be focused on locating objects; after about two months, their focus changes to identifying objects.
- Babies appear to attend to and discriminate among speech contrasts present in all possible languages. Babies also attend to and discriminate among different patterns of sounds, such as melodies or speech inflections.
- Intermodal perception is the formation of a single perception of a stimulus that is based on information from two or more senses.
- The nativist/empiricism controversy is a central issue in the study of perceptual development.

AS YOU READ . . . LEARNING OBJECTIVES

After completing Chapter 4, you should be able to answer the following questions:

4.1   What important changes in the brain take place during infancy?
4.2   How do babies' reflexes and behavioral states change?
4.3   How do infants' bodies change, and what is the typical pattern of motor skills development in the first 2 years?
4.4   What are the nutritional needs of infants?
4.5   How does malnutrition affect infants' development?
4.6   What are infants' health care and immunization needs?
4.7   What have researchers learned about sudden infant death syndrome?
4.8   How do infant mortality rates vary across groups?
4.9   How do infants' visual abilities change across the first months of life?
4.10   How do infants' senses of hearing, smell, taste, touch, and motion compare to those of older children and adults?
4.11   How do researchers study perceptual development?
4.12   How do depth perception and patterns of looking change over the first two years?
4.13   How do infants perceive human speech, recognize voices, and recognize sound patterns other than speech?
4.14   What is intermodal perception?
4.15   What arguments do nativists and empiricists offer in support of their theories of perceptual development?

AS YOU READ . . . TERM IDENTIFICATION

Adaptive reflexes (p. 99)
Auditory acuity (p. 108)
Colic (p. 100)
Dishabituation (p. 109)
Dynamic systems theory (p. 101)
Empiricists (p. 113)
Habituation (p. 109)
Infant mortality (p. 104)

Intermodal perception (p. 113)
Myelinization (p. 98)
Nativists (p. 113)
Plasticity (p. 96)
Preference technique (p. 109)
Primitive reflexes (p. 99)
Pruning (p. 96)
Reticular formation (p. 98)

Sudden infant death syndrome
  (SIDS) (p. 105)
Synapses (p. 96)
Synaptogenesis (p. 96)
Tracking (p. 107)
Visual acuity (p. 107)

AS YOU READ . . . GUIDED STUDY QUESTIONS

PHYSICAL CHANGES

The Real World: A Day in the Life of a Baby? (p. 97)

1.   Summarize the typical daily activities of a six-month-old baby.

The Brain and the Nervous System (pp. 96-98)

4.1   *What important changes in the brain take place during infancy?*

2.   What do the midbrain and the medulla regulate?

3.   The least-developed part of the brain at birth is the _____, the convoluted gray matter that wraps around the midbrain and is involved in _____.

4.   Define the following terms:
        a.   synapses (p. 96)

        b.   synaptogenesis (p. 96)

        c.   pruning (p. 96)

        d.   plasticity (p. 96)

5.   Describe the pattern of brain development (creation of synapses and pruning).

6.   Define the following terms:
        a.   myelinization (p. 96)

        b.   reticular formation (p. 96)

7.   The sequence of myelinization follows both _____ and _____ patterns.

Development in the Information Age: Is Television Harmful to the Developing Brain? (p. 98)

8.   List possible flaws in the research about the relationship between television watching and ADHD (attention-deficit hyperactivity disorder).

Reflexes and Behavioral States (pp. 98-99)

4.2   How do babies' reflexes and behavioral states change?

9.   Define the following terms:
        a.   adaptive reflexes (p. 99)

        b.   primitive reflexes (p. 99)

10.   Give examples of the two types of reflexes.

Type of Reflex	Example
Adaptive Reflexes	
Primitive Reflexes	

11.   Weak or absent adaptive reflexes in neonates suggest that _____.

12.   Define colic (p. 100).

13.   List the states of consciousness.
▪

▪

▪

▪

▪

14.   Research suggests that prompt attention to a crying baby in the first three months actually leads to

_____.

Growth, Motor Skills,, and Developing Body Systems (pp. 100-102)

4.3   How do infants' bodies change, and what is the typical pattern of motor skill development in the first 2 years?

15.   Describe growth during the first two years after birth.

16.   Distinguish between gross motor skills and fine motor skills by giving an example of each.

Type of Motor Skill	Example
Gross Motor Skills	
Fine Motor Skills	

17.   What are the gender differences in motor skill development?

18.   Despite gender differences in the rate of physical development, the _____ of motor skill development is virtually the same for all children.

19.   Define dynamic systems theory (p. 101).

20.   Explain how experience influences motor development.

21.   How do bones change during infancy?

22.   Explain how motor development is dependent on ossification.

23.   Describe the changes in muscle composition during infancy.

24.   How is stamina related to the lungs and heart?

AFTER YOU READ . . . PRACTICE TEST #1
PHYSICAL CHANGES

1. **The connections between neurons are called _____.**
    a.   synapses
    b.   pruning
    c.   glial cells
    d.   myelin sheaths

2. **What is "pruning" as it relates to development?**
    a.   a surgical technique for compensating for brain damage
    b.   elimination of redundant neural pathways
    c.   slowly easing the child off of the bottle and onto solid food
    d.   a surgery that may alleviate epileptic seizures

3. **Reflexes such as sucking are called _____.**
    a.   states of consciousness
    b.   primitive reflexes
    c.   adaptive reflexes
    d.   neurological reflexes

4. **The typical sequence of the infant's behavioral states is _____.**
    a.   deep sleep, crying and fussing, lighter sleep, and quiet awake
    b.   light sleep, deep sleep, crying and fussing, active awake, quiet awake
    c.   active awake, quiet awake, quiet sleep, crying and fussing
    d.   deep sleep, lighter sleep, alert wakefulness, and fussing

5. **_____ are also called fine motor skills.**
    a.   Manipulative skills
    b.   Locomotor skills
    c.   Nonlocomotor skills
    d.   Gross motor skills

6. **The process of bone hardening is called _____.**
    a.   the proximodistal pattern
    b.   locomotor skills
    c.   stamina
    d.   ossification

HEALTH AND WELLNESS

Nutrition (pp. 102-104)

4.4 What are the nutritional needs of infants?

25.   What are the benefits of breast milk over bottle-feeding?

26.   Describe some special circumstances in which breast milk may need to be supplemented or replaced?

Malnutrition (pp. 103-104)

4.5 How does malnutrition affect infants' development?

27.   How can malnutrition in infancy impair an infant's brain?
28.   Define the following terms and describe how each is harmful to children:

Nutritional Problem	Definition	Potential Harm to Child
Macronutrient Malnutrition		
Marasmus		
Kwashikor		
Micronutrient Malnutrition		

Health Care and Immunizations (p. 104)

4.6 What are infants' health care and immunization needs?

29.   How can the timing of respiratory infections that lead to ear infections be important?

30.   List the immunizations included in a "full set."

AFTER YOU READ . . . PRACTICE TEST #2
HEALTH AND WELLNESS

Indicate whether each of the following statements is true or false.

_____ 1. For most infants, breastfeeding is substantially superior nutritionally to bottle-feeding.

_____ 2. On average, breastfed infants are more likely to suffer from such problems as diarrhea, gastroenteritis, bronchitis, ear infections, and colic.

_____ 3. There are situations in which breast milk is not sufficient to meet babies nutritional needs.

_____ 4. There is strong evidence to support the belief that solid food encourages babies to sleep through the night.

_____ 5. Micronutrient malnutrition results from a diet that contains too few calories.

_____ 6. When the calorie deficit is severe, a disease called marasmus results.

_____ 7. One of the most important elements of well baby care is vaccination of the infant against a variety of diseases.

_____ 8. In the U.S., the average baby has seven respiratory illnesses in the first year of life.

INFANT MORTALITY

Sudden Infant Death Syndrome (SIDS) (p. 105)

4.7   What have researchers learned about sudden infant death syndrome?

31.   Define the following terms:
       a.   infant mortality (p. 104)

       b.   sudden infant death syndrome (SIDS) (p. 105)

32.   List some of the evidence or recommendations physicians have found as to the causes of SIDS.

Contributor	Evidence or Recommendation
Season of the Year	
Apnea	
Sleeping Position	
Smoking in the Home	
Delayed Brain Maturation	

Group Differences in Infant Mortality (pp. 105-106)

4.8   ***How do infant mortality rates vary across groups?***

33.   Discuss the factors related to group differences in infant mortality.

AFTER YOU READ . . . PRACTICE TEST #3
INFANT MORTALITY

Indicate whether each of the following statements is true or false.

_____ 1.   Researchers formally define infant mortality as death within the first year after birth.

_____ 2.   The U.S. consistently has a lower infant mortality than other industrialized nations.

_____ 3.   Babies with a history of apnea are less likely to die from SIDS.

_____ 4.   Smoking by the mother during pregnancy is an important contributor to SIDS.
_____ 5.   Myelinization progresses at a slower rate in children who display apnea in the early days of life.
_____ 6.   The link between poverty and infant mortality is clear cut and simple.

_____ 7.   Access to prenatal care is a factor that distinguishes ethnic groups in the U.S. in regards to infant mortality.
_____ 8.   Mortality rates among the babies of immigrants of all groups are lower than those of U.S.-born infants.

SENSORY SKILLS

Vision (p. 107)

4.9   ***How do infants' abilities change across the first months of life?***

34.   Define the following terms:
a.   visual acuity (p. 107)

b.   tracking (p. 107)

35.   Describe the changes in an infant's visual acuity during the first two years after birth.

36.   Describe infants' ability to sense color.

37.   Why is "tracking" an important skill for infants to develop?

Hearing and Other Senses (p. 108)

4.10   How do infants' senses of hearing, smell, taste, and motion compare to those of older children and adults?

38.   Define auditory acuity (p. 108).

39.   How does the auditory acuity of an infant compare to that of an adult?

40.   Describe how the ability to determine the location of a sound develops during infancy.

41.   Summarize the development of the following senses by completing the table.

Sense	Summary of Development in Infancy
Smell	
Taste	
Touch	
Motion	

AFTER YOU READ . . . PRACTICE TEST #4
SENSORY SKILLS

Indicate whether each of the following statements is true or false.

_____ 1. Newborns and young infants have far more sensory capacity than physicians or psychologists thought.

_____ 2. Most children reach the level of 20/20 vision by about two years of age.

_____ 3. The types of cells in the eyes are necessary for perceiving red and green are not present in infants until six months after birth.

_____ 4. Infants younger than two months show some tracking for brief periods if the target is moving slowly.

_____ 5. Children's hearing improves up to adolescence.

_____ 6. Because your two ears are separated from one another, sounds arrive at one ear slightly before the other, which allows you to judge location.

_____ 7. In infants, the sense of smell and taste are not related to each other.

_____ 8. Reflexes related to feeding are associated with the sense of touch.

PERCEPTUAL SKILLS

Studying Perceptual Development (p. 109)

4.11 How do researchers study perceptual development?

42. Define the following terms:
    a. preference technique (p. 109)

    b. habituation (p. 109)

    c. dishabituation (p. 109)

43. Give an example of each of the three methods for studying perceptual development.

Method	Example
Preference Technique	
Habituation/Dishabituation	
Operant Conditioning	

Looking (pp. 110-112)

4.12   How do depth perception and patterns of looking change over the first two years?

44.   Why does an infant need depth perception?

45.   Distinguish among the three kinds information that may be used to judge depth.

Binocular	*Monocular*	*Linear Perception*

46.   Describe how depth perception develops.

47.   Trace the development of what babies look at in the first few months, including faces.

Research Report: Langlois's Studies of Babies' Preferences for Attractive Faces (p. 111)

48.   What were the results of Langlois' study of babies' preferences for attractive faces?

Listening (p. 112)

4.13   How do infants perceive human speech, recognize voices, and recognize sound patterns other than speech?

49.   Describe how infants develop abilities to discriminate speech sounds, including individual voices.

50.   Describe the evidence that infants pay attention to patterns or sequences of sounds.

51.   Describe infants' abilities to discriminate between individual voices.

Combining Information from Several Senses (pp. 112-113)

4.14   What is intermodal perception?

52.   Define intermodal perception (p. 113).

53.   Trace the development of infants; intermodal perception.

Explaining Perceptual Development (pp. 113-114)

4.15   What arguments do nativists and empiricists offer in support of their theories of perceptual development?

54.   Define the following terms:
    a.   nativists (p. 113)

    b.   empiricists (p. 113)

55.   State the arguments for nativism.

56.   State the arguments for empiricism.

57.   State the arguments for the interactionist position.

AFTER YOU READ . . . PRACTICE TEST #5: PERCEPTUAL SKILLS

1. **Responding to a familiar stimulus as if it is new is called _____.**
   a. dishabituation
   b. interposition
   c. intersensory integration
   d. habituation

2. **Pictorial information, sometimes called _____, requires input from only one eye.**
   a. linear perspective
   b. binocular cues
   c. monocular cues
   d. kinetic cues

3. **If you move your head, objects near you seem to move more than objects further away, a phenomenon called _____.**
   a. linear perspective
   b. motion parallax
   c. monocular cues
   d. binocular cues

4. **A baby's visual attention is guided by a search for meaningful patterns _____.**
   a. in the first two months
   b. between two and three months
   c. between four and six months
   d. after six months

5. **Before two months, babies seem to look mostly at _____.**
   a. a person's mouth
   b. a person's eyes
   c. the internal part of a face
   d. the edges of faces

6. **By age _____, a baby's ability to discriminate non-heard consonant contrasts begins to fade**
   a. one year
   b. six months
   c. three months
   d. two months

7. **The transfer of information from one sense to another is called _____.**
   a. intersensory perception
   b. motion parallax
   c. intermodal perception
   d. habituation

8. **_____ argue that perceptual skills are learned.**
   a. Interactionists
   b. Nativists
   c. Habituationists
   d. Empiricists

AFTER YOU READ . . . CRITICAL REFLECTION EXERCISES

What Babies Do

1.   How would you respond to the following comment from a student colleague? "Babies drive me nuts; all they can do is eat and sleep. They can't do anything for themselves."

2.   Your friend has a 10-month-old girl whom she is trying to get to feed herself. She is expressing her frustration to you because her daughter keeps throwing her food utensils on the floor. Explain to her why her child might be doing this. What suggestions would you have for how your friend can encourage the child to learn, yet keep the floor clean?

3.   How could you design a study to see if an infant remembers a toy she saw an hour ago?

Advice for Young Parents

Imagine that you are a Social Worker. You have been assigned the following case. Sara and her husband Jim are both seventeen. They are the proud parents of Katie, a four-month-old daughter. Sara and Jim do not have much money, but they are interested in providing as well as possible for their girl. Utilizing information from the chapter, give at least five pieces of advice to these young parents. For each piece of advice you give, cite specific information from the textbook to support that advice.

AFTER YOU READ . . . COMPREHENSIVE PRACTICE TEST
MULTIPLE CHOICE QUESTIONS

1. **The part of the newborn brain that is the LEAST developed is the _____.**
   a. brainstem
   b. hypothalamus
   c. cortex
   d. thyroid

2. **Neurons that are insulated with the myelin sheath _____.**
   a. cannot form new neural connections
   b. can conduct the neural impulse faster
   c. become nerve muscle cells
   d. become rigid and less efficient

3. **If an infant's primitive reflexes do not disappear by around six months of age, _____.**
   a. we might suspect a neurological problem
   b. there is nothing to worry about since they never disappear
   c. the infant is more likely to be a boy since boys mature more slowly
   d. it means the infant is not getting enough intellectual stimulation

4. **The ability to maintain activity is called _____.**
   a. nativism
   b. auditory acuity
   c. cross-modal transfer
   d. stamina

5. **Which of the following statements about infant nutrition is true?**
   a. Viruses cannot be transmitted through breast milk.
   b. Babies need solid foods to supplement breast milk or formula beginning at two months of age.
   c. Breast milk provides important antibodies for the infant against many kinds of diseases.
   d. Solid foods encourage babies to sleep through the night.

6. **When an infant's diet contains almost enough calories, but not enough protein, it may lead to _____.**
   a. micronutrient malnutrition
   b. macronutrient malnutrition
   c. marasmus
   d. kwashikor

7. **Infants _____ are more likely than their peers to have learning disabilities and language deficits during the school years.**
   a. who have been exposed to measles
   b. who have chronic ear infections
   c. who have not had flu shots
   d. who attend day care

8.   **The leading cause of death between one month and one year of age is _____.**
   a.   ossification
   b.   micronutrient malnutrition
   c.   sudden infant death syndrome
   d.   habituation

9.   **The ability to see details at a distance is called _____.**
   a.   visual acuity
   b.   dishabituation
   c.   myelinization
   d.   auditory acuity

10.   **Each of the following is one of the four basic tastes registered by the tongue EXCEPT _____.**
   a.   salty
   b.   bland
   c.   sweet
   d.   bitter

11   **Babies appear to be especially sensitive to touches on each of the following EXCEPT:**
   a.   the abdomen
   b.   the soles of the feet
   c.   the face
   d.   the legs

12.   **Which of the following correctly illustrates the concept of habituation?"**
   a.   learning habits simply by being exposed to them
   b.   no longer noticing a ticking clock after a few moments of exposure
   c.   hearing someone whisper your name across a loud and crowded room
   d.   learning how to categorize information into schemes through practice

13.   **Each of the following is a possible way to judge depth EXCEPT _____.**
   a.   binocular cues
   b.   pictorial information
   c.   habituation
   d.   kinetic cues

14.   **Babies seem to prefer the mother's face _____.**
   a.   from the earliest hours of life
   b.   from one month after birth
   c.   from three months after birth
   d.   from six months after birth

15.   **Empirical findings show that intermodal perception is possible as early as _____ and becomes common by _____.**
   a.   three months; one year
   b.   six months; one year
   c.   one month; nine months
   d.   one month; six months

TRUE-FALSE QUESTIONS

_____ 1. The reticular formation is the part of the brain responsible for keeping your attention on what you are doing and for helping you sort out important and unimportant information.

_____ 2. Sixty to eighty percent of infants develop colic.

_____ 3. One of the most important elements of well baby care is vaccination of the infant against a variety of diseases.

_____ 4. Infant mortality rates vary little across groups in the U.S.

_____ 5. Infants' ability to sense color, even in the earliest weeks after birth, is almost identical to that of adults.

_____ 6. Newborns' auditory acuity is better than their visual acuity.

_____ 7. The preference is used to keep track of how long a baby listen to each pattern of sounds.

_____ 8. Newborns are unable to tell their mother's voice from another female voice.

ESSAY QUESTIONS

1. Discuss the relationship between brain development and good nutrition for infants.

2. How is visual acuity related to synaptogenesis, pruning, and myelinization?

3. Discuss the relationship between the fading of infants' ability to discriminate non-heard consonant contrasts and synaptogenesis and pruning.

WHEN YOU HAVE FINISHED . . . PUZZLE IT OUT

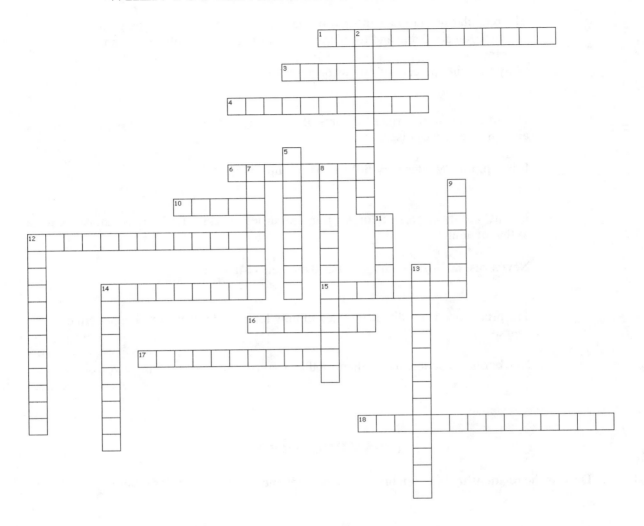

Across
1. The sheaths of axons are covered/ insulated
3. Connections between neurons
4. Disease resulting from insufficient protein
6. Disease resulting from severe calorie deficiency
10. Brief periods when breathing stops
12. Malnutrition from deficiency of certain vitamins or minerals
14. Reflexes that disappear during the first year after birth
15. Visually following a moving object
16. The ability to maintain activity
17. Decline in attention to a familiar stimulus
18. The process of synapse development

Down
2. Claim that perceptual abilities are learned
5. Claim that perceptual abilities are inborn
7. Reflexes such as sucking
8. Malnutrition resulting from a diet with too few calories
9. The process of eliminating unused synapses
11. Intense daily bouts of crying
12. Also called fine motor skills
13. Responding to a familiar stimulus as if new
14. The ability of the brain to change in response to experience

Created by Puzzlemaker at DiscoverySchool.com

WHEN YOU HAVE FINISHED . . . RESEARCH PROJECT

Student Project 6: Observation In A Newborn Nursery

You can get a feeling for what newborn babies are like, as well as learn something about observational techniques, by arranging to visit a newborn nursery in a local hospital. Your instructor will have made arrangements with one or more hospitals for permission for such observations. You will need to sign up for a specific observation time.

At all times, remember that newborn nurseries are complex, busy, and they cannot tolerate lots of questions or extra getting in the way. So be unobtrusive, non-demanding, and do what you are told.

Procedure

Position yourself at one side of the window outside the newborn nursery, leaving room at the window for others to see their newborns. From this vantage point, observe one baby for approximately half an hour. Proceed in the following way:

BABY'S STATES

30-second intervals	Deep Sleep	Active Sleep	Quiet Awake	Active Awake	Crying & Fussing
1					
2					
3					

1.   Set up a score sheet that looks something like the one shown above, continuing the list for sixty 30-second intervals.

2.   Reread the material in Table 4.2 in the text until you know the main features of the five states as well as possible. You will need to focus on the eyes (open versus closed, rapid eye movement), the regularity of the baby's breathing, and the amount of body movement.

3.   Select an infant in the nursery and observe that infant's state every 30 seconds for half an hour. For each 30-second interval, note on your score sheet the state that best describes the infant over the proceeding 30 seconds. Do not select an infant to observe who is in deep sleep at the beginning. Pick an infant who seems to be in an in-between state (active sleep or quiet awake), so that you can see some variation over the half hour observation.

4.   If you can arrange it, you might do this observation with a partner, each of you scoring the same infant's state independently. When the half hour is over, compare notes. How often did you agree on the infant's state? What might have been producing the disagreements?

5.   When you discuss or write about the project, consider the following issues: Did the infant appear to have cycles of states? What were they? What effect, if any, do you think the nursery environment might have had on the baby's state? If you worked with a partner, how much agreement or disagreement did you have? Why?

You may find yourself approached by family members of the babies in the nursery, asking what you are doing, why you have a clipboard and a stopwatch. Be sure to reassure the parents or grandparents that your presence does not in any way suggest that there is anything wrong with any of the babies. Let them know that you are doing a school project on observation. You may even want to show them the text describing the various states.

Alternate Project

The same project can be completed in a home setting with any infant under one or two months of age, with appropriate permission obtained from the baby's parents. You should observe the infant when he or she is lying in a crib or another sleeping location where it is possible for the child to move fairly freely (an infant seat won't do, nor will a baby carrier of any kind).

CHAPTER 4 ANSWER KEY

Practice Test #1 Physical Changes

1. a   2. b   3. c   4. d   5. a   6. d

Practice Test #2 Health and Wellness

1. T   2. F   3. T   4. F   5. F   6. T   7. T   8. T

Practice Test #3 Infant Mortality

1. T   2. F   3. F   4. T   5. T   6. F   7. T   8. T

Practice Test #4 Sensory Skills

1. T   2. T   3. F   4. T   5. T   6. T   7. F   8. T

Practice Test #5 Perceptual Skills

1. a   2. c   3. b   4. a   5. d   6. a   7. c   8. d

Comprehensive Practice Test

Multiple Choice Questions

1. c   2. b   3. a   4. d   5. c   6. d   7. b   8. c   9. a   10. b
11. d   12. b   13. c   14. a   15. d

True-False Questions

1. T   2. F   3. T   4. F   5. T   6. T   7. F   8. F

Essay Questions

- ▪ The nervous system is the most rapidly developing body system in the first two years after birth.
- ▪ Adequate nutrition is essential for the brain's development.

2.
- ▪ Visual acuity improves rapidly during the first year as a result of synaptogenesis, pruning, and myelinization in the neurons that serve the eyes and the brain's vision processing centers.

3.
- ▪ At about six months, infants begin to lose the ability to distinguish pairs of vowels that do not occur in the language they are hearing.
- ▪ By age one, the ability to discriminate non-heard consonants begins to fade.
- ▪ These findings are consistent with what we know about the pattern of rapid, apparently preprogrammed, growth of synapses in the early months after birth, followed by synaptic pruning.
- ▪ Many connections are initially created, permitting discriminations along all possible sound continua, but only those pathways that are actually used in the language the child hears are strengthened or retained.

Puzzle It Out

Across

1. myelinization
3. synapses
4. kwashiorkor
6. marasmus
10. apnea
12. micronutrient
14. primitive
15. tracking
16. stamina
17. habituation
18. synaptogenesis

Down

2. empiricists
5. nativists
7. adaptive
8. macronutrient
9. pruning
11. colic
12. manipulative
13. dishabituation
14. plasticity

COGNITIVE DEVELOPMENT IN INFANCY

BEFORE YOU READ . . . CHAPTER SUMMARY

Cognitive development in infancy includes thinking changes, learning and remembering, and the emergence of language skills. Measuring intelligence in infancy is also discussed.

Cognitive Changes

- In Piaget's sensorimotor stage, infants begin with schemes they are born with and accommodate them to their experiences. The development of object permanence is the most important cognitive milestone.
- Recent research suggests that Piaget underestimated infants' capabilities and their inborn abilities.
- Developmentalists such as Spelke and Baillargeon have studied object permanence within the context of infants' global understanding of objects. Their research shows that Piaget underestimated how much younger infants know about objects and their movements.

Learning, Categorizing, and Remembering

- From the first moments following birth, babies are capable of learning in a variety of ways, such as classical and operant conditioning and schematic learning.
- Infants use categories to organize information.
- Babies as young as three months of age can remember specific objects and their own actions with those objects over periods of as long as a week. With age, their memories become less and less tied to specific cues or contexts.

The Beginnings of Language

- Behaviorists claim that babies learn language by being reinforced for making word-like sounds. Nativists, on the other hand, argue that children's comprehension and production of language is innate. Interactionists say that language development is a sub-process of cognitive development.
- Developmentalists better understand how the environment affects language development.
- Babies' earliest sounds are cries, followed by cooing, then by babbling. At 9 months, babies typically use meaningful gestures and can understand more words than they can produce.
- The first spoken words typically occur at about 1 year, after which children acquire words slowly. At about 24 months, they add new words rapidly and generalize them to many more situations.
- Simple two-word sentences appear in children's expressive language at about 18 months of age.
- The rate of language development varies from one child to another. Some toddlers display an expressive style in early word learning while others show a referential style.
- The sequence of language development seems to hold true for babies in all cultures. The child's word order of a child's telegraphic speech depends on which language she is speaking.

Measuring Intelligence in Infancy

- Infant intelligence tests are not strongly related to later measures of intelligence. Basic information-processing skills, such as the rate of habituation at four months, are correlated with later intelligence test scores.

AS YOU READ . . . LEARNING OBJECTIVEQUESTIONS

After completing Chapter 5, you should be able to answer the following questions:

5.1   What are the important milestones of Piaget's sensorimotor stage?
5.2   What are some of the challenges offered to Piaget's explanation of infant cognitive development?
5.3   What does research tell us about infants' understanding of objects?
5.4   How do infants learn through conditioning and modeling?
5.5   How does categorical understanding change over the first 2 years?
5.6   How does memory function in the first 2 years?
5.7   What are the behaviorist, nativist, and interactio0nist explanations of language development?
5.8   What are some of the environmental influences on language development?
5.9   How do infants' sounds, gestures, and understanding of words change in the early months of life?
5.10   What are the characteristics of toddlers' first words?
5.11   What kinds of sentences do children produce between 18 and 24 months of age?
5.12   What kinds of individual differences are evident in language development?
5.13   How does language development vary across cultures?
5.14   How is intelligence measured in infancy?

AS YOU READ . . . TERM IDENTIFICATION

A-not-B error (p. 124)
Babbling (p. 134)
Bayley Scales of Infant Development (p. 140)
Cooing (p. 134)
Deferred imitation (p. 124)
Expressive language (p. 135)
Expressive style (p. 138)
Holophrases (p. 136)
Infant directed speech (p. 132)
Inflections (p. 136)
Intelligence (p. 140)
Interactionists (p. 131)
Language acquisition device (LAD) (p. 131)
Mean length of utterance (MLU) (p. 137)

Means-end behavior (p. 123)
Naming explosion (p. 136)
Object Concept (p. 126)
Object permanence (p. 123)
Primary circular reaction (p. 122)
Receptive language (p. 134)
Referential style (p. 139)
Schematic learning (p. 129)
Secondary circular reaction (p. 123)
Sensorimotor stage (p. 122)
Telegraphic speech (p. 136)
Tertiary circular reaction (p.123)
Violation of expectations method (p. 126)

AS YOU READ . . . GUIDED STUDY QUESTIONS

COGNITIVE CHANGES

Piaget's View of the First 2 Years (pp. 122-124)

5.1   *What are the important milestones of Piaget's sensorimotor stage?*

1.   Define the following terms:
    a.   sensorimotor stage (p. 122)

    b.   primary circular reactions (p. 122)

    c.   secondary circular reactions (p. 123)

    d.   means-end behavior (p. 123)

    e.   tertiary circular reactions (p. 123)

    f.   object permanence (p. 123)

    g.   A-not-B error (p. 124)

    h.   deferred imitation (p. 124)

2.   Fill in the following table indicating the name of each of the sensorimotor substages and characteristics of each:

Substage	Characteristics
1 (0-1 month)	
2 (1-4 months)	
3 (4-8 months)	
4 (8-12 months)	

Substage	Characteristics
5 (12-18 months)	
6 (18-24 months)	

3.   Describe the development of object permanence across the first year.

4.   Trace the development of deferred imitation in infancy.

Challenges to Piaget's View (pp. 124-126)

5.2   What are some of the challenges offered to Piaget's explanation of infant cognitive development?

5.   Describe the recent research about object permanence that challenges Piaget's findings.

6.   List two important exceptions to the general confirmation of Piaget's sequence of imitation.

7.   List three reasons why the findings about deferred imitation are significant.

Alternative Approaches (pp. 126-128)

5.3   What does research tell us about infants' understanding of objects?

8.   Define the following terms:

    a.   object concept (p. 126)

    b.   violation of expectations method (p. 126)

9.   Describe Elizabeth Spelke's research on the object concept.

10.   Describe the Spelke's research using the violation of expectations method.

11.   Describe Renee Baillargeon's research on the object concept.

AFTER YOU READ . . . PRACTICE TEST #1
COGNITIVE CHANGES

Match the term in the right hand column with its definition in the left column.

_____ 1.	The many simple repetitive actions that center around a baby's own body.	a. accommodation
_____ 2.	An infant's understanding of the nature of objects and how they behave.	b. assimilation
_____ 3.	Repeating a behavior in the absence of the model who first demonstrated it.	c. connected surface principle
_____ 4.	The baby repeats some action in order to trigger a reaction outside her own body.	d. deferred imitation
_____ 5.	Incoming information is added to the limited array of a baby's schemes.	e. means-end behavior
_____ 6.	Assumption that when two exterior areas are joined to each other, they belong to the same object.	f. object concept
_____ 7.	The ability to manipulate mental symbols occurs.	g. object permanence
_____ 8.	The understanding that objects continue to exist when they can't be seen.	h. primary circular reactions
_____ 9.	A research strategy in which researchers move an object on one way after having taught an infant to expect it to move in another.	i. secondary circular reactions
_____ 10.	The deliberate experimentation with variations of previous actions.	j. sensorimotor stage

a. accommodation
b. assimilation
c. connected surface principle
d. deferred imitation
e. means-end behavior
f. object concept
g. object permanence
h. primary circular reactions
i. secondary circular reactions
j. sensorimotor stage
k. substage 2
l. substage 3
m. substage 4
n. substage 5
o. substage 6
p. tertiary circular reaction
q. violation of expectations method

LEARNING, CATEGORIZING, AND REMEMBERING

Conditioning and Modeling (pp. 128-129)

5.4   How do infants learn through conditioning and modeling?

12.   Give examples of the ways infants learn through classical conditioning, operant conditioning, and modeling.

Schematic Learning (p. 129)

5.5   How does categorical understanding change over the first 2 years?

13.   Define schematic learning (p. 129).

14.   Describe how infants build and use categories as they take in information, including the concepts of superordinates and hierarchical categorization.

Memory (pp. 129-130)

5.6   How does memory function in the first 2 years?

15.   Briefly describe the research on infants' memory. What do the findings demonstrate?

AFTER YOU READ . . . PRACTICE TEST #2
LEARNING, CATEGORIZING, AND REMEMBERING

Indicate whether each of the following statements is True or False.

_____ 1.   Generally, the term learning is used to denote temporary changes in behavior that result from experience.

_____ 2.   Learning of emotional responses through classical conditioning processes may begin as early as the first week of life.

_____ 3.   Both the sucking response and head turning have been successfully increased by the use of reinforcements such as sweet liquids or the sound of the mother's voice.

_____ 4.   The mother's voice and the father's voice are equally effective reinforcers for virtually all babies.

_____ 5.   Schemas help the baby to distinguish between the familiar and the unfamiliar.

_____ 6.   By seven months of age, infants actively use categories to process information.

_____ 7.   Infants respond to superordinate categories before they display reactions to basic-level categories.

_____ 8.   The concept that smaller categories are nested within larger ones is demonstrated to some degree by one-year-olds.

_____ 9.   Babies as young as three months can remember specific objects and their own actions with those objects over periods as long as a week.

_____ 10.   With age, babies' memories become more and more tied to specific cues or contexts.

THE BEGINNINGS OF LANGUAGE

Theoretical Perspectives (pp. 130-132)

5.7   What are the behaviorist, nativist, and interactionist explanations of language development?

16.   Define the following terms:
    a.   language acquisition device (LAD) (p. 131)

    b.   interactionists (p. 131)

17.   Distinguish among the following perspectives on the development of language. Include examples of each.

Theory	Proponent(s)	Description and Examples
Behaviorist		
Nativist		
Interactionist		

18.   List two examples of evidence in support of the interactionist view.
-
-
-

Influences on Language Development (pp. 132-133)

5.8   What are some of the environmental influences on language development?
19.   Define infant directed speech (p. 132).

20.   List 5 characteristics of infant directed speech (formerly called "motherese").
-
-
-
-
-

21.   How does the sheer quantity of language a child hears impact language development?

22.   Describe the effects of poverty on exposure to language.

The Real World: The Importance of Reading to a Toddler (p. 133)

23.   Describe and give examples of dialogic reading.

Early Milestones of Language Development (pp. 133-135)

5.9   How do infants' sounds, gestures, and understanding of words change in the early months of life?

24.   Define the following terms:
        a.   cooing (p. 134)

        b.   babbling (p. 134)

        c.   receptive language (p. 134)

25.   List two important reasons for babies' babbling.

26.   List the series of changes that seem to come together at nine or ten months.

Research Report: Early Gestural "Language"
in the Children of Deaf Parents (p. xx)

27.   Describe the language development of deaf children of deaf parents, and of hearing children of deaf parents.

The First Words (pp. 135-136)

5.10   What are the characteristics of toddlers' first words?

28.   Define the following terms and give examples of each:
    a.   expressive language (p. 135)

    b.   holophrases (p. 136)

    c.   naming explosion (p. 136)

29.   Distinguish expressive language from receptive language.

The First Sentences (pp. 136-137)

5.11   What kinds of sentences do children produce between 18 and 24 months of age?

30.   Define the following terms:
    a.   telegraphic speech (p. 136)

    b.   inflections (p. 136)

31.   List the distinguishing features of babies' first sentences.

Individual Differences in Language Development (pp. 137-139)

5.12   What kinds of individual differences are evident in language development?

32.   Define the following terms:
    a.   mean length of utterance (MLU) (p. 137)

    b.   expressive style (p. 138)

    c.   referential style (p. 139)

33.   Describe the subset of children who talk late and who do not catch up.

34.   Distinguish between expressive style and referential style, and give examples of how they are related to a child's cognitive development.

No Easy Answers: One Language or Two? (p. 137)

35.   List at least five advantages of growing up bilingual.

36.   List at least three disadvantages of growing up bilingual.

Language Development across Cultures (p. 139)

5.13   How does language development vary across cultures?

37.   List four similarities in language development across cultures.

38.   Give examples of cross-cultural differences

AFTER YOU READ . . . PRACTICE TEST #3
THE BEGINNINGS OF LANGUAGE

1. **Chomsky called the innate language processor _____.**
   a. receptive language
   b. expressive language
   c. dialogic device
   d. the language acquisition device

2. **The pattern of speech characterized by a higher pitch than that which is exhibited by adults and children when they are not speaking to an infant is called _____.**
   a. infant-directed speech
   b. metalinguistic ability
   c. babbling
   d. referential style

3. **Each of the following is a characteristic of children whose parents talk to them often and read to them regularly EXCEPT _____.**
   a. learn to read more easily when they reach school age
   b. develop larger vocabularies
   c. use simpler sentences
   d. talk sooner

4. **When adults repeat the child's own sentences but in slightly longer, more grammatically correct forms, the speech is called _____.**
   a. the language acquisition device
   b. receptive style
   c. recasting
   d. expressive style

5. **Which is of following is the typical sequence of language development in infancy?**
   a. babbling, cooing, telegraphic speech, holophrases
   b. cooing, babbling, gestural language, holophrases
   c. gestural language, babbling, telegraphic speech, cooing
   d. holophrases, gestural language, cooing, telegraphic speech

6. **Which of the following is TRUE about babbling?**
   a. Babbling is preparation for spoken language.
   b. Babbling includes only the sounds that the baby hears.
   c. Babbling is repetitive vowel sounds.
   d. Babbling begins at about two months.

7. **Each of the following is part of the series of changes in language that converge by about nine or ten months EXCEPT _____.**
   a. imitative gestural games
   b. the first comprehension of individual words
   c. the beginning of meaningful gestures
   d. the drift of babbling toward the non-heard language sounds

8.   Between 16 and 24 months, most children begin to add new words rapidly. This is called
        _____.
        a.   expressive language
        b.   the naming explosion
        c.   telegraphic speech
        d.   expressive style

9.   **Inflections are** _____.
        a.   examples of the dialogic reading style
        b.   grammatical markers
        c.   metalinguistic ability
        d.   recasting

10.   **The average sentence length is referred to as** _____.
        a.   a referential style
        b.   a holophrase
        c.   the mean length of utterance
        d.   adult-directed speech

MEASURING INTELLIGENCE IN INFANCY (p. 140)

5.14   *How is intelligence measured in infancy?*

39.   Define the following terms:
    a.   intelligence (p. 140)

    b.   Bayley Scales of Infant Development (p. 140)

40.   State how the Bayley Scales of Infant Development useful and what are its drawbacks?

Usefulness	*Drawbacks*

41.   How have habituation tasks been of value as measures of infant intelligence?

42.   Describe the usefulness of the Fagan Test of Infant Intelligence for special populations.

AFTER YOU READ . . . PRACTICE TEST #4
MEASURING INTELLIGENCE IN INFANCY

Indicate whether each of the following statements is True or False.

_____ The ability to take in information and use it to adapt to the environment is called
1. intelligence.

_____ It is quite easy to create a test that can effectively measure intelligence in infants.
2.

_____ The Bayley Scales of Infant Development measure primary reflexes.
3.

_____ What is being measured on typical infant intelligence tests is not the same as what is
4. tapped by the commonly used childhood or adult intelligence tests.

_____ Individual differences in rate of habituation in the early months of life are unlikely to
5. predict later intelligence test scores.

AFTER YOU READ . . . COMPREHENSIVE PRACTICE TEST
MULTIPLE CHOICE QUESTIONS

1. Piaget's first stage during which infants use information from their senses and motor actions to learn about the world is called _____.
   a. sensorimotor stage
   b. preoperational stage
   c. concrete operational stage
   d. formal operational stage

2. The understanding that a toy exists even if we roll it under the couch is called _____.
   a. object permanence
   b. conservation
   c. concept consistency
   d. schematic processing

3. Each of the following statements is true of the recent findings about deferred imitation EXCEPT _____.
   a. Infants can and do learn specific behaviors through modeling, even when they have no chance to imitate the behavior immediately.
   b. Babies may be more skillful than Piaget thought.
   c. Deferred imitation begins at 14 months.
   d. More abilities than Piaget suggested may be built in from the beginning and may develop continuously, rather than in stages, throughout infancy.

4 An infant's understanding of the nature of objects and how they behave is called _____.
   a. means-end behavior
   b. object concept
   c. deferred imitation
   d. object permanence

5. Infants learn by each of the following methods EXCEPT _____.
   a. modeling
   b. classical conditioning
   c. operant conditioning
   d. expressive imitation

6. Schematic learning assumes that _____.
   a. babies attempt to categorize their experiences
   b. children cannot learn unless the information is organized for them
   c. babies will only learn if they are reinforced for exploring
   d. learning is sequential and orderly

7. Which of the following is an accurate statement about infant memory?
   a. Infants younger than six months do not retain memories.
   b. The expansion of memory is preprogrammed.
   c. Infants develop very general memories for information.
   d. Early infant memory is specific to the context in which it was learned.

8.   **Theorists who argue that language development is part of the broader process of cognitive development are called _____.**
        a.   nativists
        b.   interactionists
        c.   behaviorists
        d.   psychoanalysists

9.   **A child understands a word that is spoken before she can say the word. This is called _____.**
        a.   expressive language
        b.   receptive language
        c.   imitation
        d.   innate vocalization

10.   **Combinations of gestures and single words that convey more meaning than just the word alone are termed _____.**
        a.   expressive linguistics
        b.   babbles
        c.   holophrases
        d.   infant-directed speech

11.   **Telegraphic speech typically includes each of the following parts of speech EXCEPT _____.**
        a.   nouns
        b.   verbs
        c.   adjectives
        d.   adverbs

12.   **Children's early vocabulary that uses words linked to social relationships rather than objects is called _____.**
        a.   hierarchical style
        b.   referential style
        c.   expressive style
        d.   metalinguistic ability

13.   **Each of the following statements about language development across cultures is true EXCEPT _____.**
        a.   babies the world over coo before they babble
        b.   telegraphic speech precedes holophrases in every language
        c.   all babies understand language before they can speak it
        d.   babies in all cultures begin to use their first words at about 12 months

14.   **Which of the following is an accurate statement about infant intelligence tests?**
        a.   Babies who habituate quickly when they are four or five months old are likely to have higher intelligence test scores at later ages.
        b.   The Bayley Scales of Infant Development accurately predict a child's intelligence at age ten.
        c.   None of the infant intelligence tests correlate with intelligence test scores at later ages.
        d.   Infant intelligence tests are based on individual differences in cognitive abilities.

15. **Tests of _____ are also known as novelty preference and visual recognition.**
   a.   reflex tests
   b.   habituation
   c.   motor skills
   d.   expressive style

TRUE-FALSE QUESTIONS

Indicate whether each of the following statements is True or False.

_____
1.
One consequence of the drive to explore is means-end behavior, or the ability to keep a goal in mind and devise a plan to achieve it.

_____
2.
Piaget argued that deferred imitation was possible as early as substage three.

_____
3.
The concept that smaller categories are nested within larger ones, or hierarchical categorization, is demonstrated to some degree by two-year-olds.

_____
4.
Newborns do not appear to be able to remember auditory stimuli to which they are exposed while sleeping.

_____
5.
Expressive language is the ability to produce as well as understand and respond to words.

_____
6.
Children who use a referential style have vocabularies made up predominantly of names for things or people.

_____
7.
The Bayley Scales of Infant Development measure primarily language development.

_____
8.
Individual differences in rate of habituation in the early months after birth may predict later intelligence test scores.

ESSAY QUESTIONS

1.   Using Piaget's six sensorimotor substages as your guide, trace the cognitive development of infants. Include the approximate ages of each substage and the distinguishing characteristics of each. Include specific examples of each.

2.   Discuss the importance of reading to toddlers.

3.   Discus the pros and cons to measuring intelligence in infancy.

WHEN YOU HAVE FINISHED . . . PUZZLE IT OUT

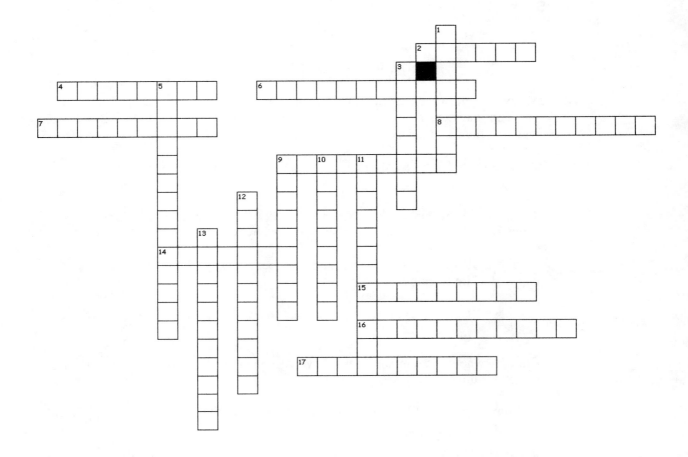

Across
2. Repetition of vowel sounds
4. View that language comprehension and production is innate
6. Combinations of gestures and single words
7. Learning involving the organization of experiences into expectancies
8. Grammatical markers
9. Adults expand on a child's own sentence in a more grammatically correct form
14. Conditioning in which infants learn by reinforcement
15. Infant-directed speech
16. Speech that uses simple, two-word sentences
17. Ability to produce as well as understand and respond to words

Down
1. Learning by watching others
3. Repetition of combination of consonant and vowel sounds
5. View that language development is part of broader process
9. Ability to understand language
10. Conditioning in which infants learn emotional responses
11. Piaget's first stage
12. View that language is learned by reinforcement
13. Language style made up of names for things or people

Created by Puzzlemaker at DiscoverySchool.com

WHEN YOU HAVE FINISHED . . . RESEARCH PROJECT

Student Project 7: Development of the Object Concept

For this project, you will need to locate an infant between 6 and 12 months of age. Obtain permission from the baby's parents, following whatever procedure your instructor requires, and ask one of them to be there while you present materials to the baby.

Procedure

Obtain from the parents one of the baby's favorite toys. Place the baby in a sitting position or on his stomach in such a way that he can reach for the toy easily (as in figure 5.2). Then perform the following steps:

Step 1: While the baby is watching, place the toy in full view and easy to reach. See if the infant reaches for the toy.

Step 2: In full view of the infant, cover part of the toy with a handkerchief, so that only part is visible. Does the baby reach for the toy?

Step 3: While the infant is reaching for the toy (you'll have to pick your moment), cover it completely with the handkerchief. Does the baby continue reaching?

Step 4: In full view of the baby, while he is still interested in the toy, cover the whole toy with the cloth. Does the baby try to pull the cloth away or search for the toy in some way?

You may need to use more than one toy to keep the baby's interest and/or spread the test over a period of time.

Analysis and Report

Jackson, Campos, and Fischer (1978) report that step 2 (continuing to reach for the partly covered toy) is typically "passed" at about 26 weeks, step 3 at about 28 or 29 weeks, and the final step (reaching for the toy that was fully covered before the child began to reach) at about 30 or 31 weeks. The closer to these ages your infant is, the more interesting your results are likely to be.

Did your subject's performance conform to those expectations? If not, why do you think it was different? You might read the Jackson, Campos, and Fischer paper to see some of the reasons they give for differences in results from several studies. Do you think it mattered, for example, that a familiar toy was used? Did it matter that the mother or father was present?

Reference
Jackson, E., Campos, J. J., & Fischer, K. W. (1978). The question of decalage between object permanence and person permanence. *Developmental Psychology, 14*, 1-10.

CHAPTER 5 ANSWER KEY

Practice Test #1 Cognitive Changes
1. h   2. f   3. d   4. i   5. b   6. c   7. o   8. g   9. q   10. p

Practice Test #2 Learning, Categorizing, and Remembering
1. F   2. T   3. T   4. F   5. T   6. T   7. T   8. F   9. T   10. F

Practice Test #3 The Beginnings of Language
1. d   2. a   3. c   4. c   5. b   6. a   7. d   8. b   9. b   10. c

Practice Test #4 Measuring Intelligence in Infancy
1. T   2. F   3. F   4. T   5. F

Comprehensive Practice Test
Multiple Choice Questions
1. a   2. a   3. c   4. b   5. d   6. a   7. d   8. b   9. b   10. c
11. d   12. c   13. b   14. a   15. b

True-False Questions
1. T   2. F   3. T   4. F   5. T   6. T   7. F   8. T

Essay Questions
1.
- Substage 1: Birth to on month. Built-in reflexes.
- Substage 2: One to four months. Primary circular reactions—repeating pleasurable actions involving the infant's own body. Beginning of coordination between looking and listening, between reaching and looking, and between reaching and sucking.
- Substage 3: Four to eight months. Secondary circular reactions—repeating some action to trigger a reaction outside the baby's body.
- Substage 4: Eight to 12 months. Beginning of causal connections resulting in mean-end behavior.
- Substage 5: Twelve to 18 months. Tertiary circular reactions—trying out variations of original behavior. Purposeful, experimental behavior.
- Substage 6: Eighteen to 24 months. Ability to manipulate mental symbols, such as words or images, allowing the infant to generate solutions to problems simply by thinking about them.

2.
- Children gain a wide range of words in their speech. They talk sooner, develop larger vocabularies, use more complex sentences, and learn to read more readily when they reach school age.

3.
- Pro: Helps heath care professionals identify infants who require special interventions to support cognitive development.
- Con: Can result in "labeling" children as "smart" or "slow."

Puzzle It Out

Across	**Down**
2. cooing	1. modeling
4. nativist	3. babbling
6. holophrases	5. interactionist
7. schematic	9. receptive
8. inflections	10. classical
9. recasting	11. sensorimotor
14. operant	12. behaviorist
14. motherese	13. referential
16. telegraphic	
17. expressive	

SOCIAL AND PERSONALITY DEVELOPMENT IN INFANCY

BEFORE YOU READ . . . CHAPTER SUMMARY

Developmentalists of diverse theoretical orientations agree that the formation of a strong emotional connection to a primary caregiver early in life is critical to healthy child development and has important implications across the entire lifespan.

Theories of Social and Personality Development
- Freud believed that the weaning process in the oral stage of development influenced the development of personality. Erikson emphasized the role of the family in providing for all of the infant's needs, thereby instilling a sense of trust.
- Ethologists believe that the first two years constitute a sensitive period for attachment in human infants and that infants who fail to form a close relationship with a primary caregiver are at risk for future social and personality problems.

Attachment
- The development of synchrony, a set of mutually reinforcing and interlocking behaviors that characterize most interactions between parent and infant, is essential to the development of the parents' attachment to the infant.
- According to Bowlby, the baby's attachment to the parents emerges gradually across three stages.
- Children differ in the security of their first attachments and in the internal working model that they develop. The secure infant uses the parent as a safe base for exploration and can be readily consoled by the parent.
- Caregiver characteristics such as the caregivers' emotional responses to the infant,, their marital and socioeconomic status, and their mental health.
- Children who were securely attached to their mothers in infancy are more sociable and more positive in their behavior toward friends and siblings than those who were insecurely attached. The internal model of attachment that individuals develop in infancy affects how they parent their own babies.
- Studies in many countries suggest that a secure attachment is the most common pattern everywhere, but cultures differ in the frequency of different types of insecure attachment.

Personality, Temperament, and Self-Concept
- A few key dimensions of temperament tend to cluster into three types: easy children, difficult children, and slow-to-warm-up children.
- Heredity, neurological processes, and environment contribute to individual differences in temperament. Infant temperament may affect security of attachment. The goodness-of-fit between an infant's temperament and the ways her environment responds to her is the real factor in correlations between temperament and attachment.
- The infant develops the awareness of a separate self and the understanding of self-permanence (called the subjective self), and an awareness of himself as an object in the world (the objective self). An

emotional self develops in the first year as the range of emotions develops, as well as the ability to use information about emotions.

Effects of Nonparental Care

- Comparing parental care to nonparental care is difficult because there are so many kinds of non-parental care arrangements.
- High-quality daycare has beneficial effects on many children's overall cognitive development, especially on disadvantaged children.
- Some studies show that children with a history of daycare are more aggressive in their social relationships whereas other studies show them to be more socially skillful.
- Factors such as stress hormones, individual differences, and gender differences may affect a child in nonparental care.

AS YOU READ . . . LEARNING OBJECTIVES

After completing Chapter 6, you should be able to:

6.1   How do Freud's and Erikson's views of personality development in the first 2 years differ?
6.2   What are the main ideas of attachment theory?
6.3   How does synchrony affect parent-infant relations?
6.4   What are the four phases of attachment and the behaviors associated with them?
6.5   What are the variables that contribute to the development and stability of the four types of attachment?
6.6   What variables might affect a parent's ability to establish an attachment relationship with an infant?
6.7   What are the long-term consequences of attachment quality?
6.8   In what ways do patterns of attachment vary across cultures?
6.9   On which dimensions of temperament do most developmentalists agree?
6.10   What are the roles of heredity, neurological processes, and environment in the formation of temperament?
6.11   How do the subjective self, the objective self, and the emotional self development during the first 2 yeas?
6.12   Why is it difficult to study the effects of nonparental care on development?
6.13   What might be the effects of nonparental care on cognitive development?
6.14   What does research suggest about the risks of nonparental care with respect to social development?
6.15   What variables should be taken in to account in interpretations of research on nonparental care?

AS YOU READ . . . TERM IDENTIFICATION

Attachment (p. 150)   Personality (p. 157)
Attachment theory (p. 148)   Secure attachment (p. 152)
Goodness-of-fit (p. 160)   Separation anxiety (p. 152)
Insecure/ambivalent attachment (p. 152)   Social referencing (p. 152)
Insecure/avoidant attachment (p. 152)   Stranger anxiety (p. 152)
Insecure/disorganized attachment (p. 152) Subjective self (p. 160)
Niche-picking (p. 154)   Synchrony (p. 150)
Objective (categorical) self (p. 160)   Temperament (p. 157)

AS YOU READ . . . GUIDED STUDY QUESTIONS

THEORIES OF SOCIAL AND PERSONALITY DEVELOPMENT

Psychoanalytic Perspectives (p. 148)

6.1   How do Freud's and Erikson's views of personality development in the first 2 years differ?

1.   What was Freud's belief about the importance of the oral stage? Why was the weaning process important?

2.   Describe the importance of the symbiotic relationship between the mother and the infant.

3.   How does Erikson's theory differ from Freud's? Why is the trust versus mistrust stage so important?

Ethological Perspectives (pp. 148-149)

6.2   What are the main ideas of attachment theory?

4.   Define the following terms:
    a.   attachment theory (p. 148)

    b.   attachment (p. 148)

5.   According to John Bowlby, why are internal models important to attachment?

No Easy Answers: Adoption and Development (p. 149)

6.   Why are the child's circumstances prior to adoption important to consider?

AFTER YOU READ . . . PRACTICE TEST #1
THEORIES OF SOCIAL AND PERSONALITY DEVELOPMENT

Indicate whether each of the following statements is true or false.

_____ 1. Freud proposed a series of psychosexual stages that extend from birth through old age.

_____ 2. According to Freud, the consequences of overgratification or undergratification at the oral stage would be fixation.

_____ 3. Freud emphasized the symbiotic relationship between the mother and the young infant, in which the two behave as if they were one.

_____ 4. Erikson claimed that responding to the infant's needs by talking to her and comforting her were just as important to development as nursing and weaning.

_____ 5. Ethologists claim that attachment behaviors are learned behaviors, not instinctive.

_____ 6. An attachment is a type of affectional bond in which a person's sense of security is bound up in the relationship.

_____ 7. When you are securely attached, you can use the other as a "safe base" from which to explore the rest of the world.

ATTACHMENT

The Parents' Attachment to the Infant (p. 150)

6.3   *How does synchrony affect parent-infant relations?*

7.   Define synchrony (p. 150), and give examples.

8.   Describe the importance of synchrony to the parents' attachment to the infant.

9.   How do infants respond differently to mothers than to fathers?

Response to Mothers	*Response to Fathers*

The Infant's Attachment to the Parents (pp. 150-152)

6.4   What are the four phases of attachment and the behaviors associated with them?

10.   What are Bowlby's four phases in the development of the infant's attachment?

Phase	Name of Phase	Age	Description
1			
2			
3			
4			

11.   Define the following terms:
       a.   stranger anxiety (p. 152)

       b.   separation anxiety (p. 152)

       c.   social referencing (p. 152)

12.   How do infants express stranger anxiety?

13.   How do infants express separation anxiety?

14.   Give an example of social referencing.

15.   How do infants use social referencing to regulate their own emotions?

Variations in Attachment Quality (pp. 152-153)

6.5   What are the variables that contribute to the development and stability of the four types of attachment?

16.   Define the following terms:
       a.   secure attachment (p. 152)

       b.   insecure/avoidant attachment (p. 152)

c.   insecure/ambivalent attachment (p. 152)

d.   insecure/disorganized attachment (p. 152)

17.   List, in order, the eight episodes in the Strange Situation.
-
-
-
-
-
-
-
-

18.   What may happen to the consistency of security or insecurity if the child's circumstances change in some major way? Give examples.

19.   How does the quality of the child's relationship with each parent determine the child's security with that specific adult?

Caregiver Characteristics and Attachment (00. 154-155)

6.6   What variables might affect a parent's ability to establish an attachment relationship with an infant?

20.   How does a caregiver's emotional availability impact secure attachment?

21.   What is contingent responsiveness?

22.   How might marital and socioeconomic status affect attachment?

23.   How might the caregiver's age predict the attachment quality?

24.   How might marital conflict pose risks for the development of attachment?

25.   How might a mother's depression affect an infant's nutrition?

26.   Identify three problematic behavior patterns in depressed mothers, and how they might interact with their infants.

Category	Mother's Behavior toward the Infant
Withdrawn or Detached	
Overly Involved with Infant	
Overreaction and Anger	

27. When depressed mothers exhibit the same kind of parenting behaviors as most nondepressed mothers, their emotional status _____.

28. How does the behavior of a mother with panic disorder affect the synchrony with her infant?

Long-Term Consequences of Attachment Quality (pp. 155-156)

6.7   What are the long-term consequence of attachment quality?

29. List six behaviors of children who were rated as securely attached to their mothers in infancy.
   -
   -
   -
   -
   -
   -

30. List four behaviors of adolescents who were rated as securely attached to their mothers in infancy.
   -
   -
   -
   -

31. List two behaviors of adolescents who were rated as insecure attachments—particularly those with avoidant attachments—in infancy.
   -
   -

32. How does attachment in infancy predict sociability in adulthood?

33. Give examples of how an adult's internal model of attachment affects his or hr parenting behaviors.

34. How does attachment history affect parental attitudes?

Cross-Cultural Research on Attachment (pp. 156-157)

6.8   In what ways do patterns of attachment vary across cultures?

35.   What does the research show about secure attachment in a culture in which the child's early care is much more communal?

AFTER YOU READ . . . PRACTICE TEST #2
ATTACHMENT

1.   For an adult, the critical ingredient for the formation of a bond with an infant seems to be the opportunity to develop _____.
   a.   affect dysregulation
   b.   nonfocused orienting
   c.   synchrony
   d.   contingent responsiveness

2.   During which of Bowlby's phases in the development of the infant's attachment will the baby use a set of innate behavior patterns that orient her toward others and signal her needs?
   a.   phase 4, reactive attachment
   b.   phase 3, secure base behavior
   c.   phase 2, focus on one or more figures
   d.   phase 1, nonfocused orienting and signaling

3.   Expressions of discomfort, such as crying, when separated from an attachment figure is called _____.
   a.   stranger anxiety
   b.   separation anxiety
   c.   social referencing
   d.   separation distress

4.   A child who shows contradictory behavior patterns simultaneously is probably _____.
   a.   securely attached
   b.   insecurely attached/avoidant
   c.   insecurely attached/ambivalent
   d.   insecurely attached/disorganized/disoriented

5.   Parents who are sensitive to the child's cues and respond appropriately are demonstrating _____.
   a.   contingent responsiveness
   b.   reactive attachment
   c.   nonfocused orienting
   d.   social referencing

6.   Each of the following is a problematic behavior pattern in depressed mothers EXCEPT _____.
   a.   mothers overreact and respond angrily to babies' undesirable behaviors
   b.   mothers are sensitive to the babies' needs
   c.   mothers are overly involved with their infants
   d.   mothers are withdrawn or detached

7. **Each of the following behaviors of children is correlated to secure attachment in infancy EXCEPT _____.**
    a.   more sociable
    b.   more positive in their behavior towards friends and siblings
    c.   more aggressive and disruptive
    d.   more empathetic

8. **Secure attachment in infancy has been linked to _____ in adolescence.**
    a.   self-esteem problems
    b.   rebellious backlash
    c.   earlier sexual experience
    d.   more intimate friendships

PERSONALITY, TEMPERAMENT, AND SELF-CONCEPT

Dimensions of Temperament (pp. 157-158)

6.9   *On which dimensions of temperament do most developmentalists agree?*

36.   Define the following terms:
    a.   personality (p. 157)

    b.   temperament (p. 157)

37.   List and describe the three types of temperament proposed by Thomas and Chess.

Temperament Type	*Description*

38.   How do researchers who examine temperament from a trait rather than a categorical perspective view an infant's temperament?

39.   Describe each of the following key dimensions of temperament:

Dimension of Temperament	*Description*
Activity Level	
Approach/Positive Emotionality	
Inhibition	
Negative Emotionality	
Effortful Control/Task Persistence	

Origins and Stability of Temperament (pp. 158-160)

6.10   What are the roles of heredity, neurological processes, and environment in the formation of temperament?

40.   Describe the evidence that each of the following factors affects the formation of temperament..

Factor	Evidence
Heredity	
Neurological Processes	
Environment	

41.   Define niche-picking (p. 159) and give examples.

42.   Define goodness-of-fit (p. 160), and give examples of its importance in attachment.

Research Report: Gender Differences in Temperament (p. 160)

43.   List the gender differences in temperament found in some research studies.

44.   How might temperamental stereotyping affect the quality of the parent-infant relationship?

Self-Concept (pp. 160-162)

6.11   How do the subjective self, the objective self, and the emotional self develop during the first 2 years?

45.   Define the following terms:
        a.   subjective self (p. 160)

        b.   objective (categorical) self (p. 160)

46.   Give examples of each of the following terms to distinguish among them.

Sense of Self	Examples
Subjective Self (Existential Self)	
Objective Self (Categorical Self)	
Emotional Self	

47.   Describe the research to determine just when a child has developed the initial self-awareness that defines the beginning of the objective self.

48.   Trace the development of the emotional self by completing the following table:

Age	Behavior	Expression of Emotions
2-3 months		
5-7 months		
End of the First Year		
Near the Middle of the Second Year		

AFTER YOU READ . . . PRACTICE TEST #3
PERSONALITY, TEMPERAMENT, AND SELF-CONCEPT

Match the letter of the term in the right column with its description in the left column.

_____ 1. A tendency to respond with fear or withdrawal to new people, new situations, new objects—the flip side of approach.

_____ 2. Try new foods without much fuss, regular sleeping and eating cycles, usually happy, adjust easily to change.

_____ 3. The process of selecting experiences on the basis of temperament.

_____ 4. Inborn predispositions that form the foundations of personality.

_____ 5. The degree to which an infant's temperament is adaptable to his or her environment, and vice versa.

_____ 6. A pattern of responding to people and objects in the environment.

_____ 7. Sometimes called the categorical self.

_____ 8. Exhibit higher levels of arousal in the right frontal lobe than the left hemisphere.

_____ 9. Neurotransmitters that regulate the brain's responses to new information and unusual situations.

_____ 10. Sometimes called the existential self.

a. Activity level
b. Difficult child
c. Dopamine and serotonin
d. Easy child
e. Emotional self
f. Frontal lobe asymmetry
g. Goodness-of-fit
h. Inhibition
i. Negative emotionality
j. Niche-picking
k. Objective self
l. Personality
m. Slow-to-warm-up child
n. Subjective self
o. Temperament

EFFECTS OF NONPARENTAL CARE

Difficulties in Studying Nonparental Care (pp. 163-164)

6.12 Why is it difficult to study the effects of nonparental care on development?

49. List at least four factors that may be involved in the issue of daycare that confound the question of how much impact non-parental care has on infants and young children.

-
-
-
-

50. What is the most common pattern of nonparental care?

Effects on Cognitive Development (p. 164)

6.13   What might be the effects of nonparental care on cognitive development?

51.   Describe the evidence that high-quality daycare has beneficial effects on many children's overall cognitive development.

52.   Describe the studies that point to possible negative effects of daycare experience on cognitive development in some children, particularly middle-class children.

53.   How can these conflicting findings be reconciled?

Effects on Social Development (pp. 164-165)

6.14   What does research suggest about the risks of nonparental care with respect to social development?

54.   What evidence is there that nonparental care has a negative impact on social development?

Interpreting Research on Nonparental Care (pp. 165-166)

6.15   What variables should be taken in to account in interpretation of research on nonparental care?

55.   List and describe at least three variables that may affect the interpretation of research on nonparental care.

Variable	*Description*

The Real World: Parenting: Choosing a Daycare Setting (p. 166))

56.   Identify and describe six criteria for choosing a high-quality daycare setting.

Criteria	Description

AFTER YOU READ . . . PRACTICE TEST #4
EFFECTS OF NONPARENTAL CARE

Indicate whether each of the following statements is true or false.

_____
1.   The mother's attitudes toward the child care arrangements they have made may affect the overall experience.

_____
2.   Children from poor families are most likely to have negative experiences in nonparental care.

_____
3.   Infants whose parents exhibit behaviors associated with insecure attachment are more likely to be negatively affected by nonparental care.

_____
4.   Children who have spent ten hours or more per week in nonparental care appear to be at low risk from difficulties in social relationships.

_____
5.   The levels of the stress hormone cortisol increased from morning to afternoon in infants who were enrolled in center-based care.

_____
6.   Family variables are more important than the type of day care arrangements a family chooses.

AFTER YOU READ . . . CRITICAL REFLECTION EXERCISE

Attachment

Imagine that you work in a daycare center. You notice that one parent is having a difficult time dropping off his son. The child clings to the father in apparent fear about being dropped off, kicks and screams when the father walks away, and then seems fine. You also notice that the child seems very "mad" at his father when the father returns to pick him up. The boy refuses to look his father in the eye, does not want to be picked up, and will not answer the father's questions about how the boy's day went. Utilizing information from the text, provide answers for the following questions:

1.   According to Ainsworth's categories of attachment, what kind of attachment bond seems to have developed between this parent and child?

2.   What types of interactions between the parent and child seem to lead to this type of attachment bond?

3.   What effects might this attachment bond have on the child's developing sense of self? Why?

4.   What things might you do when interacting with this child in the daycare to ensure that this same type of relationship does not develop between you and this child? Discuss at least four things that you might do.

AFTER YOU READ . . . COMPREHENSIVE PRACTICE TEST
MULTIPLE-CHOICE QUESTIONS

1.   The theorist who proposed that infants must resolve the conflict of trust versus mistrust was
     _____.
     a.   Ainsworth
     b.   Bowlby
     c.   Erikson
     d.   Freud

2.   The view that infants are biologically predisposed to form emotional bonds with caregivers
     and that the characteristics of those bonds shape later social and personality development is
     called _____.
     a.   trust versus mistrust
     b.   attachment theory
     c.   personality theory
     d.   reactive attachment

3.   The mutual, interlocking pattern of attachment behaviors between a parent and an infant is
     called _____.
     a.   synchrony
     b.   attachment
     c.   temperament
     d.   conversation

4.   During which phase of attachment will the child show attachment behaviors that are more
     narrowly focused on select persons?
     a.   Phase 4, reactive attachment
     b.   Phase 3, secure base attachment
     c.   Phase 2, focus on one or more figure phase
     d.   Phase 1, non-focused orienting and signaling

5.   A child who does not seek much contact with the mother after she returns from a short
     absence is probably _____.
     a.   securely attached
     b.   insecurely attached/avoidant
     c.   insecurely attached/ambivalent
     d.   insecurely attached/disorganized/disoriented

6.   Which of the following statements about the relationship between the mother's age and
     attachment is accurate?
     a.   The mother's age is not a factor in attachment.
     b.   Adolescent mothers are more likely to describe their babies as "difficult."
     c.   Mothers in their 30s are more likely to describe their babies as "difficult."
     d.   Training in child development has no effect on the mother's ability to interpret an infant's
          behavior.

7.   An adult's _____ of attachment affect his or her parenting behaviors.
    a.   internal model
    b.   activity level
    c.   nonfocused orientation
    d.   symmetry

8.   *What type of attachment is the most common across cultures?*
    a.   It differs greatly from culture to culture.
    b.   It depends on the gender of the children.
    c.   insecure attachment
    d.   secure attachment

9.   Which of the following is NOT a dimension of temperament described by many of the key researchers?
    a.   activity level
    b.   emotional maturity
    c.   inhibition
    d.   negative emotionality

10.   Which statement is an accurate statement about where temperament qualities come from?
    a.   Temperament is developed in response to parental style.
    b.   Gender differences can account for most differences in temperament.
    c.   Both nature and nurture contribute to individual differences in temperament.
    d.   Early differences in temperament are a combination of the infant's mood and parental style.

11.   People of all ages choose their experiences, a process Sandra Scarr calls _____.
    a.   temperament
    b.   niche-picking
    c.   affectional bonds
    d.   heredity

12.   Another name for the objective self is _____.
    a.   existential self
    b.   categorical self
    c.   emotional self
    d.   subjective self

13.   Each of the following is an issue impacting the study of nonparental care EXCEPT _____.
    a.   most children have the same nonparental care arrangements for many years
    b.   an enormous range of different care arrangements are all lumped under the title of "nonparental care"
    c.   infants enter nonparental care arrangements at different ages and stay for varying lengths of time
    d.   nonparental care varies widely in quality

14.   What has been discovered about the effects of daycare on cognitive development?
    a.   Children spending time in daycare exhibit more emotional problems.
    b.   Children from poorer families are especially disadvantaged by daycare.
    c.   There are no consistent findings about the effects of daycare.
    d.   Cognitively enriched daycare experiences tend to positively affect children.

15.   **When children reach school age, those who entered nonparental care during the early months of life and who spent 20 or more hours per week in such care throughout early childhood are more likely to experience _____ than children who spent less time in nonparental care.**
        a.   increased activity level
        b.   increased emotionality
        c.   increased social problems
        d.   increased intelligence

TRUE-FALSE QUESTIONS

Indicate whether each of the following statements is true or false.

_____
1.   Freud believed that the weaning process should be managed in such a way that the infant's need to suck is neither frustrated nor overgratified.

_____
2.   Ethologists claim that the first five years constitute a sensitive period for attachment in human infants.

_____
3.   The father's bond seems to depend more on the development of synchrony than on contact immediately after birth.

_____
4.   Babies will look first at Mom's or Dad's face to check for the adult's emotional expression, a behavior called social referencing.

_____
5.   Generally speaking, difficult infants, as defined by Thomas and Chess, are more likely to be securely attached than babies in those theorists other two categories.

_____
6.   Near the middle of the first year, such self-conscious emotional expressions as embarrassment, pride, or shame emerge.

_____
7.   The most common pattern of nonparental care is for a child to be cared for by a family member in her own or in a relative's home.

_____
8.   When a daycare setting provides more enrichment than the child would have received at home, then daycare attendance has some beneficial cognitive effects.

ESSAY QUESTIONS

1.   Discuss the importance of synchrony with the infant.

2.   Thomas and Chess found that "easy" babies were more likely to be securely attached than "difficult" babies or "slow-to-warm-up" babies. Discuss the factors that might contribute to that attachment.

3.   Based on the research about nonparental care in the text and your own experience, what conclusions can you draw?

WHEN YOU HAVE FINISHED . . . PUZZLE IT OUT

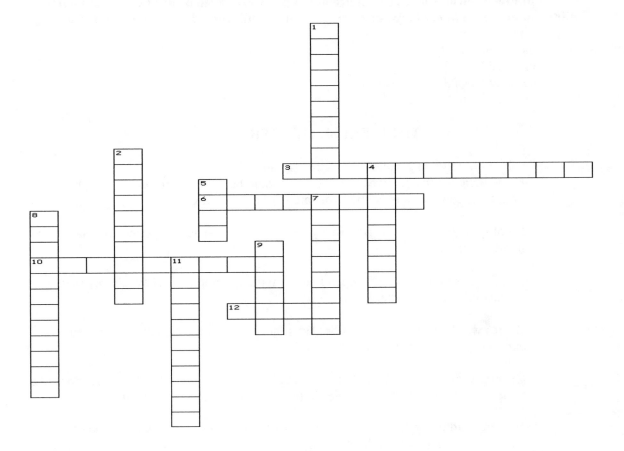

Across

3. A pattern of responding to people and objects in the environment
6. Pattern of attachment in which the infant show no preference for the parent over others
10. Also known as the categorical self
12. First stage of Freud's theory

Down

1. Also known as the existential self
2. The emotional tie to a parent from which an infant derives security.
4. A mutual, interlocking pattern of attachment behaviors
5. Infants who approach new events positively, and have good sleeping and eating cycles
7. Infants who are slow to develop regular sleeping and eating cycles
8. Pattern of attachment in which the infant shows contradictory behavior
9. Pattern of attachment in which the infant uses the parent as a safe base for exploration
11. Inborn predispositions that form the foundations of personality

Created by Puzzlemaker at DiscoverySchool.com

WHEN YOU HAVE FINISHED . . . INVESTIGATIVE PROJECT

Student Project 8: Observation of Turn Taking

This observation is designed to examine "turn taking" in the feeding interaction. You will observe a single feeding—breast or bottle—of an infant not older than one month, preferably younger. Naturally, you will need to obtain the appropriate written permission from the parents for this observation. Tell them that the purpose of your observation is simply for you to develop better observational skills. You will not be interfering in any way, and there are no "right" or "wrong" ways to go about the task.

Procedure

Observe for a total of about ten minutes, keeping a running record of behaviors by the child and by the parent. To make the task manageable, focus on only three behaviors for each member of the pair, listed below with an appropriate abbreviation letter for each:

Infant behaviors:
- sucking (S)
- fussing or crying (C)
- other vocalizing (grunt, any other non-crying sounds) (V)

Parent behaviors:
- jiggling (J)
- vocalizing (any talking to the infant, other sounds such as singing or cooing) (V)
- stroking or touching (T)

To record these behaviors, you will need a sheet with two columns of boxes on it: one column for the infant and one for the parent, such as:

Infant	Parent

Begin your observation a few minutes after the feeding has begun so that the infant and parent can adapt a bit to your presence and settle into some kind of pattern of interaction. Then start recording whatever behavior is occurring.
- If the infant is doing nothing, but the parent is jiggling or talking or touching, then put the relevant letter in the parent box for the first row.
- If the infant is doing something and the parent is simultaneously doing something, record each in the adjacent boxes in a single row.
- If the infant is doing something but the parent is not, then put the relevant letter in the infant box for that row and leave the parent box blank.

When either member of the pair changes behavior, move to the next row in your record sheet.

- If the baby sucks and then stops, and after the baby stops the mother jiggles and then says something, and then the baby sucks again, the chart would look like this:

Infant	Parent
S	
	J
	V

- If the baby sucks and the mother talks at the same time, and then the infant stops sucking and the mother keeps talking, it would look like this:

Infant	Parent
S	V
	V

For this observation, you should pay no attention to the duration of an activity. For the purposes of this exercise, it doesn't matter if the child sucks for three seconds or for 30 seconds before some change occurs.

When you have completed ten minutes of observation, or when the feeding is completed, whichever comes first, stop recording. You will need to remain seated and quiet until the feeding is over so as not to distract the parent or the infant. Be sure to thank the parent, and feel free to show the parent your observational record if he or she asks.

Analysis and Report

In examining your observational record, see if you can detect any signs of "turn taking" in the patterns of interaction. Does the parent jiggle or talk primarily in the pauses of the infant's sucking? Or does the parent talk and jiggle at the same time as the sucking? Can you devise some way of scoring the sequence of interactions that would yield a measure of "turn taking?" What are the difficulties involved in such a score?

WHEN YOU HAVE FINISHED . . . RESEARCH PROJECT
Student Project 9: Assessment of Daycare Centers

You will have a far better sense of the variation in quality of daycare centers if you visit some yourself. Your instructor may have arranged for visits to several such centers, and you may need to sign up for designated times. If you have a choice, try to visit a least one for-profit center and at least one that is run by a charitable or educational organization (e.g., a church-run or university center).

Procedure

You should of course present yourself to the office in each center when you arrive, identifying yourself as a student in Professor _____'s _____ class. Find out whether there are any special ground rules, such as places you may not go. Arrange to spend at least an hour in each center, sitting as unobtrusively as possible at the side of the room or on the edge of the playground. If you need to walk around so that you can see the full setting, feel free to do so, but do not intrude on the process. As you observe, imagine that you are a parent of a youngster, and you are looking for a care setting for that child.

With that frame of reference, record the following information for each center:
- What is the teacher/child ratio? Does this vary depending on the age of the child?
- How many children are cared for in each group in the center? (Some centers will care for all children as a single "group." Others will have separate rooms for children of different ages. What you want to know is the number of children cared for together.)

In addition, you should rate each center on a series of five-point scales, where a score of 1 always means "poor" or "low" and a score of 5 always means "optimum" or "high":

	Rating
Amount of individual one-on-one contact between adults and children	1 2 3 4 5
Amount of verbal stimulation from adults to children	1 2 3 4 5
Richness and complexity of verbal stimulation from adults to children	1 2 3 4 5
Cleanliness of environment	1 2 3 4 5
Colorfulness of environment	1 2 3 4 5
Adequacy of space	1 2 3 4 5
Summary rating of center	1 2 3 4 5

Analysis

Compare the results for several centers which you observed. If you had a young child, would you be willing to place your child in any of these centers? Why or why not? Having observed these centers, can you suggest other criteria that might be helpful for a parent? What sort of research would be needed to determine the importance of any of these features for a child's development?

WHEN YOU HAVE FINISHED . . . INVESTIGATIVE PROJECT

Student Project 10: Investigation of Daycare Options

Any parent can tell you that it is not easy to obtain good information about available daycare options. The purpose of this investigation project is therefore not only to discover as much as possible about the options in your community, but to identify good sources and good strategies for obtaining such information.

Basic Questions to Answer

- What center-care settings are available?
- Who runs the centers? For-profit companies? Churches? Schools? Others?
- How many and what ages of children do these centers accommodate? What are the costs of such center care?
- What is the best way for someone to find out about these care options?
- What family daycare options are available, and how does one locate them? Is there a registry? A licensing process? Are all family daycare providers listed in such registries or licensed?
- Are after-school care settings available as well? Who runs them? How much do they cost?
- Is care available for children in the evening and at night (as might be needed by a parent who works evenings or on the night shift)?

Sources

Much of the information you'll need can be gleaned on the phone, or from the phone book. The Yellow Pages will list daycare centers, usually under "Child-Care." Data on family daycare is much more difficult to come by (both for you and for parents). For information on licensing, especially the licensing of home-care or family daycare providers, you will want to talk to local or state government agencies. To locate individual care providers, bulletin boards are often the best data source—those located in places parents are likely to be, such as colleges or universities, on grocery store bulletin boards, in Laundromats, etc. A person or group doing this project will need to sample such stores in some systematic fashion, and then call the providers whose names they find in this way to find out how many children are cared for, what age, for what hours, and what fee is charged.

Analysis and Report

Your instructor may want you to prepare an oral or a written report for your class. In any case, you should prepare a written description of the steps you followed and the answers to the questions listed above.

CHAPTER 6 ANSWER KEY

Practice Test #1 Theories of Social and Personality Development
1. F   2. T   3. T   4. T   5. F   6. T   7. T

Practice Test #2 Attachment
1. c   2. d   3. b   4. d   5. a   6. b   7. c   8. d

Practice Test #3 Personality, Temperament, and Self-Concept
1. h   2. d   3. j   4. o   5. g   6. l   7. k   8. f   9. c   10. n

Practice Test #4 Effects of Nonparental Care
1. T   2. F   3. T   4. F   5. T   6. T

Comprehensive Practice Test
Multiple Choice Questions
1. c   2. b   3. a   4. c   5. b   6. b   7. a   8. d   9. b   10. c
11. b   12. b   13. a   14. d   15. c

True-False Questions
1. T   2. F   3. T   4. T   5. F   6. F   7. T   8. T

Essay Questions
1.
- Bonding of the adult with the infant.
- Imitative conversation style—language development
- Cognitive development

2.
- Difficult babies actively resist comfort, consequently, synchrony may lead a parent to make less effort to establish a nurturing relationship with a difficult infant.
- Slow-to-warm-up babies are less responsive to parental behaviors directed toward them. Synchrony causes the parents of these unresponsive infants to reduce the frequency of behaviors directed toward them.
- The kind of give-and-take relationships most easy infants experience with their parents never develop for babies who are difficult or slow-to-warm-up.

3.
- Children who enter day care before their first birthday may be at greater risk for insecure attachment.
- Children who stay in nonparental care for more than two hours per week are at greater risk for negative affects to social development.
- The quality of the nonparental care is essential, whether it is care by a relative or is center-based care or some combination.
- Quality care is likely to be especially beneficial to children from poor families.

Puzzle It Out

Across	Down	
3. personality	1. subjective	7. difficult
6. avoidant	2. attachment	8. disorganized
10. objective	4. synchrony	9. secure
12. oral	5. easy	11. temperament

CHAPTER 7

PHYSICAL AND COGNITIVE DEVELOPMENT IN EARLY CHILDHOOD

BEFORE YOU READ . . . CHAPTER SUMMARY

In the years from two to six, the period known as early childhood, the child changes from being a dependent toddler, able to communicate only in very primitive ways, to being a remarkably competent, communicative social creature, ready to begin school. Subtle physical changes happen during this period as well as a number of advances in cognitive and language development. Issues involved in intelligence testing are also discussed.

Physical Changes

- Changes in height and weight are far slower in the preschool years than in infancy. Motor skills continue to improve gradually, with marked improvement in large muscle skills (gross motor skills) and slower advances in small muscle skills (fine motor skills).
- Brain growth, synapse formation, and myelinization continue in early childhood, although at a pace slower than in infancy. Neurological milestones, such as lateralization and handedness, happen between two and six.
- Health and wellness issues include diet, illness, stress, and accidents.
- Two-to-nine-year-olds are more likely to be abused or neglected than infants or older children. Characteristics of the child and the abuser increase the risk of abuse. Education, identification of families at risk, and keeping abused children from further injury are three ways to prevent abuse.

Cognitive Changes

- According to Piaget, the 18- to 24-month-old child begins to use symbols and enters the preoperational stage. Despite this advance, the preschool child still lacks many sophisticated cognitive characteristics. This age child is still egocentric and lacks an understanding of conservation.
- Research challenging Piaget's findings makes it clear that young children are less egocentric than Piaget thought.
- By age four or five, the child has developed a new and quite sophisticated theory of mind. They understand that other people's actions are based on the child's own thoughts and beliefs.
- Information-processing theory explains early childhood cognitive development in terms of limitations on young children's memory systems. Vygotsky's socio-cultural theory asserts that children's thinking is shaped by social interaction through the medium of language.

Changes in Language

- Fast-mapping enables language development to increase at a rapid pace between ages two and four
- Between ages three and four, children's advances in grammar are extraordinary. Inflections, questions and negatives, and overregularization lead to the use of complex sentences.
- Phonological awareness, a child's sensitivity to the sound patterns that are specific to her own language, is key to the child's ability to learn to read and write. Children seem to acquire this skill through word play.

Differences in Intelligence

- Scores on early childhood intelligence tests are predictive of later school performance and are at least moderately consistent over time.
- Arguments about the origins of difference in IQ nearly always boil down to a dispute about nature versus nurture.
- Several kinds of racial differences in IQ or test performance have been consistently found. Such differences seem most appropriately attributed to environmental variation, rather than genetics.

AS YOU READ . . . LEARNING OJECTIVE QUESTIONS

After completing Chapter 7, you should be able to answer the following questions:

7.1   What are the major milestones of growth and motor development between 2 and 6?
7.2   What important changes happen in the brain during these yeas?
7.3   What are the nutritional and health care needs of young children?
7.4   What factors contribute to abuse and neglect, and how do these traumas affect children's development?
7.5   List the characteristics of children's thought during Piaget's preoperational stage?
7.6   How has recent research challenged Piaget's view of this period?
7.7   What is a theory of mind, and how does it develop?
7.8   How do information-processing and sociocultural theorists explain changes in young children's thinking?
7.9   How does fast-mapping help children learn new words?
7.10   What happens during the grammar explosion?
7.11   What is phonological awareness, and why is it important?
7.12   What are the strengths and weaknesses of IQ tests?
7.13   What kinds of evidence support the nature and nurture explanations for individual differences in IQ?
7.14   What theories and evidence have been offered in support of genetic and cultural explanations of group differences in IQ scores?

AS YOU READ . . . TERM IDENTIFICATION

Centration (p. 185)
Conservation (p. `85)
Corpus callosum (p. `78)
Egocentrism (p. 183)
False belief principle (p. 187)
Fast-mapping (p. 191)
Handedness (p. 179)
Hippocampus (p. 179)
Intelligence quotient (IQ) (p. 194)
Invented spelling (p. 193)
Lateralization (p. 178)

Metacognition (p. 190)
Metamemory (p. 190)
Operational efficiency (p. 189)
Overregularization (p. 192)
Phonological awareness (p. 193)
Preoperational stage (p. 183)
Reaction range (p. 198)
Semiotic (symbolic) function (p. 183)
Short-term storage space (STSS) (p. 189)
Theory of mind (p. 187)

AS YOU READ . . . GUIDED STUDY QUESTIONS

PHYSICAL CHANGES

Growth and Motor Development (pp. 177-178)

7.1   What are the major milestones of growth and motor development between 2 and 6?

1.   What are the typical changes in height and weight in the preschool years?

2.   Compare the milestones of motor development from age two to age six by completing the following table:

Age	Gross Motor Skills	Fine Motor Skills
18-24 months		
2-3 years		
3-4 years		
4-5 years		
5-6 years		

3.   How does training in writing and drawing affect physical and cognitive development?

The Brain and Nervous System (pp. 178-179)

7.2   What important changes happen in the brain during these years?

4.   Define the following terms:
    a.   corpus callosum (p. 178)

    b.   lateralization (p. 178)

    c.   hippocampus (p. 179)

    d.   handedness (p. 179)

5.   Describe the interaction of maturation and experience in the development of lateralization.

6.   How is the hippocampus involved in memory?

7.   What is infantile amnesia?

8.   How does handedness develop?

Health and Wellness (pp. 180-181)

7.3   What are the nutritional and health care needs of young children?

9.   For each of the following health issues of children in early childhood, identify possible causes of concern.

Issue	Possible Causes of Concern
Medical Check-ups	
Eating Problems	
Illness	
Stress	
Accidents	

10.   What is the leading cause of death of preschoolers?

11.   What are some precautions that parents can implement to help prevent accidents?

The Real World: Good Night's Sleep for Kids (and Parents, Too!) (p. 181)

12.   Explain how operant conditioning may be involved in children sleeping in their parents' bed.

13.   List five recommended bedtime practices.
-
-
-
-
-

Abuse and Neglect (pp. 181-192)

7.4   What factors contribute to abuse and neglect, and how do these traumas affect children's development?

14.   What is the legal definition of child abuse?

15.   What is neglect?

16.   List at least two reasons why it is difficult to define child abuse and neglect in a practical sense.

17.   List six types of child abuse.
-
-
-
-
-
-

18.   Give examples of each of the following broad categories of explanations of why abuse happens.

Categories	Examples
Sociocultural Factors	
Characteristics of the Child	
Characteristics of the Abuser	
Family Stresses	

19.   What is post-traumatic stress disorder (PTSD), why do some abused children develop it?

20.   List ways each of the following may help prevent abuse:

Categories	Ways to Prevent Abuse
Education	
Identification of Families at Risk	
Protection from Further Injury	

AFTER YOU READ . . . PRACTICE TEST #1
PHYSICAL CHANGES

1. **During the preschool years, children add about _____ in height and about _____ in weight.**
    a. 1-3 inches; 4 pounds
    b. 2-4 inches; 8 pounds
    c. 2-3 inches; 6 pounds
    d. 3-5 inches; 10 pounds

2. **Running, jumping, hopping, and skipping are examples of _____.**
    a. fine-muscle skills
    b. gross muscle skills
    c. manipulative skills
    d. nonlocomotor skills

3. **The brain structure through which the left and right sides of the cerebral cortex communicate is called _____.**
    a. the corpus callosum
    b. lateralization
    c. handedness
    d. brain maturation

4. **The process through which brain functions are divided between the two hemispheres of the cerebral cortex is called _____.**
    a. brain maturation
    b. myelinization
    c. the corpus callosum
    d. lateralization

5. **The tendency to rely primarily on the right or left hand is called _____.**
    a. the reticular formation
    b. handedness
    c. brain maturation
    d. myelinization

6. **Children living in single-parent homes are more likely (than children living with both biological parents) to experience each of the following EXCEPT _____.**
    a. more headaches
    b. more asthma
    c. less stress
    d. higher vulnerability to illness

7. **Each of the following is a type of child abuse EXCEPT _____.**
    a. providing adequate supervision
    b. drugging or poisoning children
    c. failure to obtain medical attention for an illness or injury
    d. underfeeding an infant

8.   **Post-traumatic stress disorder involves each of the following EXCEPT _____.**
        a.   nightmares
        b.   flashback memories
        c.   sleep disturbances
        d.   low levels of anxiety

COGNITIVE CHANGES

Piaget's Preoperational Stage (pp. 183-185)

7.5   List the characteristics of children's thought during Piaget's preoperational stage.

21.   Define the following terms:
    a.   semiotic (symbolic) function (p. 183)

    b.   preoperational stage (p. 183)

    c.   egocentrism (p. 183)

    d.   centration (p. 185)

    e.   conservation (p. 185)

22.   Explain Piaget's use of the following terms, and give examples of each:

Locomotion	*Animism*

23.   Explain how children demonstrate their understanding of conservations by using each of the characteristics listed in the table.

Characteristic	*Explanation of Conservation*
Identity	
Compensation	
Reversibility	

Research Report: Children's Play and Cognitive Development (p. 184)

24.   Complete the following table with a description of each of the six play behaviors:

Type of Play	Play Behavior
Constructive Play	
First Pretend Play	
Substitute Pretend Play	
Sociodramatic Play	
Rule-governed Play	

Challenges to Piaget's View (pp. 185-187)

7.6   How has recent research challenged Piaget's view of this period?

25.   List and give examples of the two levels of perspective-taking ability proposed by John Flavell.

  ▪

  ▪

26.   Give an example of how preschoolers' understanding of emotion has challenged Piaget's description of the young child's egocentrism.

Theories of Mind (pp. 187-189)

7.7   What is a theory of mind, and how does it develop?

27.   Define the following terms:
  a.   theory of mind (p. 187)

  b.   false belief principle (p. 187)

28.   Describe the progression of children's understanding of thoughts, desires, and beliefs by completing the following table:

Age	Examples of Understanding
3	

Age	Examples of Understanding
4-5	
5-7	

29.   List at least four correlates of a child's theory of mind.
-
-
-
-

30.   Give examples of how certain aspects of theory of mind develop across cultures.

Alternative Theories of Early Childhood Thinking (pp. 189-191)

7.8   How do information-processing and sociocultural theorists explain changes in young children's thinking?

31.   Define the following terms:
       a.   short-term storage space (STSS) (p. 189)

       b.   operational efficiency (p. 189)

       c.   metamemory (p. 190)

       d.   metacognition (p. 190)

32.   How does Robbie Case's Neo-Piagetian theory explain why the seven-year-old is better able to handle the processing demands of conservation than the four-year-old?

33.   Describe the research on training children in matrix classification skills.

34.	Give examples of how children's metamemory and metacognitive skills improve during the early childhood period.

35.	Briefly describe Vygotsky's views on development using the example of the puzzle.

36.	Vygotsky proposed four stages that represent steps toward the child's internalization of the ways of thinking used by adults in her society. Complete the following table to trace this development:

Stage	Examples of Internalization
Primitive Stage	
Naïve Psychology Stage	
Private Speech Stage	
Ingrowth Stage	

AFTER YOU READ . . . PRACTICE TEST #2
COGNITIVE CHANGES

Match the letter of the term in the right column with its description in the left column.

_____ 1.	A set of ideas constructed by a child or adult to explain other people's ideas, beliefs, desires, and behavior.	a. Animism
_____ 2.	Play that develops by age 5 or 6 in which children prefer formal games.	b. Centration
_____ 3.	The young child's tendency to think of the world in terms of one variable at a time.	c. Compensation
_____ 4.	The capacity to mentally compare the transformed appearance of a given quantity of matter to its original appearance.	d. Constructive
_____ 5.	An understanding that enables a child to look at a situation from another person's point of view and cause that person to have a false belief	e. Conservation
_____ 6.	A neo-Piagetian term that refers to the maximum number of schemes that can be processed in working memory at one time.	f. Egocentrism
_____ 7.	The knowledge about how the mind thinks and the ability to control and reflect on one's own thought processes.	g. False belief principle
_____ 8.	The stage of Vygotsky's theory in which the child learns to use language to communicate but still does not understand it's symbolic character.	h. First pretend
_____ 9.	Product of preoperational logic when children believe that objects are alive.	i. Identity
_____ 10.	Play between ages 2 and 3 when children begin to use objects to stand for something altogether different.	j. Ingrowth

a. Animism
b. Centration
c. Compensation
d. Constructive
e. Conservation
f. Egocentrism
g. False belief principle
h. First pretend
i. Identity
j. Ingrowth
k. Locomotion
l. Matrix classification
m. Metacognition
n. Metamemory
o. Naïve psychology
p. Operational efficiency
q. Preoperational
r. Primitive
s. Private speech
t. Reversibility
u. Rule-governed
v. Semiotic function
w. Short-term storage space
x. Sociodramatic
y. Substitute pretend
z. Theory of mind

CHANGES IN LANGUAGE

Fast-Mapping (pp. 191-192)

7.9   How does fast-mapping help children learn new words?

37.   Define fast-mapping (p. 191).

38.   How does fast-mapping enables preschool children to learn new words.

The Grammar Explosion (p. 292)

7.10   What happens during the grammar explosion?

39.   Children seem to add inflections and more complex word orders in fairly predictable sequences. Give examples of each of the following:

Inflection	Example
Adding *–ing* to a verb	
Prepositions	
Plural *–s* on nouns	
Possessives	
Irregular Past Tense	
Articles	
Plural *–s* to Third Person Verbs	
Regular Past Tense	
Auxiliary Verbs	

40.   List the sequence in the child's developing use of questions and negatives.

41.   Define overregularization (p. 192), or overgeneralization, and give examples.

Phonological Awareness (pp. 192-193)

7.11   What is phonological awareness, and why is it important?

42.   Define the following terms, and give examples of each:

a.   phonological awareness (p. 193)

b.   invented spelling (p. 193)

43.   What are the benefits to the child of developing phonological awareness in early childhood?

44.   Describe how phonological awareness develops through word play.

45.   What are the benefits to the child of using invented spelling as a preschooler?

AFTER YOU READ . . . PRACTICE TEST #3
CHANGES IN LANGUAGE

Indicate whether each of the following statements is true or false.

_____
1.
Piaget recognized that the overriding theme of cognitive development in the early childhood years is language acquisition.

_____
2.
By the time a child goes to school at age 5 or 6, her total vocabulary has risen to perhaps 50,000 words.

_____
3.
Children learning English typically add the –s to third person verbs before they add –ing to a verb.

_____
4.
When a child says, "I go-ed to the store with Mommy," he is using overregularization.

_____
5.
Phonological awareness in the early childhood years is related to rate of literacy in languages as varied as English, Punjabi, and Chinese.

_____
6.
Reciting nursery rhymes is an example of word play that contributes to phonological awareness.

DIFFERENCES IN INTELLIGENCE

Measuring Intelligence (pp. 193-195)

7.12   *What are the strengths and weaknesses of IQ tests?*

46.   Define intelligence quotient, or IQ (p. 194).

47.   Who designed the first modern intelligence test that was published in 1905?

48.   What was the practical purpose of the first test?

49.   How was IQ computed from the Stanford-Binet? State the formula and give examples.

Formula	*Examples*

50.   What is the current process for IQ score calculations?

51.   What are the scores for "gifted" and for "retarded?"

"Gifted"	*"Retarded"*

52.   Describe the intelligence test designed by David Wechsler.

53.   What negative long-term outcomes are associated with low intelligence?

54.   How does IQ correlate to resilience?

Level of IQ	*Resilience*
High IQ	
Low IQ	

55.   What is the general rule of thumb regarding age and the stability of IQ scores?

56.   What are some limitations of IQ tests?

Origins of Individual Differences in Intelligence (pp. 196-198)

7.13   What kinds of evidence support the nature and nurture explanations for individual differences in IQ?

57.   What do both twin studies and studies of adopted children show?

58.   Give examples of five behaviors of family interactions that foster higher scores.

Behavior	Example

59.   How do programs like Head Start or other quality preschool experiences supplement home environments and family interactions? Include IQ scores as well as other measures in your answer.

60.   Define reaction range (p. 198), and give examples.

Group Differences in Intelligence Test Scores (pp. 198-199)

7.14   What theories and evidence have been offered in support of genetic and cultural explanations of group differences in IQ scores?

61.   How do many developmentalists use reaction range to explain differences in IQ scores of African-American and White children?

62.   Describe the Flynn effect, and give examples.

63.   Give examples of Flynn's belief that many theorists have neglected a consideration of cultural beliefs in their search for a heredity basis for intelligence.

No Easy Answers: To Test or Not to Test? (p. 200)

64.   How can intelligence testing benefit children?

65.   Why is routine testing of young children who have no disabilities more controversial?

AFTER YOU READ . . . PRACTICE TEST #4
DIFFERENCES IN INTELLIGENCE

1. **Psychologists can devise tests of intelligence for preschoolers that measure _____ .**
   a.   vocabulary and reasoning skills
   b.   only vocabulary
   c.   mathematical ability
   d.   reasoning skills and mathematical ability

2. **The practical use of the first modern intelligence test was to _____ .**
   a.   sort out children who were gifted and needed extra assignments
   b.   label children as "smart" and "not smart"
   c.   place children in "tracks" for their school career
   d.   identify children who might have difficulty in school.

3. **Children who score above _____ are often called gifted.**
   a.   100
   b.   110
   c.   120
   d.   130

4. **_____ scales on intelligence tests provide psychologists with information about a child's short-term memory capacity.**
   a.   Performance
   b.   Verbal
   c.   Working memory
   d.   Processing speed

5. **Intelligence is likely to add to a child's _____ .**
   a.   resilience
   b.   secular effect
   c.   reaction range
   d.   Flynn effect

6. **Low intelligence is associated with a number of negative long-term outcomes, including all of the following EXCEPT _____ .**
   a.   delinquency in adolescence
   b.   increased self-esteem
   c.   adult illiteracy
   d.   criminal behavior in adulthood

7. **Children who go through Head Start or other quality preschool experience _____**
   a.   are more likely to be place in special education classes than their peers
   b.   have poorer immunization rates than their peers
   c.   are more likely to repeat a grade than their peers
   d.   have better school adjustment than their peers

8.   _____ is a range between upper and lower boundaries for traits such as intelligence, which is established by one's genes; one's environment determines where, within those limits, one will be.
a.   Flynn effect
b.   Reaction range
c.   Intelligence quotient
d.   The gifted-retarded dichotomy

AFTER YOU READ . . . CRITICAL REFLECTION EXERCISES

Kindergarten

You are about to enter your first day of teaching Kindergarten. Based on the information provided in the text, provide detailed responses to the following questions:

1. At what level of language development will most of these children be? What language skills will they have?

2. How might the child's perception of you and the classroom experience be related to culture? What things might you do to minimize any potential negative effects of cultural differences, yet support these differences at the same time?

3. How would a child's cognitive development influence his or her play?

Intelligence

Based on the discussion of intelligence in the text, how would you define "intelligence"? There is not a "right versus wrong" definition. Utilizing the concepts discussed, what definition makes sense to you? Why? How would you utilize this definition if you were raising a child in the two to six age range?

AFTER YOU READ . . . COMPREHENSIVE PRACTICE TEST
MULTIPLE CHOICE QUESTIONS

1. **Which of the following statements is TRUE concerning growth and motor skill development in the preschool years?**
   a. Changes in height and weight are at the same rate as in infancy.
   b. Changes in motor development are as dramatic as in infancy.
   c. The most impressive changes are in small muscle skills.
   d. Changes in height and weight are far slower in the preschool years.

2. **The _____ is involved in the transfer of information to long-term memory.**
   a. corpus callosum
   b. hippocampus
   c. cerebral cortex
   d. cerebellum

3. **_____ are the major cause of death in preschool and school-age children.**
   a. Automobile accidents
   b. Chronic illnesses
   c. Acute illnesses
   d. Stressful situations

4. **Which of the following is NOT one of the four broad categories of risk factors for abuse?**
   a. socio-cultural factors
   b. family stresses
   c. responsive parenting
   d. characteristics of the child

5. **According to Piaget, the preschool child is in the _____ stage of cognitive development.**
   a. sensorimotor
   b. preoperational
   c. concrete operational
   d. formal operational

6. **A set of ideas that explains other people's ideas, beliefs, desires, and behaviors is called _____.**
   a. false belief principle
   b. theory of mind
   c. metamemory
   d. matrix classification

7. **An understanding that enables a child to look at a situation from another person's point of view and determine what kind of information will cause that person to have a false belief is called _____.**
   a. the theory of mind
   b. conservation
   c. egocentrism
   d. the false belief principle

8. Knowledge about how memory works and the ability to control and reflect on one's own memory function is called _____.
   a. metamemory
   b. metacognition
   c. metaprocessing
   d. metaknowledge

9. The ability to categorically link new worlds to real-world objects or events is called _____.
   a. fast-tracking
   b. categorizing
   c. fast-mapping
   d. invented spelling

10. Which of the following inflections is the child likely to add first to his words?
    a. the suffix –ing
    b. the suffix –ed
    c. auxiliary verbs
    d. plurals

11. A child who says "foots" instead of "feet" is _____.
    a. probably in danger of developing language deficits
    b. exhibiting overregularization
    c. not a native speaker of English
    d. at least five years old

12. A child's sensitivity to the sound patterns that are specific to her own language is called _____.
    a. metacognition
    b. overregularization
    c. metamemory
    d. phonological awareness

13. Which of the following correctly illustrates the formula use to calculate IQ?
    a. chronological age + mental age ÷ 100
    b. mental age ÷ chronological age x 100
    c. chronological age – mental age + 100
    d. chronological age ÷ mental age ‑ 100

14. Which of the following family characteristics tends to lead to children having higher IQs?
    a. families that avoid excessive restrictiveness
    b. families that set extremely high performance standards
    c. families that do not place high demands on their children
    d. families that encourage competition between siblings

15. Each of the following statements is true about IQ testing EXCEPT _____.
    a. Labels based on IQ testing at an early age may be detrimental to young children's future development.
    b. IQ testing of children is always reliable.
    c. IQ tests are important tools for identifying children who have special educational needs.
    d. Using IQ tests to classify normal young children is of little value.

TRUE-FALSE QUESTIONS

Indicate whether each of the following statements is true or false.

_____
1. Brain growth, synapse formation, and myelinization continue in early childhood at the same rate as in infancy.

_____
2. Food aversions rarely develop during the preschool years.

_____
3. Piaget used the term animism to refer to the aspect of preoperational logic in which children believe that inanimate objects are alive.

_____
4. Robbie Case theorized that there is a limit on how many schemes can be attended to in short-term storage space (STSS).

_____
5. After children have figured out inflections and the basic sentence forms using negatives and questions, they begin to create remarkably complex sentences.

_____
6. Children who use invented spelling strategies before school-based instruction in reading and writing are more likely to become poor spellers and poor readers later in childhood.

_____
7. When an enrichment program such as Head Start is begun in infancy rather than at age 3 or 4, IQ scores remain elevated into adulthood.

_____
8. Significant differences in IQ scores between African-American and White children are not found on infant tests of intelligence or on measures of infant habituation rate.

ESSAY QUESTIONS

1. The text states that the difference between abusive and non-abusive parents is the presence of a number of risk factors that show how the parents respond to the ordinary stresses of parenting. Discuss the risk factors and how they interact to affect whether or not parents abuse their children.

2. Compare Piaget's concept of egocentrism with the theory of mind. Are they mutually exclusive or can a child be egocentric as well as the theory of mind? Give examples to support your answer.

3. Choose a book, story, or nursery rhyme that preschoolers might enjoy that uses word play to increase their phonological awareness. Give examples of how it would increase a child's phonological awareness.

WHEN YOU HAVE FINISHED . . . PUZZLE IT OUT

Across
1. Knowledge about how the mind thinks
5. The young child's tendency to think of the world in terms of one variable at a time
7. Range between upper and lower boundaries which is established by one's genes
8. A brain structure that is important in learning
9. Knowledge about how memory works
10. The process through which brain functions are divided between the two hemispheres of the cerebral cortex
11. Piaget's second stage of cognitive development

Down
2. Attachment of regular inflections to irregular words
3. The understanding that matter can change in appearance without changing in quantity
4. The young child's belief that everyone sees the world that everyone sees the world the way he does
6. A strong preference for using one hand or the other

Created by Puzzlemaker at DiscoverySchool.com

WHEN YOU HAVE FINISHED . . . INVESTIGATIVE PROJECT

Student Project 11: Assessing the Child's Theory of Mind

For this project, you will need to locate a child between the ages of three and five. You must obtain written permission from the child's parents, following by whatever procedure your instructor specifies. The testing should be done in a quiet place in the child's home.

The task that has most often been used to assess the child's theory of mind has been called the Smarties task because it uses a box of a type of candy called "Smarties," common in England and Canada where much of this research has been done. United States children, however, are not going to be familiar with Smarties, so we need to revise the procedure, using an M&M bag filled with small rocks.

Procedure

Find a quiet place where you and the child can sit down at a table or on the floor. Tell the child:

> We're going to play a game where I show you some things and ask you questions about them.

Bring out your M&M bag and ask the child to look at it. Then open the bag and show the child that there are rocks inside. Ask:

> What's inside the bag?

If the child doesn't say "rocks," ask again, *What are they?* When it is clear that the child knows that they are really rocks, put the rocks in the bag and close it. Now ask the child the following questions (all adapted from the procedure used by Gopnik & Astington, 1988) and write down the child's answers carefully.

> Does it look like this bag has rocks in it or does it look like it has candies in it?

> What's really inside the bag? Are there really rocks inside it, or are there really candies inside it?

> When you first saw the bag, before we opened it, what did you think was inside it? Did you think there were rocks inside it, or did you think there were candies inside it?

> Your Mom hasn't seen inside this bag. If your Mom sees the bag all closed up like this, what will she think is inside it? Will she think there are rocks inside it, or will she think there are candies inside it?

When you are done, thank the child, compliment the child on his or her answers, and stay long enough to play with the child at some game the child chooses.

Analysis and Report

In analyzing and reporting on your result, compare your child's answers to those reported in the text. Did your child understand the difference between appearance and reality? Did she or he understand false belief?

Reference

Gopnik, A., & Astington, J. W. (1988). Children's understanding of representational change and its relation to the understanding of false belief and the appearance-reality distinction. *Child Development, 59,* 26-37.

WHEN YOU HAVE FINISHED . . . RESEARCH PROJECT

Student Project 12: Beginning Two-Word Sentences

Some of you have been around young children a lot, and already have some sense for the delightful quality of their early language, but all of you would benefit from some additional listening. Locate a child who is still in the earliest stages of sentence formation, or just beginning to add a few inflections. This is most likely to be a child of 20 to 24 months, but a child between 24 and 30 months may do fine, too. The one essential aspect is that the child must be speaking at least some two-word sentences. If you are unsure, ask the parent; they can nearly always tell you whether the child has reached this stage or not.

Procedure

As usual, begin by following whatever procedures your instructor requires for obtaining appropriate informed consent from the parents of your subject for you to observe. Then arrange to spend enough time with the child at his or her home, or in any other convenient setting, so that you can collect a list of 50 different spontaneous utterances, including both one-word and two-word sentences. By spontaneous, I mean those that the child speaks without prompting; try to avoid getting into a situation in which the mother or some other adult actively tries to elicit language from the child, although it is certainly acceptable if you collect a sample from a time when the child is playing with an adult, or doing some activity with a parent or older sibling. The most fruitful time is likely to be when the child is playing with someone, and it is fine to ask the mother to play with the child, but not to play the sort of game in which the object is to get the child to talk. Whenever you can, make notes about the context in which each sentence occurred so that you can judge the meaning more fully.

Analysis and Report

When you have your list of 50 utterances, try describing the child's language in any terms from the text. For example, is the child using any grammatical inflections? Which ones? Does the pattern conform to what was described? What about questions or negatives? And what about the different meanings expressed? What is the child's mean length of utterance (MLU)? To calculate the MLU you will need to count the number of meaningful units in each sentence. Each word is a meaningful unit, but so is each grammatical inflection, like the *-s* for a plural, the *-ed* ending for a past tense, etc. Some specific rules to follow in calculating the MLU are:

1. Do not count such sounds as "uh," or " "um," "oh," but do count "no," "yeah," and "hi."
2. All compound words, like "birthday," "choo-choo," "night-night," and "pocketbook" should be counted as single words.
3. Count all irregular past tenses as single words, such as "got," "did," "want," and "saw," but count as two words any regular past tense, such as "play-ed," or any erroneous extension of the past tense, such as "went-ed."
4. Count as one all diminutives, such as "doggie" or "mommy."
5. Count as one all combinations, such as "gonna," "wanna," or "hafta."
6. Count as one each auxiliary, such as "is," "have," "will," "can," and "must," and as one each inflection, such as the "s" for plural or possessive, the "s" for third person singular verb form, and the "ing" on a verb.

WHEN YOU HAVE FINISHED . . . RESEARCH PROJECT

Student Project 13: Conversation between Mother and Child

This project focuses on the social environment—what is said to the child as well as the child's response. Again, find a child around age two, though it's acceptable to go up to about three and a half. (It can be the same child you listened to in project 12, but you should collect the two sets of observations separately.)

Procedure

After obtaining the appropriate informed consent, spend some time with the child while the mother or father is around. As with project 12, the interaction should be as spontaneous as possible. It is fine if the adult and child play together as long as they aren't playing "repeat after me" naming games.

Record the conversation between the parent and the child, making sure that you have the sentences of the two people in the right order. Continue to record the conversation until you have at least 25 sentences for each. You may use a tape recorder if you wish, but you'll find it helpful to write down the sentences as they occur as well.

Analysis and Report

Did the adult adapt his or her language to that of the child? Did the adult repeat the child's utterances with minor modifications? Was there any obvious reinforcement or shaping going on? Did the adult attempt to correct the child's speech, and if so, what was the effect? Include your record of the conversation in your report, along with a page or two of comments.

CHAPTER 7 ANSWER KEY

Practice Test #1 Physical Changes

1. c   2. b   3. a   4. d   5. b   6. c   7. a   8. d

Practice Test #2 Cognitive Changes

1. z   2. u   3. b   4. t   5. g   6. p   7. m   8. o   9. a   10. y

Practice Test #3 Changes in Language

1. T   2. F   3. F   4. T   5. T   6. T

Practice Test #4 Differences in Intelligence

1. a   2. d   3. d   4. c   5. a   6. b   7. d   8. b

Comprehensive Practice Test

Multiple Choice Questions

1. d   2. b   3. a   4. c   5. b   6. b   7. d   8. a   9. c   10. a

11. b   12. d   13. b   14. a   15. b

True-False Questions

1. F   2. F   3. T   4. T   5. T   6. F   7. T   8. T

Essay Questions

1.
- Socio-cultural factors: Personal or cultural values that regard physical abuse of children as morally acceptable.
- Characteristics of the child: Children with physical or mental disabilities or those who have difficult temperaments.
- Characteristics of the abusers: Parents who are depressed, lack parenting skills and knowledge, have a history of abuse themselves, or are substances abusers.
- Family stresses: Factors such as poverty, unemployment, and inter-parental conflict

2.
- Egocentrism: The preoperational child's tendency to look at things entirely from her own point of view.
- Theory of mind: A set of ideas constructed by a child or adult to explain other people's ideas, beliefs, desires, and behavior.

3.
- Choose a favorite and include specific examples.

Puzzle It Out

Across
1. metacognition
5. centration
7. reaction
8. hippocampus
9. metamemory
10. lateralization
11. preoperational

Down
2. overregularization
3. conservation
4. egocentrism
6. handedness

CHAPTER 8

SOCIAL AND PERSONALITY DEVELOPMENT IN EARLY CHILDHOOD

BEFORE YOU READ . . . CHAPTER SUMMARY

Children between ages two and six undergo remarkable changes in their social skills. They go from being nay-saying, oppositional toddlers who spend most of their play times alone to being skilled, cooperative playmates by age five or six.

Theories of Social and Personality Development

- Freud and Erikson each described two stages of personality development in early childhood. Both suggest that the key to this period is the balance between the child's emerging skills and desire for autonomy, and the parent's need to protect and control the child's behavior. More recent psychoanalytic approaches, however, include relationships with peers and siblings.
- Social-cognitive theorists emphasize that advances in social and personality development are associated with cognitive development. They focus on three areas of interest: person perception, understanding of intentions, and understanding of different kinds of rules.

Personality and Self-Concept

- As young children gain more understanding of the social environment, their temperaments ripen into true personalities.
- Two aspects of self-concept, the categorical self and the emotional self, continue to develop between ages two and six, and the social self is added. Children make major strides in self-control and in their understanding of their own social roles.

Gender Development

- Neither Freud's nor Erikson's explanations of gender development has fared well. Social learning theory explanations are more persuasive but ignore the role of cognitive development. Social-cognitive theories explain and predict gender-related understanding and behavior better then psychoanalytic or learning theories.
- Children seem to develop gender constancy, the understanding that gender is an innate characteristic that cannot be changed, in three steps: labeling their own and others' gender, understanding the stability of gender, and comprehending the constancy of gender at about age five or six.
- In these same years, children begin to learn what goes with being a boy or a girl in a given culture. By age five or six, most children have developed fairly rigid rules about what boys or girls are supposed to do or be.
- Sex-typed behavior, different patterns of behavior among girls and boys, develops earlier than ideas about sex roles, beginning as early as 18 to 24 months of age. Girls tend to adopt an enabling style of behavior whereas boys are likely to show a constricting or restrictive style.

Family Relationships and Structure

- Although the child's attachment to the parents remains strong, many attachment behaviors become less visible. Young preschoolers may show more refusals and defiance of parental influence attempts than infants, but as they gain language and cognitive skills, they generally comply fairly readily.
- Different approaches to parenting result in differences in children's development. Authoritative parenting, combining warmth, clear rules, and communication with high maturity demands, is associated with the most positive results.
- Ethnicity and socio-economic class are linked to parenting style. Studies of parenting style and developmental outcomes suggest that in some situations, authoritative parenting may not always be the "best" style for Asian Americans, African Americans, and children of poor parents.
- Family structure affects social and personality development. Data from studies in the U.S. indicate that more positive outcomes are associated with two biological parents than any other family structure.
- Following a divorce, children typically show declines in school performance and show more aggressive, negative, or depressed behavior. Many effects of divorce are associated with problems that existed before the marriage ended.
- A number of variables are involved with family structure and divorce, such as a change in family income, the upheaval of subtracting or adding new adults to the family system, and the possible shift away from authoritative parenting. Ultimately, it is the process within the family, rather than any particular disruption, that is significant for the child.

Peer Relationships

- Preschoolers participate in various kinds of play that are related to the development of social skills. Children who are unskilled at the social skill of group entry are often rejected by their peers.
- Physical aggression toward peers increases and then declines during these years, whereas verbal aggression increases among older preschoolers. Some children develop a pattern of aggression that creates problems for them throughout childhood and adolescence.
- Children display prosocial behavior as young as age two, and the behavior seems to grow as the child's ability to take another's perspective increases. Parents and teachers can encourage the development of altruistic behavior. Stable friendships develop between children in this age range.

AS YOU READ . . . LEARNING OBJECTIVES

After completing Chapter 8, you should be able to answer the following questions:

8.1   What major themes of development did the psychoanalytic theorists propose for the early childhood period?
8.2   What are the findings of social-cognitive theorists with respect to young children's understanding of the social world?
8.3   How does temperament change in early childhood?
8.4   What changes take place in the young child's categorical, emotional, and social selves during the preschool years?
8.5   How do the major theoretical orientations explain gender development?
8.6   Describe the development of gender identity, gender stability, and gender constancy?
8.7   What are the characteristics of young children's sex-role knowledge?
8.8   How is the behavior of young children sex-typed?
8.9   How does attachment change during the early childhood years?
8.10   How do parenting styles affect children's development?
8.11   How are ethnicity and socioeconomic status related to parenting style?
8.12   How is family structure related to children's development?

8.13   How does divorce affect children's behavior in early childhood and in later years?

8.14   What are some possible reasons for the relationship between family structure and development?

8.15   What are the various kinds of play that are exhibited by preschoolers?

8.16   What is the difference between instrumental and hostile aggression, and which is more prevalent during early childhood?

8.17   How do prosocial behavior and friendship patterns change during early childhood?

AS YOU READ . . . TERM IDENTIFICATION

Aggression (p. 232)

Authoritarian parenting style (p. 221)

Authoritative parenting style (p. 221)

Cross-gender behavior (p. 219)

Emotional regulation (p. 212)

Empathy (p. 213)

Extended family (p. 230)

Gender (p. 214)

Gender constancy (p. 215)

Gender identity (p. 216)

Gender schema theory (p. 215)

Gender stability (p. 216)

Hostile aggression (p. 232)

Inductive discipline (p. 223)

Instrumental aggression (p. 233)

Parenting styles (p. 220)

Permissive parenting style (p. 221)

Person perception (p. 209)

Prosocial behavior (p. 234)

Sex-typed behavior (p. 218)

Social skills (p. 231)

Social-cognitive theory (p. 208)

Uninvolved parenting style (p. 221)

AS YOU READ . . . GUIDED STUDY QUESTIONS

THEORIES OF SOCIAL AND PERSONALITY DEVELOPMENT

Psychoanalytic Perspectives (p. 208)

8.1   What major themes of development did the psychoanalytic theorists propose for the early childhood period?

1.   List and describe the two stages of Freud's theory during the preschool years.

Stage	Description

2.   List and describe the two stages of Erikson's theory during the preschool years.

Stage	Description

3.   According to Erikson, what is the key to healthy development during this period?

Social-Cognitive Perspectives (pp. 208-210)

8.2   What are the findings of social-cognitive theorists with respect to young children's understanding of the social world?

4.   Define the following terms:
        a.   social-cognitive theory (p. 208)

        b.   person perception (p. 209)

5.   Give examples of how young children's observations and categorizations of people are far less consistent than those of older children.

6.   Describe how children demonstrate the cross-race effect.

7.   Explain and give an example of a social convention.

8.   Give examples of how young children demonstrate their understanding of intentions.

Research Report: Racism in the Preschool Classroom (p. 210)

9.   How do young children form race schemas?

10.   What is the key to preventing racial awareness from developing into racism? Give examples.

AFTER YOU READ . . . PRACTICE TEST #1
THEORIES OF SOCIAL AND PERSONALITY DEVELOPMENT

Fill in the blanks with the best answer.

1. Freud described two stages during the preschool years, the _____ stage and the

    _____ stage.

2. Erikson described two stages in the preschool period, the _____ stage and the

    _____ stage.

3. In contrast to the psychoanalytic tradition, _____ assumes that social and
    emotional changes in the child are the result of—or at least facilitated by—the enormous growth
    in cognitive abilities that happens during the preschool yeas.

4. _____ is the ability to classify others according to categories such as age,
    gender, and race.

5. A phenomenon in which individuals are more likely to remember the faces of people of their own

    race than those of a different race is called the _____ .

6. Research suggests that children know more about _____ than Piaget thought,
    but they are still limited in their ability to base judgments entirely on them.

PERSONALITY AND SELF-CONCEPT

From Temperament to Personality (p. 211-212)

8.3   How does temperament change in early childhood?

11. Describe the link between a difficultness of temperament and concurrent and future behavior
    problems.

12. How is the transition from temperament to personality influenced by parental responses to a
    young child's temperament?

Self-Concept (pp. 212-214)

8.4   What changes take place in the young child's categorical, emotional, and social selves during the preschool years?

13.   Define the following terms:
a.   emotional regulation (p. 212)

b.   empathy (p. 213)

14.   How does a child's temperament affect the process of gaining emotional regulation?

15.   List the two aspects involved in empathy.
■

■

16.   Give examples of the following moral emotions.

Moral Emotion	*Example*
Guilt	
Shame	
Pride	

17.   How does the interplay among guilt, shame, and pride and young children's awareness of them influence "morally acceptable" behavior?

18.   Give an example of a social "script."

19.   Give examples of how role scripts help young children become more independent.

AFTER YOU READ . . . PRACTICE TEST #2
PERSONALITY AND SELF-CONCEPT

Fill in the banks with the best answer.

1.   Children with difficult temperaments learn that the behaviors associated with difficultness, such

   as complaining, often result in _____.

2.   _____ represents the combination of the temperament with which children are
   probably born and the knowledge they gain about temperament-related behavior during
   childhood.

3.   The transition from temperament to personality is also influenced by _____ to
   the young child's temperament.

4.   _____ is the ability to control emotional states and emotion-related behavior.

5.   The process of acquiring emotional regulation is one in which control shifts slowly from the

   _____ to the _____.

6.   Empathy involves two aspects: _____ and then

   _____.

7.   _____ help young children become more independent as they gain an
   increasing awareness of themselves as players in the social game.

GENDER DEVELOPMENT

Explaining Gender Development (pp. 214-216)

8.5   How do the major theoretical orientations explain gender development?

20.   Define the following terms:
   a.   gender (p. 215)

   b.   gender constancy (p. 215)

   c.   gender schema theory (p. 215)

21.　　Summarize the theoretical views of gender development by completing the following table:

Psychoanalytic Explanations
Freud
Difficulty of Freud's Theory

Social-Learning Explanations
Role of Parents
Evidence that Social-Learning Theory is Insufficient

Social-Cognitive Explanations
Kohlberg's Theory
Difficulty with Kohlberg's Theory

Gender Schema Theory
Gender Schema Theory
Key Difference between Gender Schema and Kohlberg's Theory

Biological Approaches
Prenatal Exposure to Testosterone
Support for View that Hormones Affect Gender Development

The Gender Concept (pp. 216-217)

8.6　Describe the development of gender identity, gender stability, and gender constancy.

22.　　Define the following terms:
　　a.　　gender identity (p. 216)

　　b.　　gender stability (p. 216)

23.   Describe the three steps in the development of gender constancy.
       ▪

       ▪

       ▪

24.   How is gender constancy related to the concept of conservation?

Sex-Role Knowledge (pp. 217-218)

8.7   What are the characteristics of young children's sex-role knowledge?
25.   What are gender stereotypes?

26.   Give examples of commonly stereotyped traits for men and for women.

Sex-Typed Behavior (pp. 218-219)

8.8   How is behavior of young children sex-typed?
27.   Define the following terms:
       a.   sex-typed behavior (p. 218)

       b.   cross-gender behavior (p. 219)

28.   Give examples of sex-stereotyped toys.

29.   Give examples of girls' use of the enabling style, and boys' use of the restrictive style.

Style	*Examples*
Girls' Use of Enabling Style	
Boys' Use of Restrictive Style	

30.   Give examples of cross-gender behavior of girls and boys, and adults' reactions to it.

Cross-Gender Behavior	*Adults' Reaction*
Girls	
Boys	

31.   It cannot be assumed that the prevalence of sex-typed play among boys is strictly the result of adult and peer influence. List four pieces of evidence for the statement.

-

-

-

-

AFTER YOU READ . . . PRACTICE TEST #3
GENDER DEVELOPMENT

Indicate whether each of the following statements is true or false.

_____
1.
According to Freud, children learn acquire gender through the process of rationalization.

_____
2.
Social learning theorists emphasize the role of parents in shaping children's sex-role behavior and attitude.

_____
3.
Kohlberg suggested that the crucial aspect of the process is the child's understanding of his sex role.

_____
4.
Gender constancy is the understanding that gender is an innate characteristic that can't be changed.

_____
5.
The gender scheme begins to develop as soon as the child notices the differences between male and female, knows her own gender, and can label the two groups with some consistency

_____
6.
The final step in the development of true gender constancy is the recognition that someone stays the same gender even though he may appear to change by changing his hair length.

_____
7.
Sex-typed behavior is different patterns of behavior among girls and boys.

FAMILY RELATIONSHIPS AND STRUCTURE

Attachment (p. 220)

8.9   How does attachment change during the early childhood years?

32.   Compare a two- or three-year-old child's attachment to her parents with that of an infant.

Age	Attachment
2- or 3-year old	
Infant	

33.   Give examples of how attachment quality predicts behavior during the preschool years.

34.   According to Bowlby, how does the attachment relationship change at about age four? Give examples.

35.   How do advances in the internal working model lead to new conflicts?

Parenting Styles (pp. 220-223)

8.10 *How do parenting styles affect children's development?*

36.   Define the following terms:
   a.   parenting styles (p. 220)

   b.   permissive parenting style (p. 221)

   c.   authoritarian parenting style (p. 221)

   d.   authoritative parenting style (p. 221)

   e.   uninvolved parenting style (p. 221)

   f.   inductive discipline (p. 223)

37.   Complete the following table by listing the four aspects of family functioning, and stating how each is related to various child behaviors:

Aspect of Family Functioning	*Relationship to Child's Behavior*

38.   According to Maccoby and Martin, what are the two dimensions of family characteristics?
▪

▪

39. Complete the following table to describe how parenting style affects the child's behavioral outcomes:

Parenting Style	Likely Behavioral Outcomes
Authoritarian	
Permissive	
Authoritative	
Uninvolved	

40. Describe some of the complexities of the effects of parenting styles.

41. Give examples of inductive discipline.

Ethnicity, Socioeconomic Status, and Parenting Styles (pp. 223-225)

8.11 How are ethnicity and socioeconomic status related to parenting style?

42. Summarize the results of the study of 10,000 high school students representing four ethnic groups.

43. List some reasons why Asian-American parents and African-American parents tend to use the authoritarian parenting style.

The Real World: To Spank or Not to Spank? (p. 225)

44. List two likely outcomes of spanking in the short term.

▪

▪

45.   List four longer term negative effects of spanking.
■

■

■

■

■

46.   List three recommendations if spanking is used.
■

■

■

■

47.   What is the Premack principle?

Family Structure (pp. 223-225)

8.12   How is family structure related to children's development?

48.   Describe the diversity in two-parent families.

49.   List and describe two reasons why single-parent families are far more common among African
        Americans and Native Americans.
■

■

50.   Describe the type of research available on custodial grandparenting.

51.   Describe the research available on gay and lesbian parenting.

52.   Describe the research available on children who were conceived by artificial insemination.

Divorce (pp. 228-229)

8.13   *How does divorce affect children's behavior in early childhood and in later years?*

53.   List four divorce-related factors that may affect the results of research.
-
-
-
-

54.   List several negative effects of divorce for children, adolescents, and adults.

Age Group	Effects
Children	
Adolescents	
Adults	

55.   How might divorce affect boys and girls differently?

Understanding the Effects of Family Structure and Divorce (pp. 229-230)

8.14   *What are some possible reasons for the relationship between family structure and development?*

56.   In the U.S., what does research suggest as the optimum situation for children?

57.   List and describe three key reasons explaining the negative findings about divorce.

Reason	Description

58.   Define extended family (p. 230)

No Easy Answers: When Divorce is Unavoidable (p. 230)

59.   List and describe six specific things that parents can do that are likely to soften or shorten the effects of divorce.

Factor	Description

AFTER YOU READ . . . PRACTICE TEST #4
FAMILY RELATIONSHIPS AND STRUCTURE

1. **Four- and five-year-olds who are securely attached to their parents are _____ to have positive relationships with their preschool teachers than their insecurely attached peers.**
   a. equally as likely
   b. ten times as likely
   c. more likely
   d. less likely

2. **Developmental psychologists believe that two-year-olds _____.**
   a. are more compliant than at any other age
   b. comply with parents' requests more often than not
   c. are more likely to comply with self-care requests than other requests
   d. will generally say "no" to everything but then comply

3. **The permissive parental style includes _____.**
   a. low nurturance and high communication
   b. high control and low communication
   c. low maturity demands and low nurturance
   d. high nurturance and low control

4. **In a large-scale study of 10,000 high school students representing four ethnic groups, the _____ was more common among white families and more common among the middle class.**
   a. authoritative parenting style
   b. authoritarian parenting style
   c. uninvolved parenting style
   d. permissive parenting style

5. **Each of the following is a negative effect of spanking EXCEPT _____.**
   a. spanking leads to a family climate that is characterized by emotional rejection
   b. spanking is associated with lower levels of aggression among children
   c. spanking models infliction of pain as a means of getting someone to do what you want them to do
   d. spanking associates the parent who spanks with the child's experience of physical pain

6. **Each of the following is a negative effect of divorce on children EXCEPT _____.**
   a. declines in school performance
   b. increased aggression
   c. more defiance
   d. decreased likelihood of depression

7. **Each of the following is an accurate statement about extended families EXCEPT _____.**
   a. extended families include parents, grandparents, aunts, uncles, cousins, and so on
   b. grandmothers seem to be the most important sources of emotional warmth for the children of teenaged mothers
   c. extended family members rarely help single and divorced mothers with financial and emotional support as well as with child care
   d. in the U.S., extended family networks are more common among minorities than among whites.

8. **What do we know about the effects of different family structures?**
    a. The structure does not matter, but the temperament of the child does.
    b. The optimum family structure in the U.S. appears to be being reared by both natural parents.
    c. Who reared the child does not matter, but how the child is reared does.
    d. Family structure appears to affect girls more negatively than it does boys.

PEER RELATIONSHIPS

Relating to Peers Through Play (pp. 231-232)

8.15 *What are the various kinds of play that are exhibited by preschoolers?*

60. Define social skills (p. 231).

61. Distinguish among the following types of play:

Type of Play	Description
Solitary Play	
Onlooker Play	
Parallel Play	
Associative Play	
Cooperative Play	

62. How does the social skill of group entry predict children's relationships with their peers?

63. What are the sex differences in the reasons for and consequences of poor group-entry skills?

Biological Sex	Reasons for Poor Group-Entry Skills	Consequences of Poor Group Entry Skills
Girls		
Boys		

64. Describe social-skills training.

Aggression (pp. 232-234)

8.16 *What is the difference between instrumental and hostile aggression, and which is more prevalent during early childhood?*

65.   Define the following terms:
        a.   aggression (p. 232)

        b.   instrumental aggression (p. 233)

        c.   hostile aggression (p. 233)

66.   How does the emergence of dominance hierarchies affect the display of physical aggression? Why?

67.   Summarize the findings about the key factors in aggressive behaviors by completing the following table:

Factor	Research Findings
Frustration	
Reinforcement	
Modeling	

68.   Describe the research about causes of trait aggression by completing the following table:

Cause	Research Findings
Genetic Basis	
Aggressive Environment	
Reinforcement of Behavior	
Understanding o f Others' Intentions	

Prosocial Behavior and Friendships (pp. 234-235)

8.17   *How do prosocial behavior and friendship patterns change during early childhood?*

69.   Define prosocial behavior (p. 234)

70.   Give examples of prosocial behavior at age two or three and older children.

Age	*Example of Prosocial Behavior*
Age 2 or 3	
Older Children	

71.   Describe examples of parental behavior that contributes to the development of prosocial behavior by completing the following table:

Parental Behavior	*Example*
Loving and warm climate	
Providing prosocial attributions	

Parental Behavior	*Example*
Looking for opportunities for children to do helpful things	
Parental modeling of prosocial behavior	

72.   List five positive signs of the importance of having a peer friend in early childhood.
▪
▪
▪
▪

AFTER YOU READ . . . PRACTICE TEST #5
PEER RELATIONSHIPS

Match the letter of the term in the right column with its description in the left column.

_____ 1.	Aggression used to hurt another person or gain an advantage.	a. Aggression
_____ 2.	Another term for "pecking order."	b. Associative play
		c. Attributions
		d. Cooperative play
_____ 3.	A set of behaviors that usually lead to being accepted as a play partner or a friend by peers.	e. Dominance hierarchy
_____ 4.	Play in which several children work together to accomplish a goal.	f. Group entry
		g. Hostile aggression
_____ 5.	Behavior intended to help another person.	h. Instrumental aggression
		i. Parallel play
_____ 6.	Play in which toddlers pursue their own activities but also engage in spontaneous, though short-lived, social interactions.	j. Prosocial behavior
		k. Social skills
_____ 7.	Behavior intended to harm another person or an object.	l. Solitary play
_____ 8.	Aggression used to gain or damage an object.	

AFTER YOU READ . . . CRITICAL REFLECTION EXERCISE

Social and Personality Development

Based on the information in the text, respond to the following question about social and personality development during the age range of two to six years:

1. Why is the development of self-control so important during these ages? Be sure to include evidence from the text to support your answer.

2. How would you utilize the information from this chapter of the text in a preschool? What kind of issues would you confront as the teacher (discuss at least three issues)? How would you utilize the information from this chapter to address these issues?

AFTER YOU READ . . . COMPREHENSIVE PRACTICE TEST
MULTIPLE CHOICE QUESTIONS

1. **The two preschool stages that Erikson identified are _____.**
    a. trust versus mistrust and autonomy versus shame and doubt
    b. initiative versus guilt and identity versus role confusion
    c. autonomy versus shame and doubt and initiative versus guilt
    d. ego integrity versus despair and trust versus mistrust

2. **_____ is a rule that serves to regulate behavior but has no moral implications.**
    a. A moral rule
    b. A social convention
    c. Person perception
    d. Social-cognitive perception

3. **The ability to control emotional states and emotion-related behavior is called _____.**
    a. inductive discipline
    b. emotional regulation
    c. deductive discipline
    d. empathy

4. **The process of acquiring self-control requires _____.**
    a. the ability to role-play
    b. sensorimotor thought
    c. shifting control from the parents to the child
    d. a rapid shift in maturity level on the part of the child

5. **The psychological and social associates and implications of biological sex is called _____.**
    a. the sex role
    b. gender identify
    c. the gender shift
    d. gender

6. **The understanding that gender is an innate characteristic that cannot be changed is called _____.**
    a. sex role
    b. gender schema
    c. gender constancy
    d. cross-gender behavior

7. **The first step in developing gender constancy is _____.**
    a. gender stability
    b. gender identity
    c. sex-role behavior
    d. gender scripts

8. **Girls tend to use an enabling style when interacting. This means _____.**
    a.   fostering equality and intimacy
    b.   critiquing the partner so improvements can be made
    c.   discussing one's own attributes more than the partner's
    d.   contradicting, interrupting, boasting, and other forms of self-display

9. **Baumrind focused on the following four aspects of family functioning: warmth or levels of nurturance, level of expectations or "maturity demands," clarity and consistency of rules, and _____.**
    a.   communication
    b.   responsibilities
    c.   friendliness
    d.   standards

10. **A discipline strategy in which parents explain to children why a punished behavior is wrong is called _____.**
    a.   inductive discipline
    b.   authoritarian parenting
    c.   uninvolved discipline
    d.   attachment

11. **A family structure that includes parents, grandparents, aunts, uncles, cousins, and so on is called _____.**
    a.   involved parenting
    b.   single parenting
    c.   an extended family
    d.   inductive discipline

12. **Which of the following is NOT a method of softening the effects of divorce?**
    a.   The custodial parent should help children stay in touch with the non-custodial parent.
    b.   Use the children as a go-between with the ex-spouse.
    c.   Keep the conflict to a minimum.
    c.   Try to keep the number of separate changes the child has to cope with to a minimum.

13. **A set of behaviors that usually lead to being accepted as a play partner or friend by peers is called _____.**
    a.   trait aggression
    b.   altruism
    c.   solitary play
    d.   social skills

14. **When groups of children arrange themselves in well understood orders of leaders and followers, it is called _____.**
    a.   leader-follower dichotomies
    b.   dominance hierarchies
    c.   role management
    d.   interactional synchrony

15. **"You're such a helpful child!" is an example of _____.**
    a. a dominance hierarchy
    b. interactional synchrony
    c. role management
    d. a prosocial attribution

TRUE-FALSE QUESTIONS

Indicate whether each of the following statements is true or false.

_____
1.
Both Freud and Erikson emphasized the role of the child's peers in development.

_____
2.
The development of empathy is preceded by the development of sympathy.

_____
3.
The most clearly stereotyped traits for women are weakness, gentleness, appreciativeness, and soft-heartedness.

_____
4.
Children who are securely attached to their parents experience fewer behavior problems.

_____
5.
The most consistently positive outcomes have been associated with an authoritative parenting pattern in which the parent are high in both control and acceptance.

_____
6.
Children growing up in single-parent families are less likely to drop out of high school than their peers in two-parent families.

_____
7.
Teaching aggressive children how to think about others' intentions reduces aggressive behavior.

_____
8.
Like aggression, prosocial behavior is intentional and voluntary, but its purpose is to help another person in some way.

ESSAY QUESTIONS

1.   Discuss the importance of the four aspects of family functioning identified by Diana Baumrind.

2.   Research indicates that aggressive school-aged children seem to reason more like two- to three-year-olds about others' intentions. Using what you've learned about development in early childhood, design a training program for preschoolers to help decrease aggressive behavior.

3.   Which of the gender concept theories do you believe is most accurate? Defend your answer.

WHEN YOU HAVE FINISHED . . . PUZZLE IT OUT

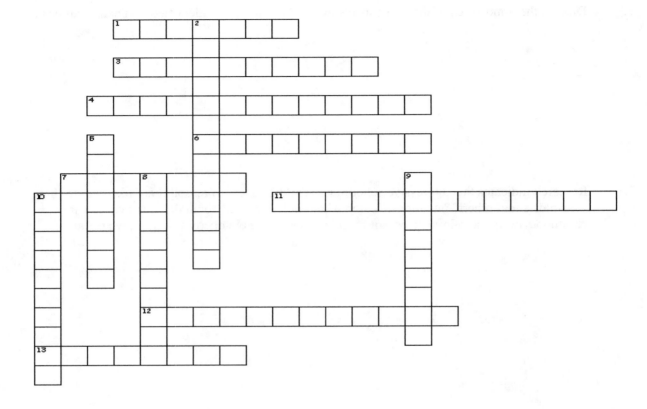

Across

1. Aggression used to hurt another person or gain an advantage
3. Parenting style high in nurturance and low in maturity demands, control, and communication
4. Parenting style high in nurturance, maturity demands, control, and communication
6. Discipline strategy in which parents explain to children why a punished behavior is wrong
7. The ability to identify with another person's emotional state
11. Parenting style low in nurturance and communication, but high in control and maturity demands
12. Aggression used to gain or damage an object
13. Family structure that includes grandparents, aunts, uncles, cousins, and so on

Down

2. Girls' preference for activities that are more typical for boys
5. A general feeling of sorrow or concern for another person
8. Behavior intended to harm another person or an object
9. Behavior intended to help another person
10. Parenting style low in nurturance, maturity demands, control, and communication

Created by Puzzlemaker at DiscoverySchool.com

Copyright © 2009 Pearson Education, Inc. Publishing as Allyn & Bacon.

WHEN YOU HAVE FINISHED . . . INVESTIGATIVE PROJECT

Student Project 14: Observation of Altruistic Behavior

In this project, take an "anthropological" approach to an observation of preschool-age children. Your instructor will have arranged for you to observe in a preschool or other group-care setting containing children between 18 months and four years of age. Permission will ordinarily have been obtained though the center itself, but you will need to follow whatever process is required to obtain the appropriate informed consent.

Procedure

For this observation, assume you are a researcher who has become interested in the earliest forms of altruistic behavior in children, and that there has not yet been any research on this subject. You want to begin simply by observing without preconceived ideas about how frequently this type of behavior might occur under what circumstances.

Observe for at least two hours in a group-care setting. Note in narrative form any episode that appears to you to fit some general criteria of "altruistic" or "compassionate" behavior. For each episode, record the circumstances involved, the gender of the child, the approximate age of the child, the other children present, and the words used (if any).

Analysis and Report

After the observation, look over your notes and try to answer the following questions:

1. What definition of altruism guided your observations? Did your definition change as a result of observing the children? Were there several types of observed "altruistic" actions that seem to be conceptually distinct?

2. Based on the episodes you have observed, what tentative hypotheses about the early development of altruism might you propose for further study? For example, are there hints of sex differences or age differences? Did the specific setting seem to have an effect? Was such behavior more common in pairs of children than in larger groups? Did this behavior occur primarily when one child was hurt or upset, or did it occur in other situations as well?

3. How might you test these tentative hypotheses with further research?

CHAPTER 8 ANSWER KEY

Practice Test #1 Theories of Social and Personality Development

1.   anal; phallic
2.   autonomy versus shame and doubt; initiative versus guilt
3.   social-cognitive theory
4.   Person perception
5.   cross-race effect
6.   social convention; moral rules

Practice Test #2 Personality and Self-Concept

1.   peer rejection
2.   Personality
3.   parental responses
4.   Emotional regulation
5.   parents; child
6.   apprehending another person's emotional stage or condition; matching that emotional state oneself
7.   role scripts

Practice Test #3 Gender Development

1. F   2. T   3. F   4. T   5. T   6. T   7. T

Practice Test #4 Family Relationships and Structure

1. c   2. b   3. d   4. a   5. b   6. d   7. c   8. b

Practice Test #5 Peer Relationships

1. g   2. e   3. k   4. d   5. j   6. b   7. a   8. h

Comprehensive Practice Test

Multiple Choice Questions

1. c   2. b   3. b   4. c   5. d   6. c   7. b   8. a   9. a   10. a
11. c   12. b   13. d   14. b   15. d

True-False Questions

1. F   2. F   3. T   4. T   5. T   6. F   7. T   8. T

Essay Questions

1. ■ Warmth or nurturance: Children show higher self-esteem, more empathy, more altruism, higher IQs, and less delinquent behavior.

   ■ Clarity and consistency of rules: Children are less likely to be defiant or non-compliant, are more competent and sure of themselves, and are less aggressive.

   ■ Levels of expectations (maturity demands): Children have higher self-esteem and show more altruism.

   ■ Communication between parent and child: Children are more emotionally and socially mature.

2. ■ The training could include the following concepts: reinforcement, modeling, parenting style, emotional regulation, etc.

3. ■ Answers should include the key principles of the theory and rationale as to why it was selected.

Puzzle It Out

Across
1. Hostile
3. Permissive
4. Authoritative
6. Inductive
7. Empathy
11. Authoritarian
12. Instrumental
13. Extended

Down
2. Tomboyishness
5. Sympathy
8. Aggression
9. Prosocial
10. Uninvolved

POLICY QUESTION II

"DEADBEAT DADS:" IRRESPONSIBLE PARENTS OR POLITICAL SCAPEGOATS?

Learning Objective: Summarize the issues about "deadbeat dads" (pp. 228-229).

1.   Define deadbeat dad.

2.   List two consequences of the efforts to keep up with child support obligations.

3.   Give examples of how custodial mothers are forced to cooperate with government officials.

4.   How has the general public been enlisted to find deadbeat dads?

5.   List two criticisms of deadbeat dad policies.

6.   State two examples of how the courts are biased against fathers.

7.   According to fathers' rights organizations and empirical research, what lies at the heart of the child support issue?

8.   Give examples of issues involved with child support awards exceeding what a non-custodial father can realistically pay.

9.   List three reforms of the judicial process that would improve child support compliance.

10.   Federal welfare reform legislation in 1992 and 1996 required every state to take steps to improve enforcement of child support orders. The states have complied in a variety of ways. Use your Internet skills to find the answers to the following questions.

    a.   What are the penalties in your state for non-payment of child support?

    b.   What efforts have been made by officials in your state to locate deadbeat dads?

    c.   Can an alleged deadbeat dad or a non-custodial father seeking a reduction in a child support award represent himself in court in your state? If not, are there agencies that provide low-cost legal assistance to such men?

    d.   Does your state have policies requiring custodial mothers to cooperate in identifying their children's fathers?

    e.   Do welfare statistics in your state indicate that deadbeat dad policies have reduced the welfare rolls?

    f.   Do you agree with your state's current approach to the deadbeat dad issue? Why or why not?

CHAPTER 9

PHYSICAL AND COGNITIVE DEVELOPMENT IN MIDDLE CHILDHOOD

BEFORE YOU READ . . . CHAPTER SUMMARY

Development in middle childhood, ages six to twelve, is marked by major physical changes, including those in the brain. Cognitive advances occur in these years, and the patterns and habits established during this time affect not only adolescent experiences, but also adulthood. Formal education impacts development and a variety of factors—such as learning disabilities, attention problems, language proficiency, sex, race, and culture—shape academic achievement.

Physical Changes

- Growth from six to twelve is steady and slow. Coordination of both large muscles and fine motor continue to improve. Sex differences in bone and skeletal maturation may lead boys and girls to pursue different activities.
- Major growth spurts occur in the brain in six- to eight-year-olds and in ten- to twelve-year-olds. Neurological development leads to improvements in selective attention, information-processing speed, and spatial perception.
- Accidents and obesity are among the most significant health hazards of this age group.

Cognitive Changes

- Language development continues at an astonishing rate with vocabulary growth, improvements in grammar, and an understanding of the social uses of language.
- The school-aged child discovers or develops a set of immensely powerful schemes that Piaget called concrete operations, such as reversibility, addition, subtraction, multiplication, division, and serial ordering. The child develops the ability to use inductive logic but does not yet use deductive logic.
- Piaget understood that it took children some years to apply the new cognitive skills to all kinds of problems, a phenomenon he called horizontal decalage. The "operations" may actually be rules for solving specific types of problems.
- Children in middle childhood clearly make improvements in processing efficiency, automaticity, executive and strategic processes, and expertise.

Schooling

- Literacy, the ability to read and write, is the focus of education in the six- to twelve-year-old period. Reading skills include improvements in phonological awareness, automaticity, learning word parts, comprehension strategies, and exposure to good literature. Writing techniques include outlining, paragraph development, language mechanics, as well as how to edit their own and others' written work.
- Children with limited English perform as well as English-speaking peers when they receive specific kinds of support in schools.
- Achievement tests are designed to assess specific information learned in school; intelligence tests are also used in schools to assess and group children for instruction. Both types of tests may ignore important aspects of intellectual functioning.

- A number of variables are associated with school performance, including sex, ethnicity, and culture.

Children with Special Needs

- In the U.S., 12 to 13 percent of all school children receive special education services; most of them are classified as learning disabled.
- Many children with attention-deficit hyperactivity disorder (ADHD) have problems in school but do not fit well into typical special education categories. The cause of ADHD is unknown. The two types of ADHD are the hyperactive/impulsive type, and the inattentive type.

AS YOU READ . . . LEARNING OBJECTIVES

After completing Chapter 9, you should be able to answer the following questions:

9.1   What kinds of physical changes occur during middle childhood?
9.2   In what ways does the brain change during these yeas?
9.3   What are the three most important health hazards for 6- to 12-year olds?
9.4   How do vocabulary and other aspects of language change during middle childhood?
9.5   What cognitive advantages do children gain as they move through Piaget's concrete operational stage?
9.6   What is horizontal decalage, and how does Siegler explain concrete operational thinking?
9.7   How do children's information processing skills improve during these years?
9.8   What should be included in an effective literacy curriculum?
9.9   How do bilingual and ESL approaches to second-language instruction differ?
9.10   What are the characteristics of effective schools?
9.11   What kinds of group differences in achievement have educational researchers found?
9.12   Why is the term "learning disability" controversial?
9.13   How does attention-deficit hyperactivity disorder affect a child's development?

AS YOU READ . . . TERM IDENTIFICATION

Achievement test (p. 259)
Analytical style (p. 263)
Association areas (p. 147)
Asthma (p. 148)
At-risk-for-overweight (p. 249)
Attention-deficit hyperactivity disorder (ADHD) (p. 268)
Automaticity (p. 254)
Balanced approach (p. 257)
BMI-for-age (p. 248)
Bilingual education (p. 258)
Class inclusion (p. 253)
Concrete operational stage (p. 251)
Decentration (p. 251)
Deductive logic (p. 252)
Dyslexia (p. 266)
English-as-a-second-language (ESL) program (p. 258)

Excessive weight gain (p. 248)
Executive processes (p. 255)
Inclusive education (p. 268)
Inductive logic (p. 252)
Learning disability (p. 266)
Memory strategies (p. 255)
Overweight (p. 249)
Processing efficiency (p. 254)
Relational style (p. 263)
Relative right-left orientation (p. 247)
Reversibility (p. 252)
Selective attention (p. 247)
Spatial cognition (p. 247)
Spatial perception (p. 247)

AS YOU READ . . . GUIDED STUDY QUESTIONS

PHYSICAL CHANGES

Growth and Motor Development (p. 246)

9.1   What kinds of physical changes occur during middle childhood?

1.   Between six and twelve, children grow _____ inches and add about _____

pounds each year.

2.   List some of the skills that improve as a result of gains in large muscle coordination and in fine
muscle coordination.

Motor Skill	Example
Large Motor Skills	
Fine Motor Skills	

3.   Give examples of how the sex differences in skeletal and muscular maturation cause girls to be
better-coordinated but slower and somewhat weaker than boys.

Biological Sex	Example
Girls	
Boys	

The Brain and Nervous System (pp. 246-247)

9.2   In what ways does the brain change during these years?

4.   Define the following terms:
    a.   selective attention (p. 247)

    b.   association areas (p. 247)

    c.   spatial perception (p. 247)

    d.   relative right-left orientation (p. 247)

    e.   spatial cognition (p. 247)

5.   Describe the site and the result of the two growth spurts by completing the following table:

Site	Result

6.   Give an example of how the myelinization of linkages between the frontal lobes and the reticular formation work together to develop selective attention.

7.   How does the myelinization of the association areas contribute to increases in information-processing speed?

8.   Give an example of the development of the lateralization of spatial perception, and describe a behavioral test of spatial perception lateralization that neuroscientists often use.

9.   What evidence suggests that visual experience affects the development of spatial perception? Give an example of how visual experiences might explain sex differences in spatial perception and spatial cognition.

Health and Wellness (pp. 248-250)

9.3   What are the three most important health hazards for 6-to 12-yewar-olds?

10.   Define the following terms:
       a.   asthma (p. 248)

       b.   excessive weight gain (p. 248)

       c.   BMI-for-age (p. 248)

       d.   overweight (p. 249)

       e.   at-risk-for-overweight (p. 249)

11.   What are the two most common causes of head injuries in children?
       ▪

       ▪

Copyright © 2009 Pearson Education, Inc. Publishing as Allyn & Bacon.

12.   Describe the "step" approach to treating asthma.

13.   What is the purpose of the BMI-for-age?

14.   List the likely causes of excessive weight gain in middle childhood.

15.   List nine ways to successfully help children lose weight.
        ▪
        ▪
        ▪
        ▪
        ▪
        ▪
        ▪
        ▪
        ▪

AFTER YOU READ . . . PRACTICE TEST #1
PHYSICAL CHANGES

1.   **Between ages six and twelve, children grow _____ inches and add about _____ pounds each year.**
        a.   one to two; ten
        b.   two to three; six
        c.   two to four; eight
        d.   three to five; four

2.   **The primary sites of brain growth during the first spurt of middle childhood are the _____.**
        a.   occipital lobes and parietal lobes
        b.   frontal lobes and temporal lobes
        c.   sensory and motor areas
        d.   medulla and the cerebellum

3.   **Parts of the brain where sensory, motor, and intellectual functions are linked are called _____.**
        a.   association areas
        b.   frontal lobes
        c.   cerebellum and brainstem
        d.   parietal lobes

4.   **The ability to identify and act on relationships between objects in space is called _____.**
        a.   metamemory
        b.   spatial cognition
        c.   metacognition
        d.   spatial perception

5.   **The ability to understand the difference between statements such as, "It's on YOUR right," and "It's on MY right," is called _____.**
        a.   handedness
        b.   spatial cognition
        c.   an executive process
        d.   relative right-left orientation

6.   **Head injuries are more common among _____ than any other age group.**
        a.   infants
        b.   preschoolers
        c.   school-aged children
        d.   teenagers

7.   **A child who is overweight is one whose BMI-for-age is at the _____.**
        a.   95th percentile
        b.   75th percentile
        c.   50th percentile
        d.   25th percentile

8.   **Experts on weight management in childhood recommend each of the following EXCEPT _____.**

   a.   limiting time playing outside
   b.   encouraging everyone in the family to drink lots of water
   c.   involving the whole family in physical activities such as walking and bicycling
   d.   limiting children's TV, video game, and computer time

COGNITIVE CHANGES

Language (pp. 250-251)

9.4   How do vocabulary and other aspects of language change during middle childhood?

16.   How many words do children add to their vocabularies per year between ages six and 12?

17.   Give examples of derived words.

18.   According to Jeremy Anglin, what do children learn about the structure of language at about age eight or nine?

Piaget's Concrete Operational Stage (pp. 251-252)

9.5   What cognitive advantages do children gain as they move through Piaget's concrete operational stage?

19.   Define the following terms:
    a.   concrete operational stage (p. 251)

    b.   decentration (p. 251)

    c.   reversibility (p. 252)

    d.   inductive logic (p. 252)

    e.   deductive logic (p. 252)

20.   To what is the concrete operational stage devoted?

21.   Give examples of decentration and reversibility.

22.   Why did Piaget believe that the concept of reversibility was the most important?

23.   Distinguish between inductive logic and deductive logic by giving examples of each.

Direct Tests of Piaget's View (pp. 252-254)

9.6   What is horizontal decalage, and how does Siegler explain concrete operational thinking?

24.   Define class inclusion (p. 253)

25.   What is horizontal decalage?

26.   Give examples of research that has found that Piaget was correct in his assertions that concrete operational schemes are acquired gradually across the six- to twelve-year-old period.

27.   Give examples of class inclusion.

28.   Describe Robert Siegler's research with a balance scale to discover the rules for problem solving.

29.   Describe the four steps of rule formation Siegler found by completing the following table:

Rule	Description
Rule I	
Rule II	
Rule III	
Rule IV	

Advances in Information-Processing Skills (pp. 254-256)

9.7   How do children's information processing skills improve during these years?

30.   Define the following terms and give an example of each:
        a.   processing efficiency (p. 254)

        b.   automaticity (p. 254)

        c.   executive process (p. 255)

        d.   memory strategies (p. 255)

31.   Give evidence that cognitive processing becomes more efficient.

32.   Explain why automaticity is critical to efficient information-processing.

33.   Give an example of how executive processes increase during middle childhood.

34.   Explain how expertise can make a difference in how efficiently the information-processing system works.

AFTER YOU READ . . . PRACTICE TEST #2
COGNITIVE CHANGES

Match the letter of the term in the right column with its description in the left column.

_____	1.	The ability to make efficient use of short-term memory capacity.	a. automaticity
			b. centration
_____	2.	Words that have a basic root to which some prefix or suffix is added.	c. class inclusion
			d. concrete operational stage
_____	3.	The inability to think of some transformed object as it was prior to the transformation.	e. decentration
_____	4.	Thinking that takes multiple variables into account.	f. deductive logic
			g. derived words
_____	5.	Learned methods for remembering information.	h. executive processes
_____	6.	Piaget's third stage of cognitive development.	i. horizontal decalage
			j. inductive logic
_____	7.	A type of reasoning based on hypothetical premises that requires predicting a specific outcome from a general principle.	k. irreversibility
			l. memory strategies
			m. metacognition
_____	8.	The understanding that subordinate classes are included in larger, superordinate classes.	n. processing efficiency
_____	9.	The ability to recall information from long-term memory without using short-term memory capacity.	o. reversibility
_____	10.	Knowing about knowing or thinking about thinking.	

SCHOOLING

Literacy (pp. 256-258)

9.8   What should e included in an effective literacy curriculum?

35.   Define balanced approach (p. 257)

36.   What is literacy?

37.   Why is phonological awareness a significant skill?

38.   Describe a guided reading session.

39.   Complete the following table by providing an example of each of the following skills:

Skill	Example
Automaticity	
Word Parts	
Comprehensive Strategies	
Good Literature	

40.   Describe the skills involved in learning to write.

41.   Describe some techniques to assist poor readers.

Second-Language Learners (pp. 258-259)

9.9   How do bilingual and ESL approaches to second-language instruction differ?

42.   Define the following terms:
    a.   bilingual education (p. 258)

    b.   English-as-a-second-language (ESL) program (p. 258)

43.   What does LEP stand for?

44.   Why is most bilingual education for Spanish-speaking children? Why is it logistically impossible for most LEP children?

45.   Why is submersion probably not the best approach for learning English?

46.   How do LEP students' performances in school compare to that of English-speaking children?

Achievement and intelligence Tests (pp. 259-262)

9.10   *What are the characteristics of effective schools?*

47.   Define achievement test (p. 259).

48.   How does an achievement test differ from an intelligence test?

49.   List at least two objections to using IQ tests in schools.
■

■

50.   Complete the following table by listing and briefly describing the eight types of intelligence, according to Howard Gardner:

Type of Intelligence	Description

51.   List and give an example of the three components of Sternberg's triarchic theory of intelligence by completing the following table:

Component	Example

52.   List and describe the three components of Goleman's theory of emotional intelligence, and explain why it is important.

Component	Importance

No Easy Answers: IQ Testing in the Schools *(p. 261)*

53.   What is a legitimate use for IQ testing in schools?

54.   List and describe three strong reasons usually given against using IQ tests to group elementary school children for instruction.

55.   What are culturally reduced tests?

The Real World: Homeschooling (p. 262)

56.   List reasons why some parents choose to homeschool their children.

Group Differences in Achievement (pp. 262-266)

9.11   What kinds of group differences in achievement have educational researchers found?

57.   Define the following terms:
        a.   analytical style (p. 263)

        b.   relational style (p. 263)

58.   What sex differences in test scores exist?

59.   State the environmental factors that shaped the sex differences in mathematics.

60.   How does an analytical style or a relational style affect achievement?

Style	Affect on Achievement
Analytical Style	
Relational Style	

61.   Describe how achievement differences may be due to philosophical beliefs.

62.   How might feelings of hopelessness on the part of some disadvantaged students be a factor?

63.   How might cultural beliefs affect achievement?

64.   Complete the following table to describe the differences in how teaching methods differ between Asian teachers and U.S. teachers:

Difference	Asian Teaching Method	U.S. Teaching Method
Theme		
Time teaching whole class		
Computational Fluency		
Use of Rewards		

65.   Give an example of computational fluency.

Research Report: Stereotype Threat (p. 264)

66.   What is stereotype threat theory?

AFTER YOU READ . . . PRACTICE TEST #3
SCHOOLING

1.   **Each of the following is a step in the process of learning to read EXCEPT _____.**
     a.   automaticity with respect to identifying sound-symbol connections
     b.   learning about word parts, such as prefixes and suffixes
     c.   attaining computational fluency
     d.   instruction in comprehension strategies

2.   **An approach to second-language education in which children receive instruction in two difference languages is called _____.**
     a.   submersion
     b.   bilingual education
     c.   immersion
     d.   aversion

3.   **A test designed to assess specific information learned in school is called _____.**
     a.   an achievement test
     b.   an intelligence test
     c.   metacognition
     d.   computational fluency

4.   **The type of multiple intelligence that deals with the ability to use language effectively is called _____ intelligence.**
     a.   linguistic
     b.   naturalistic
     c.   spatial
     d.   logical/mathematical

5.   **The type of multiple intelligence that is the ability to understand oneself is called _____ intelligence.**
     a.   musical
     b.   bodily kinesthetic
     c.   intrapersonal
     d.   interpersonal

6.   **Each of the following is a component of emotional intelligence EXCEPT _____.**
     a.   the ability to express one's emotions
     b.   awareness of the behavior, moods, and needs of others
     c.   the capacity to channel emotions into the pursuit of worthwhile goals
     d.   awareness of one's own emotions

7.   **A tendency to focus on the details of a task is called _____.**
     a.   computational style
     b.   relational style
     c.   cognitive style
     d.   analytical style

8.   **The degree to which an individual can automatically produce solutions to simple calculation problems is called _____.**
   a.   executive processes
   b.   computational fluency
   c.   metamemory
   d.   metacognition

CHILDREN WITH SPECIAL NEEDS

Learning Disabilities (pp. 266-268)

9.12 ***Why is the term "learning disability" controversial?***

67. Define the following terms:
    a.   learning disability (p. 266)

    b.   dyslexia (p. 266)

    c.   inclusion education (p. 268)

68. Describe how a neurological explanation of learning disabilities might occur.

69. Describe reciprocal teaching.

70. Give examples of the variety of inclusive education found in schools.

Attention-Deficit Hyperactivity Disorder (pp. 268-270)

9.13 ***How does attention-deficit hyperactivity disorder affect a child's development?***

71. Define attention-deficit hyperactivity disorder (ADHD) (p.)268.

72. Give examples of evidence that children with ADHD are neurologically different from their peers.

73. List four factors that are unlikely to cause ADHD.
-
-
-
-

74. List and describe the two types of ADHD.

Type	*Description*

75.   List the kinds of problems ADHD children may have in school.

76.   Describe parent training that may be useful in helping parents cope with children who have ADHD.

77.   Identify the pros and cons of giving children ADHD stimulant medication, like methylphenidate (Ritalin), by completing the following table:

Pros	Cons

AFTER YOU READ . . . PRACTICE TEST #4
CHILDREN WITH SPECIAL NEEDS

Fill in the blanks with the best answer.

1.   A disorder in which a child has difficulty mastering a specific academic skills, even though she

    possesses normal intelligence and no physical or sensory handicaps is said to have a

    _____.

2.   In _____ programs, children with learning disabilities work in pairs or groups.
    Each child takes a turn summarizing and explaining material to be learned to the others in the
    group.

3.   _____ is a mental disorder that causes children to
    have difficulty attending to and completing tasks.

4.   Psychologists are fairy sure that _____, _____, or
    _____ is not the cause of ADHD.

5.   There are two types of ADHD: _____ and _____.

AFTER YOU READ . . . CRITICAL REFLECTION EXERCISE

Developing Cognitive Skills

Imagine that you are a school teacher working with children ranging in age from six to eight years. You want to make sure that you develop classroom activities that provide children with practice with their developing cognitive skills. First, describe three skills that children are developing during these ages. Second, suggest one activity for each of these skills that you could use in the classroom to enhance the child's use of each skill.

AFTER YOU READ . . . COMPREHENSIVE PRACTICE TEST

MULTIPLE CHOICE QUESTIONS

1.   **School age children will show the most dramatic increase in _____.**
        a.   jumping ability
        b.   intelligence
        c.   running speed
        d.   fine motor coordination

2.   **The ability to focus cognitive activity on the important elements of a problem or situation is called _____.**
        a.   selective attention
        b.   myelinization
        c.   relative right-left orientation
        d.   spatial cognition

3.   **The most serious long-term health risk in the middle childhood period is _____.**
        a.   excessive weight gain
        b.   difficulty sleeping
        c.   coordination of vision with body movements
        d.   anorexia

4.   **A derived word is one that _____.**
        a.   was slang but is now considered acceptable
        b.   has a basic root to which a prefix or suffix is added
        c.   means dramatically different things in different cultures
        d.   is offensive to individuals of particular cultural groups

5.   **The understanding that both physical actions and mental operations can be reversed is called _____.**
        a.   addition and subtraction
        b.   conservation
        c.   reversibility
        d.   reverse object rotation

6.   **Piaget understood that it took children some years to apply their new cognitive skills to all kinds of problems, a phenomenon he called _____.**
        a.   automaticity
        b.   executive processes
        c.   class inclusion
        d.   horizontal decalage

7.   **The ability to recall information from long-term memory without using short-term memory capacity is called _____.**
        a.   horizontal decalage
        b.   conservation
        c.   automaticity
        d.   memory strategies

8. **The ability to read and write is called _____.**
   a. phonological awareness
   b. literacy
   c. long-term memory
   d. intelligence

9. **An approach to second-language education in which children attend English classes for part of the day and receive most of their academic instruction in English is called _____.**
   a. computational fluency
   b. emotional intelligence
   c. horizontal decalage
   d. English-as-a-second-language (ESL)

10. **The type of multiple intelligence that deals with numbers and logical problem-solving is _____.**
    a. musical intelligence
    b. logical intelligence
    c. spatial intelligence
    d. linguistic intelligence

11. **The three components of Sternberg's triarchic theory of intelligence are _____.**
    a. contextual intelligence, experiential intelligence, and componential intelligence
    b. interpersonal intelligence, intrapersonal intelligence, and musical intelligence
    c. logical/mathematical intelligence, spatial intelligence, and interpersonal intelligence
    d. linguistic intelligence, emotional intelligence, and bodily kinesthetic intelligence

12. **Focusing attention on the "big picture" instead of an individual bits of information is called a(n) _____.**
    a. individualistic style
    b. collectivist style
    c. relational style
    d. analytical style

13. **The degree to which an individual can automatically produce solutions to simple calculation problems is called _____.**
    a. computational fluency
    b. executive processes
    c. horizontal decalage
    d. metacognition

14. **The total absence of reading is the technical definition of _____.**
    a. literacy
    b. dyslexia
    c. learning disability
    d. limited English proficient

15. **Which of the following is a possible cause of attention-deficit hyperactivity disorder?**
   a. environmental toxins
   b. diet
   c. limited English proficient
   d. brain damage

TRUE-FALSE QUESTIONS

Indicate whether each of the following statements is true or false.

1. _____ The ability to infer rules from and make predictions about the movement of objects in space is called spatial cognition.

2. _____ The most frequent cause of school absence for six- to 12-year-olds is head injuries.

3. _____ Children develop the ability to use deductive logic before inductive logic.

4. _____ The understanding that subordinate classes are included in larger, superordinate classes is called class inclusion.

5. _____ The three components of emotional intelligence are awareness of one's own emotions, the ability to express one's emotions appropriately, and the capacity to channel emotions into the pursuit of worthwhile goals.

6. _____ On average, studies in the U.S. show that girls do slightly better on verbal tasks and at arithmetic computation and that boys do slightly better at numerical reasoning.

7. _____ When reading is the problem skill, the term dyslexia is often used.

8. _____ Medication always improves the grades of children with ADHD.

ESSAY QUESTIONS

1. How can parents and teachers help school-aged children gain expertise?

2. Choose one of the theories of intelligence (Gardner's, Sternberg's, or Goleman's) and give reasons why you believe it accurately represents human intelligence.

3. Compare the analytical style to the relational style. Suggest reasons why the cognitive style may impact success in school.

WHEN YOU HAVE FINISHED . . . PUZZLE IT OUT

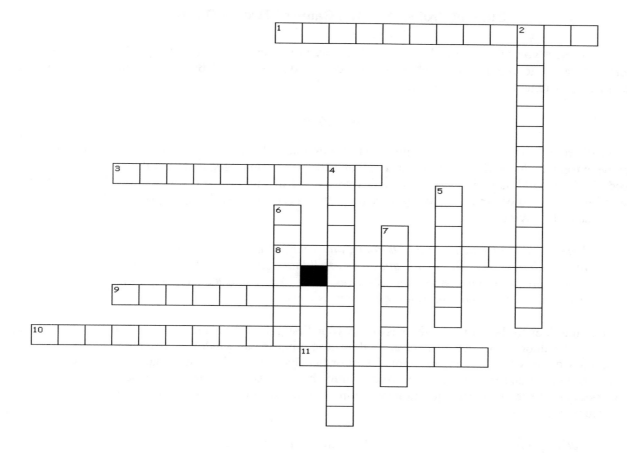

Across

1. Thinking that takes multiple variables into account
3. The ability to use language effectively
8. Style that focuses on the details of a task
9. Reasoning in which general principles are inferred from specific experiences
10. Style that focuses on the "big picture"
11. Facility with numbers and logical problem-solving

Down

2. The inability to think of some transformed object as it was prior to the transformation
4. The ability to understand oneself
5. Words that have a basic root to which some prefix or suffix is added
6. The ability to appreciate spatial relationships
7. Problems in reading or the inability to read

Created by Puzzlemaker at DiscoverySchool.com

WHEN YOU HAVE FINISHED . . . RESEARCH PROJECT

Student Project 15: The Game of Twenty Questions

For this project you will need to locate a child between the ages of six and ten, and obtain permission from the parent to research their child using the procedure specified by your instructor. Be sure to reassure the parents that you are not "testing" the child.

Procedure

Arrange a time to be alone with the child if at all possible. Having the mother, father, or siblings there can be extremely distracting, both for the child and for you. Come prepared with the equipment you will need. Tell the child that you have some games you would like to play. Play with the child for a while to establish some kind of rapport before you begin your experiment. At the appropriate moment, introduce your "game" by saying:

> *I am thinking of something in this room, and your job is to figure out what I am thinking of. To do this, you can ask any questions at all that I can answer by saying yes or no, but I can't give you any answer other than yes or no. You can ask as many questions as you need, but try to find out in as few questions as you can.*

Choose "the door to the room" as the answer to your first game. (If there is more than one door, select one particular door as correct; if there is no door, use a particular window.) If the child asks questions that cannot be answered yes or no, remind him or her that you can't answer that kind of question, and restate the kind of question that can be asked. Allow the child as many questions as needed (more than 20 if necessary). Write down each question verbatim. When the child has reached the correct answer, praise her or him and then say:

> *Let's try another one. I'll try to make it harder this time. I'm thinking of something in the room again. Remember, you ask me questions that I can answer yes or no. You can ask as many questions as you need, but try to find out in as few questions as possible.*

Use your pencil or pen as the correct answer this time. After the child has solved the problem, praise her or him. If the child has not been successful, find something to praise   (i.e., "You asked some good questions, but it's a really hard problem, isn't it?") When you are satisfied that the child's motivation is still reasonably high, continue.

> *Now we're going to play another question-asking game. In this game, I will tell you something that happened, and your job is to find out how it happened by asking questions I can answer yes or no. Here's what happened: A man is driving down the road in his car. The car goes off the road and hits a tree. You have to find out how it happened by the way I answer questions you ask me about it. But I can only answer yes or no. The object of the game is to find out the answer in as few questions as possible. Remember, here's what happened: A man is driving down the road in his car, and the car goes off the road and hits a tree. Find out what happened.*

If the child asks questions that cannot be answered yes or no, remind her or him that you cannot answer that kind of question and that you can only answer yes or no. If the child can't figure out the answer, urge him or her to try until you are persuaded that you are creating frustration, at which point you should quit with lots of positive statements. The answer to the problem is that it had been raining, the car skidded on a curve, went off the road, and hit a tree.

Scoring

Score each question asked by the child on each of the three problems as belonging to one of two categories:

1. *Hypothesis*: A hypothesis is essentially a guess that applies to only one alternative. A yes answer to a hypothesis solves the problem; with a no answer, all that has been accomplished is to eliminate one possibility. In the first two problems, a hypothesis would be any question that applied to only one alternative, only one object in the room, i.e., "Is it your hair?" or "Is it the picture?" In the third problem, a hypothesis would be any question that covered only one alternative: "Did the man get stung in the eye by a bee?" "Did he have a heart attack?" "Was there a big snow bank in the middle of the road that the car ran into so that it skidded?"

2. *Constraint*: A constraint question covers at least two possibilities, often many more. A yes answer to a constraint question must be followed up ("Is it a toy?" "Yes." "Is it a truck?") A no answer to a constrain question allows the questioner to eliminate a whole class of possibilities. On the first two problems, any of the following would be constraints: "Is it in that half of the room?" "Is it something big?" "Is it a toy?" "Is it something red?" (Assuming that there is more than one red thing in the room). For the third problem, any of the following (or equivalent) would be constraints: "Was there something wrong with the car?" "Was the weather bad?" "Did something happen to the man?"

Analysis and Report

You should examine at least the following aspects of your results.

1. How many questions did the child ask for each problem?
2. On each problem, how many of the child's questions were hypotheses, and how many were constraints?
3. Did the child do better (ask more constraints) on the "concrete operations" problems (the first two) than on the "formal operations" problem (the story)? Or was the performance the same on both?

Reference

Mosher, F. A., & Hornsby, J. R. (1966). On asking questions. In J. S. Bruner, R. R. Oliver, & P. M. Greenfield (Eds.), *Studies in cognitive growth*, pp. 68-85. New York: Wiley.

WHEN YOU HAVE FINISHED . . . RESEARCH PROJECT

Student Project 16: Conservation of Mass, Number, and Weight

For this project you need to locate a child between the ages of six and ten, and obtain permission from the parents, or from both the parents and the child, following the procedures specified by your instructor. You will be testing this child for three kinds of conservation: mass, number, and weight. Recall that the concept of conservation involves the understanding that some features of objects remain invariant despite changes in other features. The weight of an object remains the same regardless of how its shape is changed; the number of objects in a row remain the same regardless of how widely spaced the objects are. Typically, number and mass conservation are learned (or discovered) at about age five or six, while conservation of weight is learned later, at perhaps eight or nine. So if you are able to find a child between six and eight, you may find out later that he or she can manage the first two conservation tasks, but not the last.

Procedure

The testing can ordinarily be done most easily in the child's home, although other settings are also acceptable. Present the child with the three tasks in the order given here, following instructions precisely.

Conservation of Mass

You will need two equal balls of clay or play dough, each a size that can be readily handled by a child's palm. Handle them yourself, rounding them into balls, and then hand them to the child, asking: *Is there the same amount of clay in each of these balls? Are they the same?*

If the child agrees that they are the same, proceed. If not, say to the child: "Make them the same." The child may want to squish them a little or may actually shift some clay from one ball to the other. That is all right. When the child is ready, ask again: *Is there the same amount of clay in each of these balls? Are they the same?*

Once the child has agreed that they are the same, say: *Now I'm going to squash this one into a pancake.*

Squash one of the two balls into a pancake and place the two objects—the remaining ball and the pancake—in front of the child. Read the following questions exactly as written and record precisely what the child says: *Is there the same amount of clay in this one* (pointing to the ball) *as there is in this one* (pointing to the pancake), *or is there more here* (pointing to the ball) *or more here* (pointing to the pancake)?

Depending on the child's answer to the first question, follow up by asking: *Why are they the same? or Why is there more here?*

Now mold the pancake back into a ball and set the two balls aside for the moment.

Conservation of Number

For this part of the process you will need 14 pennies or identical buttons. Start with ten items and place them between yourself and the child (preferably on a table, but the floor will do), spaced in two rows of five as follows:

X X X X X
X X X X X

Ask the child: *Are there the same number of pennies* (buttons) *in this row as there are in this row, or are there more here* (pointing to the child's row) *or more here* (pointing to your row)?

The child may want to move the objects around a bit before he agrees that the two rows are the same, which is fine. Once the child has agreed that they are the same, spread the objects in your row so that it is now noticeably longer than the child's row but still contains only five objects, i.e.:

X   X   X   X   X
X X X X X

Now ask the following questions, and record the child's exact answers: *Are there the same number of pennies in this row as there are in this row, or are there more here, or more here?*

Depending on the child's answer, ask either of the following probe questions: *Why are they the same?* or *Why are there more here?*

Now spread out the child's row and add two objects to each row, so that your row and the child's row are again exactly matched, with seven items equally spaced in each. Repeat the questions above, and record the child's answer precisely. Now move the objects in your row closer together, so that the child's row is now longer. Ask the questions again, and record the answers.

Conservation of Weight

Put away the pennies (or give them to the child), and bring out the two balls of clay again, saying; *Now we're going to play with the clay again.*

Hand the balls to the child and ask: *Do these two balls weigh the same? Do they have the same amount of weight?*

If the child agrees that they weigh the same, proceed. If not, say "Make them the same," and let her manipulate the balls until she agrees. Once she has agreed say: *Now I am going to make this ball into a hot dog.*

Roll one of the two balls into a hot dog shape. When you have completed the transformation, put the two pieces of clay in front of the child and ask: *Does this one* (pointing to the hot dog) *weigh the same as this one* (pointing to the ball), *or does this one weigh more, or does this one weigh more?*

Depending on the child's answer to the question, ask one of the following probe questions and record the answers carefully: *Why do they weigh the same?* or *Why does this one weigh more?*

This ends the procedure, so you should praise and thank the child. You might also want to play a bit with the child with some other toy of the child's choosing, to make sure that the whole process is pleasant for the child.

Analysis and Report

For each of the crucial questions, decide whether or not the child "conserved." To be regarded as having conserved, the child must have said (1) the two objects were the same after transformation and (2) she must also give a valid reason, such as:

> You haven't added any or taken any away, so they have to be the same.
> One is longer, but it is also skinnier, so it is still the same.
> If I made it back into a ball, it would be the same.

Compare the child's performance on the three types of conservation. Did the child conserve in all three exercises? If not, was the child's performance consistent with the typically observed sequence of acquisition? (If the child conserved weight, but not mass or number, that would be contrary to research data). What else, other than the child's basic comprehension of conservation, might affect the child's answers in the test of this kind? Was the child interested or bored? Were there distractions in the environment? Might the sequence in which the items were given have any effect? Do you think it would have mattered, for example, if conservation of weight had been tested before conservation of mass? If one were designing a study to examine the acquisition of these conservations, would one want to have all children given the items in the same order, or should the order be randomized?

If several students have completed this project, you may want to combine your data and analyze children's success on these three conservations as a function of age. Do your collective findings match the results of existing research?

WHEN YOU HAVE FINISHED . . . INVESTIGATIVE PROJECT

Student Project 17: Investigation of IQ Testing in Local Schools

As a follow-up to the information given in the text on the pros and cons of using IQ test scores in the schools, one student, or a small group of students, may wish to investigate the policies on the uses of IQ and achievement test in your own local school districts.

Basic Questions to Answer

- Is there a state-wide policy on the use of IQ tests in public schools? Is there a local district policy instead of, or in addition to, a state policy?

- Is there a state or local policy on the use of achievement tests? Are they routinely given in specific grades? How are the scores used?

- If individual IQ tests are used in the district, who administers them? Are the scores used to help in the placement of children in special programs? What other types of information are also used as part of any placement process?

Sources

The best source will be the state department of education and local school district administrative offices. At the state level there is likely to be a public information office; large school districts may also have such a service. In smaller districts, you will have to use some ingenuity to figure out which person is the best to talk to. Naturally, you should identify yourself as a student and make it clear that this information is for a report for your class.

CHAPTER 9 ANSWER KEY

Practice Test #1 Physical Changes

1. b   2. c   3. a   4. d   5. d   6. c   7. a   8. a

Practice Test #2 Cognitive Changes

1. n   2. g   3. k   4. e   5. l   6. d   7. f   8. c   9. a   10. m

Practice Test #3 Schooling

1. c   2. b   3. a   4. a   5. c   6. b   7. d   8. b

Practice Test #4 Children with Special Needs

1. learning disability
2. reciprocal teaching
3. attention deficit hyperactivity disorder (ADHD)
4. diet, environmental toxins, brain damage
5. hyperactive/impulsive type; inattentive type

Comprehensive Practice Test

Multiple Choice Questions

1. d   2. a   3. a   4. b   5. c   6. d   7. c   8. b   9. d   10. b
11. a   12. c   13. a   14. b   15. c

True-False Questions

1. T   2. F   3. F   4. T   5. T   6. T   7. T   8. F

Essay Questions

1. ▪ Answers will vary, but should include helping the child learn the basic skills, practicing the skills, and opportunities to share the skills with others.

2. ▪ Answer should include basic premise of the selected theory and reasons for its selection.

3. ▪ Analytical: focus on the details of a task.
    ▪ Relational: focus on the "big picture" and ignore the details.
    ▪ Teachers often

Puzzle It Out

Across
1. decentration
3. linguistic
8. analytical
9. inductive
10. relational
11. logical

Down
2. reversibility
4. intrapersonal
5. derived
6. spatial
7. dyslexia

CHAPTER 10

SOCIAL AND PERSONALITY DEVELOPMENT IN MIDDLE ADOLESCENCE

BEFORE YOU READ . . . CHAPTER SUMMARY

The social and personality development in children ages six to twelve includes changes in social relationships and the expansion of the self-concept. Influences beyond the family and school include after-school care, poverty, and television.

Theories of Social and Personality Development

- Freud believed that the challenge of the middle childhood years was to form emotional bonds with peers and to move beyond those that were developed with parents in earlier years. Erikson claimed that children in middle childhood acquire a sense of industry by achieving goals determined by their culture.
- Traits contribute to the development of feelings of competence. From the social-cognitive perspective, focus is on three interacting sets of factors that shape personality: person factors, environmental factors, and behavioral factors.

Self-Concept

- The psychological self develops in middle childhood. As a result, self-descriptions begin to include traits such as intelligence and friendliness along with physical characteristics.
- The self-concept of the six- to twelve-year-old contains an evaluative aspect called self-esteem. It is shaped by the degree of discrepancy a child experiences between goals and achievements, and the degree of perceived social support from peers and parents.

Advances in Social Cognition

- Between ages six and twelve, children's understanding of others' stable, internal traits improve.
- Piaget claimed that moral reasoning develops in stages which correlate with his cognitive stages.

The Social World of the School-Aged Child

- Middle childhood is a period of increasing independence of the child from the family, yet attachment to parents and siblings continues to be important.
- The biggest shift in relationships in the middle childhood years is the increasing importance of peers, particularly close friendships.
- Gender segregation of peer groups is at its peak in the school-aged years. Boys' and girls' friendships differ in specific ways.
- Although physical aggression decreases in middle childhood, relational aggression increases, especially in girls.
- Researchers divide children into three groups based on social status: popular children, rejected children, and neglected children. Aggressive children are often rejected, but some are popular. Neglected children may suffer from loneliness and depression.

Influences beyond Family and Peers

- Self-care is associated with many negative effects, but children who have parental monitoring are less likely to be affected.
- Children who grow up in poverty do worse in school and drop out at far higher rates. Protective factors, such as secure attachment, higher IQ, authoritative parenting, and effective schools can counterbalance the effects of poverty for some children.
- Television has positive educational effects, such as learning vocabulary and prosocial behavior, but heavy TV watching is associated with lower scores on achievement tests. Experts agree that watching violence on television and playing violent video games increases the level of personal aggression shown by a child.

AS YOU READ . . . LEARNING OBJECTIVES

After completing Chapter 10, you should be able to answer the following questions:

10.1 How did the psychoanalytic theorists characterize the middle childhood years?
10.2 What are the main ideas of the trait and social-cognitive theorists?
10.3 What are the features of the psychological self?
10.4 How does self-esteem develop?
10.5 How does children's understanding of others change in middle childhood?
10.6 How do children in Piaget's moral realism and moral relativism stages reason about right and wrong?
10.7 How does self-regulation affect school-aged children's relationships with their parents?
10.8 What changes occur in children's understanding of friendships during this period?
10.9 In what ways do boys and girls interact during the middle years?
10.10 What types of aggression are most common among school-aged children?
10.11 How do popular, rejected, and neglected children differ?
10.12 How does self-care affect girls' and boys' development?
10.13 What are factors contribute to resilience and vulnerability among poor children?
10.14 How do television, computers, and video games affect children's development?

AS YOU READ . . . TERM IDENTIFICATION

Moral realism stage (p. 284)
Moral relativism stage (p. 285)
Psychological self (p. 280)
Reciprocal determinism (p. 279)

Relational aggression (p. 290)
Retaliatory aggression (p. 291)
Self-care children (p. 293)
Self-efficacy (p. 281)

Self-esteem (p. 281)
Self-regulation (p. 286)
Social status (p. 292)
Trait (p. 278)

AS YOU READ . . . GUIDED STUDY QUESTIONS

THEORIES OF SOCIAL AND PERSONALITY DEVELOPMENT

Psychoanalytic Perspectives (p. 278)

10.1   How did the psychoanalytic theorists characterize the middle childhood years?

1.   What is the focus of Freud's psychosexual theory during middle childhood?

2.   What is the focus of Erikson's psychosocial theory during middle childhood?

3.   According to Erikson, who does a child develop industry? What happens is they fail to develop industry?

Develops Industry	Fails to Develop Industry

4.   How is an emerging sense of competence related to the school experience?

The Trait and Social-Cognitive Perspectives (pp. 278-280)

10.2   What are the main ideas of the trait and social-cognitive theorists?

5.   Define the following terms:
      a.   trait (p. 278)

      b.   reciprocal determinism (p. 279)

6.   Give examples of how traits contribute to feelings of competence.

7.   How did Bandura use the following terms?

Person Component	Behavior	Environment

8.   Give an example of reciprocal determinism.

AFTER YOU READ . . . PRACTICE TEST #1
THEORIES OF SOCIAL AND PERSONALITY DEVELOPMENT

Fill in the blanks with the best answer.

1.   Freud thought that the challenge of the middle childhood years was to _____ _____ and to move beyond those that were developed with _____ in earlier years.

2.   Erikson characterized middle childhood as the period during which children experience the crisis of _____.

3.   Contemporary studies that stress the child's need to feel _____ are in tune with Erikson's views.

4.   A _____ is a stable pattern of responding to situations.

5.   Bandura proposed that the person, behavioral, and environmental components interact in a pattern he termed _____.

SELF-CONCEPT

The Psychological Self (pp. 280-281)

10.3   What are the features of the psychological self?

9.   Define the psychological self (p. 280).

10.   Give examples of how the child's self description becomes increasingly precise across the middle years.

11.   Define self-efficacy (p. 281).

12.   According to Bandura, how does self-efficacy develop?

13.   What are social comparisons?

The Valued Self (p. 281)

10.4 How does self-esteem develop?

14.   Define self-esteem (p. 281).

15.   What is the valued self?

16.   How stable are self-esteem judgments over time?

17.   According to Susan Harter, what are the two major influences of a child's self-esteem?

Influence	Example

AFTER YOU READ . . . PRACTICE TEST #2
SELF-CONCEPT

Fill in the blanks with the best answer.

1.　The _____ is a person's understanding of his or her enduring psychological characteristics.

2.　As a child moves through the concrete operational period, her psychological self becomes more _____, more _____, less tied to _____, and more centered on _____.

3.　_____ is an individual's belief in her capacity to cause an intended event to occur.

4.　_____ are the processes of drawing conclusions about the self based on comparisons to others.

5.　_____ is a global evaluation of one's own worth.

ADVANCES IN SOCIAL COGNITION

The Child as Psychologist (pp. 283-284)

10.5　How does children's understanding of others change in middle childhood?

18.　Give examples of how the child's description of others moves from the concrete to the abstract during middle childhood.

19.　How do behavioral comparisons and psychological constructs change throughout the school-years?

20.　Give an example of how school-aged children are better than younger children at predicting family roles and relationships.

Moral Reasoning (pp. 284-286)

10.6　How do children in Piaget's moral realism and moral relativism stages reason about right and wrong?

21.　Define the following terms:
　　a.　moral realism stage (p. 284)

　　b.　moral relativism stage (p. 285)

22. Describe Piaget's two-stage theory of moral development, and give examples of each stage.

Stage	Description
Moral Realism Stage	
Moral Relativism Stage	

The Real World: Encouraging Moral Reasoning (p. 285)

23. Give examples of each of Thomas Lickona's suggestions to help children achieve more mature levels of moral reasoning.

AFTER YOU READ . . . PRACTICE TEST #3
ADVANCES IN SOCIAL COGNITION

Indicate whether each of the following statements is true or false.

_____
1.
Like their understanding of the physical world, 6- to -12-yer-olds' descriptions of other people move from the abstract to the concrete.

_____
2.
A behavioral comparison was any description that involved comparing a child's behaviors or physical features with those of another child or with a norm.

_____
3.
School-aged children understand family roles and relationships much better than younger children do.

_____
4.
Moral reasoning is the process of making judgments about the rightness or wrongness of specific acts.

_____
5.
In the moral realism stage, children understand that many rules can be changed through social agreement.

THE SOCIAL WORLD OF THE SCHOOL-AGED CHILD

Relationships with Parents (pp. 286-287)

10.7   How does self-regulation affect school-aged children's relationships with their parents?

24.   Define self-regulation (p. 286).

25.   Describe the attachment between parents and school-aged children.

26.   Why does the agenda of issues between parent and child change during middle childhood?

27.   Give an example of cultural differences in parental expectations of self-regulation.

28.   Give an example of sex differences in parental expectations of self-regulation.

29.   List two parenting variables that contribute to the development of self-regulation.

▪

▪

30.   Give an example of how the parenting variables are associated with the authoritative style of parenting.

Research Report: Birth Order and Children's Development (p. 286)

31.   What is the resource dilution hypothesis?

32.   Briefly summarize the research on birth order and children's development.

Friendships (pp. 287-288)

10.8   What changes occur in children's understanding of friendships during this period?

33.   Give an example of how preschoolers and young school-aged children would describe the way that people make friends. Give an example of how a ten-year-old would describe the way people make friends.

34.   List several examples of evidence of the centrality of friends to social development in middle childhood.

Gender Segregation (pp. 288-290)

10.9   In what ways do boys and girls interact during the middle childhood years?

35.   Give examples of how shared interests and activities play a critical part of friendship in the early years of middle childhood.

36.   Compare ways that girls' and boys' friendships differ, and list characteristics that they have in common by completing the following table:

Differences	Commonalities

37.   Define "controlling speech" and give examples.

Patterns of Aggression (pp. 290-292)

10.10   What types of aggression are most common among school-aged children?
38.   Define the following terms:
   a.   relational aggression (p. 290)

   b.   retaliatory aggression (p. 291)

39.   What happens to the level of physical aggression during the middle childhood years? Describe the exception to the general pattern.

40.   How do girls tend to express aggression?

41.   How does the level of retaliatory aggression change across the middle childhood years?

42.   Describe a technique to help children learn non-aggressive ways to manage the kinds of situations that lead to retaliatory aggression.

No Easy Answers: Bullies and Victims (p. 291)

43.   List the consistent roles related to bullies and victims children assume in middle childhood.

44.   List the characteristics of victims.

Social Status (pp. 292-293)

10.11   How do popular, rejected, and neglected children differ?
45.   Define social status (p. 292).

46.   List the three groups of social status.
   ▪

   ▪

   ▪

47.   Give characteristics of each of the following groups of children by completing the following table. Include behavior as well as looks or temperament.

Group	Characteristics
Popular Children	
Withdrawn/Rejected Children	
Aggressive/Rejected Children	
Neglected Children	

48.   Describe the close friends of aggressive boys.

AFTER YOU READ . . . PRACTICE TEST #4
THE SOCIAL WORLD OF THE SCHOOL-AGED CHILD

1. **A child's ability to conform to parental standards of behavior without direct supervision is called _____.**
    a. self-efficacy
    b. self-esteem
    c. self regulation
    d. self confidence

2. **Which of the following statements is true about sex differences in mothers' expectations of self-regulatory behavior?**
    a. Mothers give girls more autonomy over their own behavior than boys.
    b. Mothers hold boys to a higher standard of accountability for failure than girls.
    c. Mothers provide more guidance for girls than for boys.
    d. Mothers make different kinds of demands on boys and girls.

3. **Which parental style is linked to self-regulation in school-aged children?**
    a. permissive
    b. authoritative
    c. authoritarian
    d. neglecting

4. **Boys' friendship groups _____ than girls'.**
    a. play more indoors
    b. are more likely to play in pairs
    c. are larger and more accepting of newcomers
    d. spend more time near home or school

5. **In middle childhood, _____ becomes even less common as children learn the cultural rules about when it is acceptable to display anger or aggression and how much of a display is acceptable.**
    a. physical aggression
    b. verbal aggression
    c. hostile aggression
    d. instrumental aggression

6. **Aggression to get back at someone who hurt you is called _____.**
    a. relational aggression
    b. retaliatory aggression
    c. hostile aggression
    d. instrumental aggression

7. **An individual child's classification as popular, rejected, or neglected is called _____.**
    a. self-regulation
    b. self-esteem
    c. social status
    d. psychological self

8.   _____ realize that they are disliked by peers.
   a.   popular children
   b.   aggressive/rejected children
   c.   retaliatory children
   d.   withdrawn/rejected children

INFLUENCES BEYOND FAMILY AND PEERS

After-School Care (pp. 293-294)

10.12 How does self-care affect girls' and boys' development?

49.   Define the term self-care children (p. 293).

50.   List three consistent findings of research about self-care children.

-

-

-

51.   Why is parental monitoring so important in self-care arrangements? Give examples of effective parental monitoring.

Poverty (pp. 294-296)

10.13 What are factors that contribute to resilience and vulnerability among poor children?

52.   Give examples of how child poverty is unequally distributed across ages, races, and family structures.

Factor	Example
Age	
Race/Ethnicity	
Family Structure	

53.   How might parents living in poverty treat their children differently than do working-class or middle-class parents?

54.   Give examples of how children in low-income families differ from their better-off peers across all developmental domains.

Domain	Example
Physical	
Cognitive/Intellectual	
Social	

55.   Why are the negative effects of poverty exacerbated for children growing up in poverty-ravaged urban areas?

56.   List the symptoms of posttraumatic stress disorder from which children may suffer.

57.   List the key protective factors of resilient children, and give an example of how each factor may offer protection.

Protective Factor	Example

Media Influences (pp. 296-298)

10.14 How do television, computers, and video games affect children's development?

58.   Describe the results of research on the effects on children of viewing aggressive behavior on television.

59.   What is meant by the "digital divide" across income and ethnic groups?

60.   Describe the relationship between violent video games and aggression.

AFTER YOU READ . . . PRACTICE TEST #5
INFLUENCES BEYOND FAMILY AND PEERS

Indicate whether each of the following statements is true or false.

_____ 1. Self-care children are those who are at home by themselves after school for an hour each week.

_____ 2. Self-care has the most negative effects for children in low-income neighborhoods with high crime rates.

_____ 3. Child poverty is equally distributed across ages, races, and family structures.

_____ 4. Parents living in poverty in the U.S. tend to treat their children differently than do working-class or middle-class parents.

_____ 5. Many children living in poor inner-city neighborhood show all the symptoms of post-traumatic stress disorder.

_____ 6. Brain imaging studies suggest that long term effects of viewing violence on television may be the result of patterns of neural activation that underlie emotionally-laden behavioral scripts that children learn while watching violent programming.

_____ 7. A "digital divide" exists across income and ethnic groups.

_____ 8. Some studies suggest that video game playing hinders children's spatial-cognitive skills.

AFTER YOU READ . . . CRITICAL REFLECTION EXERCISE

Self-Concept

Utilizing information from the text, provide detailed answers to the following questions:

1. What three factors do you think are the most important in influencing the child's developing self-concept during the six- to twelve-year-old age range? What role does each of these factors play? Why do you think they are so important?

2. You have been hired to teach a parenting class. Design an exercise that you could do with this class to illustrate the important effect that parents have on the developing self-concept of their children. List and discuss three things that parents might do that would have a negative effect on the child's self-concept. Provide suggestions for how to alter each of these negative effects into a positive one.

AFTER YOU READ . . . COMPREHENSIVE PRACTICE TEST
MULTIPLE CHOICE QUESTIONS

1. According to Freud, the challenge of the middle childhood years was to _____.
   a. form an emotional bond with peers
   b. develop an increased dependence on parents
   c. experience autonomy
   d. develop a strong sense of the id

2. According to Erikson, the psychosocial task of children between the ages of six and twelve is the development of _____, or the willingness to accomplish tasks.
   a. identity
   b. industry
   c. isolation
   d. initiative

3. Each of the following is a component of Bandura's reciprocal determinism EXCEPT _____.
   a. behavior
   b. environment
   c. person
   d. a conscience

4. Children's "Who am I?" responses become more _____ across middle childhood.
   a. positive
   b. rigid
   c. focused on physical characteristics
   d. complex and comparative

5. A global evaluation of one's own worth is called _____.
   a. self-perception
   b. self-esteem
   c. self-concept
   d. self-evaluative maintenance

6. Harter suggests that self-esteem is influenced by the _____.
   a. discrepancy between who a child feels he ought to be and who he thinks he is
   b. sum total of the assessments the child makes about her skills
   c. addition of all the positive assessments minus the negative ones
   d. relationship between physical abilities and cultural expectations

7. Which of the following statements is an example of a psychological construct?
   a. "Kermit runs faster than John."
   b. "Sarah is so kind."
   c. "Maria is the best reader in fourth grade."
   d. "Jose draws better than Joshua."

8. **The understanding that people can agree to change the rules is called _____.**
   a.   moral understanding
   b.   moral relativism
   c.   moral realism
   d.   moral relationships

9. **A parenting variable that contributes to the development is self-regulation is _____.**
   a.   consistent and severe punishment
   b.   low expectations of self-regulation
   c.   the parents' own ability to self-regulate
   d.   permissive parenting

10. **Selman suggested that older elementary school children begin to view friends as persons who _____.**
   a.   are similar to them
   b.   will do good things for them
   c.   help and trust one another
   d.   will protect each other

11. **Which of the following illustrates "controlling speech?"**
   a.   "Let's work on this together."
   b.   "If you let me borrow your toy, you can look at mine."
   c.   "That's not right!"
   d.   "I wish I had that toy, too."

12. **Which of the following is an example of relational aggression?**
   a.   "What a nut."
   b.   "Bite your tongue."
   c.   "You're stupid."
   d.   "What's your problem?"

13. **A combination of rejection and aggressiveness in childhood _____.**
   a.   has negative effects but can be easily overcome
   b.   is primarily a function of whether the child feels he fits in
   c.   has been linked to continuing aggression in adulthood
   d.   is directly linked to parental attitudes

14. **Self-care children who are monitored closely are _____.**
   a.   more likely to be involved in criminal behavior
   b.   more likely to make poor grades
   c.   less likely to experience the negative effects of self-care
   d.   less likely to complete their homework

15. **Which of the following could protect a child from the effects of a stressful environment?**
   a.   a high IQ
   b.   being of high socioeconomic status
   c.   authoritarian parenting
   d.   permissive parenting

TRUE-FALSE QUESTIONS

Indicate whether each of the following statements is true or false.

_____ 1. Contemporary studies that stress the child's need to feel competent are in tune with Erikson's views.

_____ 2. Self-efficacy is an individual's believe in her capacity to cause an intended event to occur.

_____ 3. Beginning at about age six or seven, the child begins to focus more on the inner traits or qualities of another person and to assume that those traits will be visible in many situations.

_____ 4. Moral reasoning is the process of making judgments about the rightness or wrongness of specific areas.

_____ 5. Possibly the most striking thing about peer group interactions is the elementary school years is gender-segregated they are.

_____ 6. At every age, boys show more physical aggression and more assertiveness than do girls.

_____ 7. Attractive children and physically small children are more likely to be popular.

_____ 8. Research consistently demonstrates that self-care children are more poorly adjusted in terms of both peer relationships and school performance.

ESSAY QUESTIONS

1.   What are the parenting variables that contribute to self-regulation, and why are they important?

2.   Discuss the sex differences in aggression.

3.   What behavior is characteristic of popular children?

WHEN YOU HAVE FINISHED . . . PUZZLE IT OUT

Across

1. Aggression to get back at someone who has hurt you
4. The list of "don'ts" in the superego
5. The fourth of Freud's psychosexual stages
6. Speech that includes rejecting comments, ordering, manipulating, challenging, defiance
7. Internal moral judge
8. Traits such as self-pitying, tense, touchy, unstable, worrying
9. Traits such as active, assertive, enthusiastic, outgoing
10. Traits such as affectionate, forgiving, generous, kind, trusting
11. Comparison with a description that involved comparing a child's behavior or physical features with those of another child or with a norm

Down

2. Discipline that is combined with instruction
3. Aggression aimed at damaging another person's self-esteem
4. Traits such as efficient, organized, prudent, reliable

Created by Puzzlemaker at DiscoverySchool.com

WHEN YOU HAVE FINISHED . . . RESEARCH PROJECT

Student Project 18: Understanding of Friendship

For this project you will need to locate a child between the ages of six to twelve. After obtaining the appropriate permission(s), arrange with the parents to spend some time with the child, explaining that you want to talk to the child for a school project, and that this is not a "test" of any kind. Try to find a time and a place to be alone with your subject; it will not work as well if siblings or parents are present.

Procedure

After chatting for a while to establish rapport, say to the child something like:

> *I'd like to talk to you about friends. Let me tell you a story about some children who were friends.*

Then read the following story:

> Kathy and Becky have been best friends since they were five years old. They went to the same kindergarten and have been in the same class ever since. Every Saturday they would try to do something special together, such as go to the park or the store, or play something special at home. They always had a good time with each other.
>
> One day a new girl, Jeanette, moved into their neighborhood and soon introduced herself to Kathy and Becky. Right away, Jeanette and Kathy seemed to hit it off very well. They talked about where Jeanette was from and the things she could be doing in her new town. Becky, on the other hand, didn't seem to like Jeanette very well. She thought Jeanette was a show-off, but was also jealous of all the attention Kathy was giving Jeanette.
>
> When Jeanette left the other two alone, Becky told Kathy how she felt about Jeanette. "What did you think of her, Kathy? I thought she was kind of pushy, butting in on us like that."
>
> "Come on, Becky. She's new in town and just trying to make friends. The least we can do is be nice to her."
>
> "Yeah, but that doesn't mean we have to be friends with her," replied Becky. "Anyway, what would you like to do this Saturday? You know those old puppets of mine? I thought we could fix them up and make our own puppet show."
>
> "Sure, Becky, that sounds great," said Kathy. "I'll be over after lunch. I'd better go home now. See you tomorrow."
>
> Later that evening, Jeanette called Kathy and surprised her with an invitation to the circus, the last show before it left town. The only problem was that the show happened to be at the same time Kathy had promised to go to Becky's. Kathy didn't know what to do: go to the circus and leave her best friend alone, or stick with her best friend and miss a good time (Selman, 1980, pp. 321-322).

After reading the child the story, ask the following open-ended questions, and then probe the child's understanding of friendship:

1.   What do you think the problem is in this story?

2.   What do you think Kathy will do, choose to be with her old friend Becky, or go with the new girl, Jeanette? Why? Which do you think is more important: to be with an old friend or to make new friends? Why?

3.   Do you have a best friend? What kind of friendship do you have with that person? What makes that person your best friend?

Based on the child's answers, you may then want or need to probe as follows (you probably will not need to ask all of these questions; be selective, depending on your child's comments):

1.   What kind of friendship do you think Kathy and Becky have? Do you think it is a good, close relationship? What is a really good, close relation? Does it take something special to have a very good friendship? What kinds of things do friends know about each other?

2.   What does being friends for a long time, like Kathy and Becky have been, do for a friendship?

3.   What makes good, close friendships last?

4.   What kinds of things can good friends talk about that other friends sometimes can't? What kinds of problems can they talk over?

5.   What makes two friends feel really close to each other?

6.   What is the difference between the kind of friendship Becky and Kathy have and Kathy and Jeanette's friendship? Are there different kinds of friendship? What is the difference between "regular" and "best" friendships?

7.   Is it better when close friends are like each other or different from each other friendships? Why? In what way should good friends be the same? In what way should they be different?

8.   Which is better to have (be with), one close friend or a group of regular friends? Why? (Selman, 1980, pp. 321-333).

Analysis and Report

Transcribe your child's answers as close to verbatim as you can (tape them, if that will help). Describe the child's understanding of friendship and compare it to the description of friendships in the text.

Reference

Selman, R. L. (1980). *The Growth of Interpersonal Understanding.* New York: Academic Press.

WHEN YOU HAVE FINISHED . . . AT-HOME PROJECT

Student Project 19: Television Aggression

You may want to combine this project with the next one, which involves observing sex role presentations on TV. If so, you or your instructor may wish to modify the following instructions somewhat. But if you are doing this in isolation, proceed as follows:

Procedure

Using the definition of violence offered by George Gerbner ("the overt expression of physical forces against others or self, or the compelling of action against one's will on pain of being hurt or killed"), select a minimum of four half-hour television programs normally watched by children and count the number of aggressive or violent episodes in each. Extend Gerbner's definition somewhat, however, to count verbal aggression as well as physical aggression.

You may select any four (or more) programs, but consider distributing them in the following way:
- At least one "educational" television program, such as *Sesame Street* or *Mr. Rogers' Neighborhood*.
- At least one Saturday morning cartoon.
- At least one early evening adult program that is watched by young children: a family comedy, a western, a crime film, or one of each.

For each program that you watch, record the number of violent episodes, separating the instances of verbal and physical violence.

Analysis and Report

In thinking of writing about the details of your observations, consider the following questions:

1. What kind of variation in the number of violent episodes is there among the programs that you watched?

2. Are some programs more verbally aggressive, some more physically aggressive?

3. Do the numbers of violent episodes per program correspond to the numbers found by Gerbner?

4. What about the consequences of aggression in the television films? Are those who act violently rewarded or punished? How often do reward and punishment occur?

5. What behaviors other than aggression might a child learn from watching the programs you viewed? This question is particularly relevant for *Sesame Street* or *Mr. Rogers' Neighborhood*, but applies to more traditional entertainment as well.

6. In view of the material in this chapter, and your own observations for this project, what rules or limits (if any) would you place on TV viewing for your own child? Why?

WHEN YOU HAVE FINISHED . . . AT-HOME PROJECT

Student Project 20: Sex Roles on TV

If you combine this with the preceding project, recording both aggressive episodes and sex role behavior on TV programs, you will gain a very good sense of portrayals of "real life" given on TV.

Procedure

You can gain some experience designing your own research by selection among the following options:

Option 1. Watch at least five hours of TV, spread over several time periods, and record the number of male and female characters and whether they are the central character or a minor character.

Option 2. Watch four to six hours of TV, selecting among several different types of programs, and note the activities of each male and female character in the following categories: aggression, nurturance, problem solving, conformity, and physical exertion.

Option 3. Watch and analyze the commercials on at least ten programs, making sure that the programs cover the full range of types, from sports to soap operas. You might count the number of male and female participants in the commercials and the nature of their activity in each case, using some of the same categories listed in option 2.

Analysis and Report

In preparing your report, you need to specify clearly which of these options (or some other) you chose, which programs you watched, how often you defined your terms, and what results you obtained. What do you think these results mean for the average viewer of TV?

CHAPTER 10 ANSWER KEY

Practice Test #1 Theories of Social and Personality Development

1. form emotional bonds with peers; parents
2. industry versus inferiority
3. competent
4. trait theories
5. reciprocal determinism

Practice Test #2 Self-Concept

1. psychological self
2. complex; comparative; external features; feelings and ideas
3. self-efficacy
4. social comparisons
5. self-esteem

Practice Test #3 Advances in Social Cognition

1. F   2. T   3. T   4. T   5. F

Practice Test #4 The Social World of the School-Aged child

1. c   2. d   3. b   4. c   5. a   6. b   7. c   8. d

Practice Test #5: Influences Beyond Family and Peers

1. F   2. T   3. F   4. T   5. T   6. T   7. T   8. F

Comprehensive Practice Test

Multiple Choice Questions

1. a   2. b   3. d   4. d   5. b   6. a   7. b   8. b   9. c   10. c
11. c   12. c   13. c   14. c   15. a

True-False Questions

1. T   2. T   3. F   4. T   5. T   6. T   7. F   8. T

Essay Questions

1. ▪ The parents' own ability to self-regulate provides the child with models of good or poor self-regulation.
   ▪ The degree of self-regulation expected by parents influences the child's self-regulatory behavior. Higher expectations, together with parental monitoring to make certain the expectations are met, are associated with greater self-regulatory competence.

2. ▪ Boys friendships are more focused on competition and dominance than girls.
   ▪ Girls' friendships include more agreement, more compliance, and more self-disclosure than boys.
   ▪ More "controlling" speech among boys.

3. ▪ Popular children behave in positive, supportive, non-punitive, and non-aggressive ways toward most other children.
   ▪ They explain things, take their playmates' wishes into consideration, take turns in conversation, and are able to regulate the expression of their strong emotions.
   ▪ They are often good at regulating their own emotions and accurately assessing others' feelings.

Puzzle It Out

Across
1. retaliatory
4. conscience
5. latency
6. controlling
7. superego
8. neuroticism
9. extraversion
10. agreeableness
11. behavioral

Down
2. inductive
3. relational
4. conscientiousness

CHAPTER 11

PHYSICAL AND COGNITIVE DEVELOPMENT IN ADOLESCENCE

BEFORE YOU READ . . . CHAPTER SUMMARY

Development in adolescence is marked by strides, as well as challenges. Along with physical maturity comes new health risks. Advances in cognitive functioning enable teenagers to function almost as well as adults. School experiences are critical to adolescent development.

Physical Development

- There are two major growth spurts in the brain during the teenaged years. An adolescent may grow three to six inches a year for several years, and then continue to add height and weight slowly until he or she reaches their adult size. Boys add more muscle than girls; girls add more fat than boys.
- Puberty is triggered by a complex set of hormones, beginning at about age seven or eight. Menarche, a girl's first menstrual period, typically occurs two years after the beginning of other visible changes. In boys, the peak of the growth spurt typically comes fairly late in the sequence of physical development.
- Each teenager has an internal model, or mental image, of the "normal" or "right" timing for puberty. Discrepancies between an adolescent's expectation and what actually happens determine the psychological effect of puberty.

Adolescent Sexuality

- Sexual activity among teens has increased in recent decades in the United States, but many do not use contraception consistently.
- Long-term consequences for teenaged mothers are generally negative, although some girls are able to overcome the challenges.
- Teens who are homosexual or who are unsure about their sexual orientation face many obstacles in the formation of an identity.

Adolescent Health

- In general, teenagers show heightened levels of risky behavior, such as unprotected sex, drug use, and reckless driving.
- Alcohol, drugs, and tobacco are more likely to be used by teens who show other forms of deviant or problem behavior. Sensation-seeking interacts with parenting style to increase the likelihood of drug use.
- Eating disorders such as bulimia and anorexia are among the most significant mental health problems during adolescence. Body image may be a causal factor. A general tendency toward mental illness may also be a factor in eating disorders.
- The contributing factors in completed suicides include depression, aggression, and a family history of psychiatric disorders or suicide or drug or alcohol abuse.

Changes in Thinking and Memory

▪ In Piaget's fourth stage of cognitive development, the formal operational period, teenagers learn to reason logically about abstract concepts. It is characterized by the ability to apply basic operations to ideas and possibilities—systematic problem solving—in addition to actual objects.

▪ There is clear evidence of some advanced forms of thinking in at least some adolescents, but formal operational thinking is not universal, nor is it consistently used even by those who possess the ability.

▪ Adolescents process information faster, use processing resources more efficiently, understand their own memory processes better, and have more knowledge than do elementary school children.

Schooling

▪ The transition to middle school may be accompanied by changes in children's goal orientation that result in achievement and self-esteem losses.

▪ Girls seem to be at particular risk for achievement losses after the transition to high school, especially in science and math. The ethnic variations in math performance are wide, partly because not all teens receive the necessary encouragement and/or preparation for advanced high school math classes.

▪ Adolescents who succeed academically in high school are typically from authoritative families. Those who drop out are more likely to be poor, or to be doing poorly in school.

AS YOU READ . . . LEARNING OBJECTIVES

After completing Chapter 11, you should be able to answer the following questions:

11.1 How do the brains and other body systems of adolescents differ from those of younger children?
11.2 What are the major milestones of puberty?
11.3 What are the consequences of early, "on time," and late puberty for boys and girls?
11.4 What are the patterns of adolescent sexual behavior in the United States?
11.5 Which teenaged girls are most likely to get pregnant?
11.6 What are some of the causes that have been proposed to explain homosexuality?
11.7 How does sensation-seeking affect risky behavior in adolescents?
11.8 What patterns of drug, alcohol, and tobacco use have been found among adolescents in the United States?
11.9 What are the characteristics and causes of eating disorders?
11.10 Which adolescents are at greatest risk of depression and suicide?
11.11 What are the characteristics of thought in Piaget's formal operational stage?
11.12 What are some major research findings regarding the formal operational stage?
11.13 What kinds of advances in information-processing capabilities occur during adolescence?
11.14 How do changes in students' goals contribute to the transition to secondary school?
11.15 What gender and ethnic differences in science and math achievement have been found by researchers?
11.16 What variables predict the likelihood of dropping out of high school?

AS YOU READ . . . TERM IDENTIFICATION

Ability goals (p. 328)
Adolescence (p. 327)
Anorexia nervosa (p. 321)
Bulimia nervosa (p. 321)
Formal operational stage (p. 324)
Hypothetico-deductive reasoning (p. 324)
Imaginary audience (p. 325
Menarche (p.)
Personal fable (p. 325)

Pituitary gland (p. 309)
Primary sex characteristics (p. 309)
Puberty (p. 309)
Secondary sex characteristics (p. 309)
Secular trend (p. 310)
Systematic problem-solving (p. 324)
Task goals (p. 328)
Transgendered (p. 317)

AS YOU READ . . . GUIDED STUDY QUESTIONS

PHYSICAL CHANGES

Brain Development and Physical Growth (pp. 308-309)

11.1   How do the brain and other body systems of adolescents differ from those of younger children?

1.   Define adolescence (p. 307).

2.   List and describe the two major brain growth spurts in the teenaged years.

Age	Area of Brain Growth	Result of Growth
13-15		
17-19		

3.   Give examples of how the cephalocaudal and proximodistal patterns of development are reversed in adolescence.

4.   Distinguish between the development of joints in girls and in boys.

5.   Compare the gains in muscles of boys and girls.

6.   How does the increase in the size of the heart and lungs affect endurance, size, strength, and speed?

The Milestones of Puberty (pp. 309-311)

11.2   What are the major milestones of puberty?

7.   Define the following terms:
    a.   puberty (p. 309)

    b.   pituitary gland (p. 309)

    c.   primary sex characteristics (p. 310)

    d.   secondary sex characteristics (p. 310)

    e.   menarche (p. 310)

    f.   secular trend (p. 311)

8.   List the major hormones that contribute to physical growth and development.

9.   Trace the events of sexual development of girls and boys.

Timing of Puberty (pp. 312)

11.3   What are the consequences of early, "on time," and late puberty for boys and girls?

10.   Describe why the discrepancies between an adolescent's expectation and what actually happens determine the psychological effects of puberty. Give examples for girls and for boys.

AFTER YOU READ . . . PRACTICE TEST #1
PHYSICAL CHANGES

Match the letter of the term in the right column with its description in the left column.

_____ 1. Changes in body parts during puberty such as breasts and body hair.	a. Adolescence
	b. Estradiol
_____ 2. The beginning of menstrual cycles.	c. Menarche
	d. Pituitary gland
_____ 3. The transitional period between childhood and adulthood.	e. Primary sex characteristics
_____ 4. Collective term for the physical changes which culminate in sexual maturity.	f. Puberty
	g. Secondary sex characteristics
_____ 5. Hormone in girls that causes the sex organs to develop.	h. Secular trend
_____ 6. Gland that triggers other glands to release hormones	i. Testosterone

ADOLESCENT SEXUALITY

Sexual Behavior (pp. 313-315)

11.4   What are the patterns of adolescent sexual behavior in the United States?

11.   Give examples of how sexual experience varies across racial and ethnic groups, and across age and ethnic groups.

12.   List the social factors that predict teenagers' sexual activity.

13.   Give examples of the finding that teens lack knowledge about sexually transmitted diseases (STDs).

14.   Describe a comprehensive sex education program.

Teenaged Pregnancy (pp. 315-316)

11.5   Which teenaged girls are most likely to get pregnant?

15.   List the factors that predict sexual activity in general as well the likelihood that she will become pregnant.

16.   How are the children of teenaged mothers at risk?

The Real World: Crisis Intervention for the Pregnant Teen (p. 316)

17.   List the characteristics of each phase of the intervention model, and provide suggested caregiver techniques.

Phase	Characteristics of Phase	Caregiving Techniques
Initial Phase		
Escalation Phase		
Redefinition Phase		
Dysfunctional Phase		

18.   What is the goal of crisis intervention?

Sexual Minority Youth (pp. 317-318)

11.6   *What are some of the causes that have been proposed to explain homosexuality?*

19.   Define transgendered (p. 317).

20.   State the concordant rates of homosexuality for the following groups:

Group	Concordant Rate
Identical Twins	
Fraternal Twins	
Biologically Unrelated bys Adopted in the Same Family	

21.   Describe the evidence to support the hypothesis that homosexuality is programmed in at birth.

22.   Describe evidence that environment plays a role in homosexuality.

23.   Give examples of similar concerns which homosexual adolescents share with heterosexual adolescents.

AFTER YOU READ . . . PRACTICE TEST #2
ADOLESCENT SEXUALITY

Indicate whether each of the following statements is true or false.

_____ 1. Research has found that boys are more sexually active than girls.

_____ 2. The amount of testosterone in the blood is a better predictor than social factors of teenagers' sexual activity.

_____ 3. The greater the number of risk factors present in the life of an individual teenager, the greater the likelihood that he or she will be sexually active.

_____ 4. The rate of teenaged pregnancy is lower in the U.S. than in most other Western industrialized countries.

_____ 5. The younger a girl is when she becomes sexually active, the more likely she is to become pregnant.

_____ 6. The likelihood of pregnancy is lower among teenaged girls who do well in school and have strong education al aspirations.

_____ 7. The children of teenaged mothers are more likely than children born to older mothers to grow up in poverty.

_____ 8. There is no difference in the rate of depression and attempted suicide of homosexual and heterosexual teens.

ADOLESCENT HEALTH

Sensation-Seeking (p. 318-319)

11.7 How does sensation-seeking affect risky behavior in adolescents?

24. Give examples of adolescent sensation-seeking behavior.

25. Why are risky behaviors more common in adolescence than other periods?

26. Give examples of how television and other forms of the popular media may influence teens' risky behavior.

Drugs, Alcohol, and Tobacco (pp. 319-321)

11.8 What patterns of drug, alcohol, and tobacco use have been found among adolescents in the United States?

27. What is binge drinking?

28. How does sensation-seeking interact with parenting style?

29.   What are the ages during which teens seem to be most susceptible to peer influence with regard to smoking?

30.   Give examples of how parents influence teenagers' smoking habits.

Eating Disorders (pp. 321-322)

11.9   What are the characteristics and causes of eating disorders?

31.   Define the following terms:
    a.   anorexia nervosa (p. 321)

    b.   bulimia nervosa (p. 321)

32.   Describe the following possible explanations for eating disorders.

Possible Explanation	Description
Brain Dysfunction	
Genetics	
Psychoanalytic Explanation	
Discrepancy in Perception	
Culture	
Pre-existing Psychological Health	

33.   Give an example of how the general tendency toward mental illness may be a factor in eating disorders.

34.   What is an obsessive-compulsive personality disorder?

Depression and Suicide (p. 323)

11.10 Which adolescents are at greatest risk of depression and suicide?

35.   Describe the following possible explanations for teenaged depression.

Possible Explanation	Description
Dysfunction of the Pituitary Gland	
Genetics	
Parent Depression	

36.   Give examples of family stresses that might impact adolescent depression.

37.   How does low self-esteem impact teenagers' depression?

38.   Give examples of how depression can hinder academic achievement.

39.   List and describe three factors that contribute to completed suicides.

Factor	Description

40.   Describe suicide prevention programs.

AFTER YOU READ . . . PRACTICE TEST #3
ADOLESCENT HEALTH

1.   _____ leads to recklessness, which, in turn, leads to markedly increased rates of accidents and injuries in the teen years.
   a.   Sensation seeking
   b.   Bulimia
   c.   Adolescent egocentrism
   d.   Playing violent video games

2.   Social factors that predict teenagers' risky sexual behavior include each of the following EXCEPT _____.
   a.   they come from poorer families
   b.   they come from families in which sexual activity is condoned and dating rules are lax
   c.   they were abused and/or neglected in early childhood
   d.   they are less likely to use alcohol

3.   The illicit substance that teens use most often is _____.
   a.   cocaine
   b.   heroin
   c.   marijuana
   d.   LSD

4.   Teens who are high sensation-seekers choose friends _____.
   a.   who are low sensation-seekers
   b.   who are similar
   c.   who have more money than they do
   d.   to impress with their adventures

5.   The period between ages _____ seems to be the time during which a teenager is most susceptible to peer influences with regard to smoking.
   a.   15 and 17
   b.   13 and 15
   c.   11 and 13
   d.   9 and 11

6.   An eating disorder characterized by binge eating and purging is called _____.
   a.   major depression
   b.   obsessive-compulsive personality disorder
   c.   anorexia nervosa
   d.   bulimia

7.   Each of the following is a proposed cause for eating disorders EXCEPT _____.
   a.   operant conditioning
   b.   biological
   c.   psychoanalytical
   d.   discrepancy between a teens' internal image of a desirable body and her (or his) perception of her (or his) own body

8.   **A condition characterized by an excessive need for control of the environment is called _____.**
   a.   obsessive-compulsive personality disorder
   b.   major depressive disorder
   c.   dissociative identity disorder
   d.   bipolar disorder

9.   **Teenaged girls are _____ as likely as boys to report feelings of depression.**
   a.   just
   b.   three times
   c.   twice
   d.   not

10.   **Each of the following is a contributing factor in completed suicides EXCEPT _____.**
   a.   an opportunity
   b.   special training in coping abilities
   c.   an altered mental state
   d.   some triggering stressful event

CHANGES IN THINKING AND MEMORY

Piaget's Formal Operational Stage (pp. 324-325)

11.11 What are the characteristics of thought in Piaget' formal operational stage?

41. Define the following terms:
   a. formal operational stage (p. 324)

   b. systematic problem solving (p. 324)

   c. hypothetico-deductive reasoning (p. 324)

42. Describe the methods Piaget used to test for systematic problem-solving skills. Include the pendulum problem.

43. How would an adolescent using a formal operational approach differ from a concrete-operational thinker in attempting to solve the pendulum problem?

44. Give examples of deductive reasoning, and explain how deductive reasoning is related to the scientific process.

45. What is adolescent egocentrism?

46. Give examples of the two components of adolescent egocentrism by completing the following table:

Component	Example
Personal Fable	
Imaginary Audience	

47. How can Elkind's theory be helpful in explaining adolescents' everyday behaviors?

Direct Tests of Piaget's View (pp. 325-327)

11.12 What are some major research findings regarding the formal operational stage?

48.   Give examples of how adolescents gain formal operational skills in the pendulum problem and in understanding figurative language.

Research Report: Formal Operational Thinking and Everyday Problem Solving (p. 326)

49.   Give examples of how formal operational reasoning alters the ways teenagers' make decisions.

Advances in Information-Processing (pp. 327-328)

11.13 What kinds of advances in information-processing capabilities occur during adolescence?

50.   List the gains in information-processing skills of adolescents as compared to elementary school children.

51.   Give examples of how the metacognitive and metamemory skills of adolescents far exceed those of younger children.

52.   Give examples to illustrate the difference between younger children's and adolescents' processing of a memory for text. Include the four rules that participants used in writing summaries.

AFTER YOU READ . . . PRACTICE TEST #4
CHANGES IN THINKING AND MEMORY

Indicate whether each of the following statements is true or false.

_____ 1. The formal operational stage is defined as the period during which adolescents learn to reason logically about concrete concepts.

_____ 2. Systematic problem solving is the ability to search methodically for the answer to a problem.

_____ 3. Inductive reasoning involves considering hypotheses or hypothetical premises and then deriving logical outcomes.

_____ 4. Naïve idealism is manifested when adolescent use formal operational thinking to mentally construct an ideal world and then compare the real world to it.

_____ 5. According to Elkind, an imaginary audience is the belief that the events of one's life are controlled by a mentally constructed autobiography.

_____ 6. Formal operational reasoning seems to enable adolescents to understand figurative language, such as metaphors, to a greater degree.

_____ 7. Piaget would probably argue that young teens aren't good at applying their formal operational schemes to everyday problems because they haven't had much practice using them.

_____ 8. The capacity to apply memory strategies selectively continues to improve throughout adolescence.

_____ 9. Metacognitive abilities enable younger children to benefit more from training than teenagers.

_____ 10. The ability to summarize a text improves significantly during the early half of adolescence.

SCHOOLING

Transition to Secondary School (pp. 328-330)

11.14 How do changes in students' goals contribute to the transition to secondary school?

53.   Define the following terms:
        a.   task goals (p. 328)

        b.   ability goals (p. 328)

54.   Describe two models of transitional schools from elementary school to high school.

Model	Description
8-4 System	
Junior High System	

55.   Explain how a student's goal (task or ability) influences his or her behavior.

56.   What might cause adolescents' self concept to change in middle school?

57.   How can electives in high school make the transition more positive?

Gender, Ethnicity, and Achievement in Science and Math (pp. 330-331)

11.15 What gender and ethnic differences in science and math achievement have been found by researchers?

58.   Give examples of how girls are at risk for achievement losses in science after the transition to high school. Include suggestions for lessening the gap.

59.   Give examples of ethnic variations in mathematics achievement. Include examples of preparation for college-preparatory courses.

Dropping Out of High School (pp. 331-333)

11.16 *What variables predict the likelihood of dropping out of high school?*

60. Describe the characteristics of the parents of students who achieve in high school.

61. Give examples of the following influences that predict school completion.

Influences	*Examples*
Social Class	
History of Academic Failure	
Pattern of Aggressive Behavior	
Decisions about Risky Behavior	
Peer Influence	
Family Variables	

62. List the long-term consequences of dropping out of high school.

No Easy Answers: Reaching the High School Dropout (p. 332)

63. What is a charter school?

64. Give examples of how a charter school may reach the high school dropout.

AFTER YOU READ . . . PRACTICE TEST #5
SCHOOLING

Fill in the blanks with the best answer.

1. _____ are goals based on a desire for improvement; _____ are goals based on a desire to be superior to others.

2. Task goals are associated with a greater sense of _____ and more positive attitudes about school.

3. Students with ability goals adopt _____ —that is, they view performance on a given academic task as good as long as it is better than someone else's.

4. Some schools provide students with _____, either a teacher or a volunteer from the community, to whom middle-school students are assigned.

5. One approach aimed at making middle schools truly transitional involves organizing students and teachers into _____.

6. _____ seem to be at particular risk for achievement losses after the transition to high school.

7. _____ high school students earn twice as many high school credits in advanced math courses as White students, and three to four times as many as African-American and Hispanic-American students.

8. Despite ethnic differences in drop-out rates, _____ is a better predictor of school completion than is ethnicity.

9. Longitudinal studies show that students who have _____, _____, and _____ are most likely to drop out of high school.

10. One recent educational innovation, the _____, seems to be especially promising with regard to meeting the educational needs of drop-outs.

AFTER YOU READ . . . CRITICAL REFLECTION EXERCISE

Puberty and Adolescence

Utilizing information from the text, provide answers to the following questions. Be sure and provide specific examples and evidence from the chapters to support your answers.

1. What effect does the timing of the onset of puberty have on the developing adolescent? Name and discuss three factors that influence the type of effects on early or later onset of puberty will have.

2. Why are physical and cognitive changes so closely linked during adolescent development? Provide at least three possible reasons.

3. You are conducting a parents-as-teachers session. You have been asked to explain some of the factors that influence why teens might turn to drugs and alcohol. Provide four reasons that adolescents might start drinking or using other drugs. In addition, provide four pieces of advice to these parents on how to approach the concept with their children.

AFTER YOU READ . . . COMPREHENSIVE PRACTICE TEST
MULTIPLE CHOICE QUESTIONS

1. **After puberty, _____ in endurance as well as in size, strength, and speed.**
   a.   boys have a clear advantage over girls
   b.   boys have a limited advantage over girls
   c.   boys and girls have an equal advantage
   d.   girls have a clear advantage over boys

2. **The pituitary gland _____.**
   a.   regulates bodily systems such as temperature and hunger
   b.   provides the trigger for the release of hormones from other glands
   c.   produces and releases thyroxin which regulates sexual growth
   d.   triggers the development of primary and secondary sex characteristics

3. **What effect does early pubertal development have on boys?**
   a.   It has significant negative effects on self-esteem.
   b.   There are no consistent effects of the timing of pubertal development.
   c.   It tends to have positive effects on body image and the number of friends.
   d.   It has minor negative effects on body image and school-related problems.

4. **Which of the following statements about the sexual behavior of teens is true?**
   a.   The proportion of sexually experienced teens decreases across grades 9 to 12.
   b.   Sexual experience is consistent across racial and ethnic groups.
   c.   Boys are more sexually active than girls.
   d.   Teens consistently use effective contraceptive methods.

5. **The children of teenaged mothers are more likely than children born to older mothers to _____.**
   a.   grow up in poverty
   b.   complete high school
   c.   achieve high self-esteem
   d.   delay having children of their own

6. **A desire to experience increased levels of arousal, such as those that accompany fast driving or the "highs" that are associated with drugs, is called _____.**
   a.   an extracurricular activity
   b.   socializing
   c.   independence
   d.   sensation-seeking

7. **Which of the following parenting styles seems to offer teens some protection from their sensation-seeking tendencies?**
   a.   permissive parental style
   b.   authoritarian parental style
   c.   authoritative parental style
   d.   neglecting parental style

8. **Which of the following is true about anorexia nervosa?**
   a. It is less common than bulimia nervosa.
   b. It is more common in underdeveloped countries than industrialized ones.
   c. It is fatal in about five percent of the cases.
   d. It involves bingeing but not purging.

9. **Which of the following statements is true about teenage suicide?**
   a. Native-American teenagers are the least likely to complete a suicide attempt.
   b. Hispanic-American youths are the most likely to complete a suicide attempt.
   c. Boys are more likely than girls to use self-poisoning in a suicide attempt.
   d. Boys are more likely than girls to complete a suicide attempt.

10. **The ability to derive conclusions from hypothetical premises is called _____.**
    a. hypothetico-deductive reasoning
    b. formal deductive reasoning
    c. inductive reasoning
    d. abstract thinking

11. **Which of the following statements about formal operational reasoning is true?**
    a. Piaget was overly pessimistic about adolescents' thinking abilities.
    b. People whose life situations or cultures do not require formal operational thinking do not develop it.
    c. In adulthood, rates of formal operational thinking decrease with education.
    d. Piaget was overly optimistic about adolescents' thinking abilities.

12. **Which of the following is NOT an advance in the information-processing abilities of teenagers?**
    a. understanding their own memory
    b. processing information faster
    c. understanding risky behavior
    d. metacognitive and metamemory skills

13. **Goals based on personal standards and a desire to become more competent at something are called _____.**
    a. metacognition
    b. ability goals
    c. task goals
    d. metamemory

14. **Which of the following statements about gender, ethnicity, and achievement in science and math is true?**
    a. Gender differences in achievement in math are greater than ethnic differences.
    b. Ethnic differences in achievement in math are greater than gender differences.
    c. Girls excel in math but not science.
    d. Intellectually talented girls are encouraged to take courses in sciences such as chemistry and physics rather than zoology or botany.

15. **Which of the following statements about dropping out of school is true?**
    a. Few variables are involved in school completion.
    b. Ethnicity is the strongest predictor of school completion.
    c. Academic failure is not a predictor of school completion.
    d. Social class is a better predictor of school completion than ethnicity.

TRUE-FALSE QUESTIONS

Indicate whether each of the following statements is true or false.

_____
1. Major changes in brain organization show up between ages 13 and 15 and qualitative shifts in cognitive functioning appear after age 15.

_____
2. Changes in primary sex characteristics include breast development in girls, changing voice pitch and beard growth in boys, and the growth of body hair in both sexes.

_____
3. Despite their high levels of sexual activity, teenagers know remarkably little about physiology and reproduction.

_____
4. Risky behaviors may be more common in adolescence than other periods because they help teenagers gain peer acceptance and establish autonomy with respect to parents and other authority figures.

_____
5. A child in the concrete operational stage working on the pendulum problem will usually try out many different combinations of length, weight, force, and height in an inefficient way.

_____
6. In adulthood, rates of formal operational thinking decrease with education.

_____
7. Ability-goal-oriented students are more likely than others to attribute success and failure to forces outside themselves.

_____
8. Alcohol and drug use better predict a high school student's grades than do the student's grades in elementary or middle school.

ESSAY QUESTIONS

1. Discuss how the popular media may influence teenagers' sensation-seeking behavior.

2. Discuss how Elkind's adolescent egocentrism is helpful in explaining a variety of adolescents' everyday behaviors. Give specific examples.

3. Discuss the long-term consequences that correlate with dropping out of high school.

WHEN YOU HAVE FINISHED . . . PUZZLE IT OUT

Across

3. An eating disorder characterized by self-starvation
5. The beginning of menstrual cycles
7. A sex hormone in girls
8. Goals based on a desire for self-improvement
9. Gland that triggers other glands to release hormone
10. Sex characteristics that involve body parts such as breasts and body hair
11. The transitional period between childhood and adulthood

Down

1. An eating disorder characterized by binge eating and purging
2. Sex characteristics that involve the growth of the sex organs
4. A sex hormone in males
6. Goals based on a desire to be superior to others

Created by Puzzlemaker at DiscoverySchool.com

WHEN YOU HAVE FINISHED . . . RESEARCH PROJECT

Student Project 21: The Pendulum

This is a simplified version of the Inhelder and Piaget pendulum problem. To complete this project, you should locate a child between roughly age eight and 16, obtaining the parents' permission for the testing in the prescribed way.

Equipment

Because the physical objects are so important for this problem, you need to collect your equipment carefully and test it before you start. You will need three pieces of strong, flexible string (one about 25 centimeters, one about 37 centimeters, and one 50 centimeters long). You will also need three similar objects of varying weights. Fishing sinkers work well, as do keys, but the lightest one should be heavy enough so that it will weigh down the string and allow it to swing.

If you can complete the testing in some location in which you have a chance to tie all three strings to some overhead rod or other object, that would be the best, since it leaves you free to write down what your subject does. Otherwise, you will have to hold the top of each string when your subject wishes to use that string in the test.

Procedure

Tell your subject:

> *I am doing a class project about how different people go about solving a problem. The problem I would like you to solve is to find out what makes a pendulum swing faster or slower.*

Pause at this point and demonstrate how you can attach a weight to the string, then push the weight to start the pendulum swinging. Demonstrate this with more than one weight/string combination so that it is clear that there is variability in the speed of the pendulum swing. Then say:

> *You need to figure out what makes the pendulum swing faster or slower. You can use any of these strings and these three weights to help you figure this out. I'll be taking notes about what you do and say while you are working on the problem.*

Record each combination the subject tries, in the order of the attempts. If you can, you should also record any comments the subject makes in the process. Allow the subject to continue until he or she gives you an answer; if no answer is forthcoming, after a period of time, you may ask some questions like, *"Can you figure out what makes the pendulum move fast or slow?"* If that does not elicit an answer, or if the subject seems very frustrated or bored, you may terminate the procedure and thank the subject for his or her help. If the subject has not solved the problem, you will want to reassure him or her by pointing out that this is a really hard problem and that lots of kids have a hard time figuring it out.

Analysis and Report

In reporting on your project, make sure to discuss the following points:

- Did your subject solve the problem? (That is, did he or she figure out that it is the length of the string and not the weight that determines the speed of the pendulum?)
- How many separate swing/weight combination tests did it take to reach some conclusion, whether the conclusion was correct or not?

- Did the subject try various string/weight combinations in any systematic order? Or were the various attempts more random?
- Did the subject talk to himself or herself while working on the problem? Was this self-talk directed at keeping track of things that had been tried, or at thinking through the problem?
- Did your subject's performance fit the findings form Piaget's and others' studies on the age at which formal operations develop?

WHEN YOU HAVE FINISHED . . . AT-HOME PROJECT

Student Project 22: Plotting Your Own Growth

This project will work best if your parents are among those who routinely stood you up against a convenient doorjamb and measured you—and if you still live in the house with the marked-up doorjamb. Alternatively, you may have a friend or an acquaintance who has access to doorjamb data you could use. Assuming you can locate such a set of measurements, you should plot your own (or your friend's) rate of growth over the years of childhood. Calculate the inches you grew each year (estimating when needed), plot the ages and the height, and draw a curve.

When was your maximum height spurt (the year in which you grew the most inches)? During elementary school, did you grow about the same number of inches per year? If you are a female, add to the graph a point that represents your first menstruation (to the best of your recollection). Where did menarche fall on the curve; that is, did menarche occur after your major growth spurt?

CHAPTER 11 ANSWER KEY

Practice Test #1 Physical Changes

1. g   2. c   3. a   4. f   5. b   6. d

Practice Test #2 Adolescent Sexuality

1. T   2. F   3. T   4. F   5. T   6. T   7. T   8. F

Practice Test #3 Adolescent Health

1. a   2. d   3. c   4. b   5. a   6. d   7. a   8. a   9. c   10. b

Practice Test #4 changes in Thinking and Memory

1. F   2. T   3. F   4. T   5. T   6. T   7. T   8. T   9. F   10. F

Practice Test #5 Schooling

1. task goal; ability goal
2. personal control
3. relative standards
4. an adult mentor
5. teams
6. Girls
7. Asian American
8. social class
9. a history of academic failure, a pattern of aggressive behavior, poor decisions about risky behavior
10. charter school

Comprehensive Practice Test

Multiple Choice Questions

1. a   2. b   3. c   4. c   5. a   6. d   7. c   8. a   9. d   10. a
11. b   12. d   13. c   14. b   15. d

True-False Questions

1. T   2. F   3. T   4. T   5. T   6. F   7. T   8. T

Essay Questions

1.
   - In the U.S. teens spend more time watching TV, listening to music, and playing video games than they do in school.
   - Teens who are highest in sensation-seeking behaviors are those who are most strongly influenced by media portrayals of risky behavior.
   - Television programs have an abundance of sexual incidents and the use of drug and alcohol.

2.
   - Examples of the personal fable could include ones similar to these: "You don't understand what it's like to be a teenager in love." "I can drink a six-pack of beer and drive safely—no problem." I'm not at risk for HIV/AIDS; only those other people et that."
   - Examples of the imaginary audience could include ones similar to these: "I can't go to school with my hair looking like this—everyone will laugh." "I have to have the perfect shirt to wear to the party."

3.
   - Answers should include the following: higher unemployment, lower wages, increased likelihood of depression, boys with poor self-regulatory skills are more likely to become involved in criminal behavior in early adulthood.

Puzzle It Out

Across
3. anorexia
5. menarche
7. estradiol
8. task
9. pituitary
10. secondary
11. adolescence

Down
1. bulimia
2. primary
4. testosterone
6. ability

CHAPTER 12

SOCIAL AND PERSONALITY DEVELOPMENT IN ADOLESCENCE

BEFORE YOU READ . . . CHAPTER SUMMARY

The social and personality development of adolescents is strongly influenced by the process of identity development. Other factors influencing development include changes in adolescents' self-concept and social relationships. The development of moral reasoning is also considered.

Theories of Social and Personality Development

- For Freud, the primary developmental task of the genital stage is to channel the libido into a healthy sexual relationship, whereas Erikson emphasizes the development of the identity.
- James Marcia's study of identity statuses is based on Erikson's ideas, and it includes two key parts—a crisis and a commitment. Combining these elements, four identity statuses are possible.

Self-Concept

- In adolescence, the teen's self-concept becomes more abstract and differentiated. More emphasis is placed on enduring, internal qualities and ideology.
- Self-esteem drops somewhat at the beginning of adolescence and then rises steadily throughout the teen years.
- Gender-related aspects of the psychological self are termed sex-role identity.
- Minority teenagers, especially those of color in a predominantly white culture, face the task of creating two identities in adolescence: a sense of individual identity that sets them apart from others and an ethnic identity that includes self-identification as a member of their specific group.

Moral Development

- Kohlberg proposed six stages of moral reasoning, organized into three levels. These levels are loosely correlated with age, develop in a specified order, and appear in this same sequence in all cultures studied so far.
- The acquisition of cognitive role-taking skills is important to moral development, but the social environment is important as well.
- Kohlberg's theory has been criticized by theorists who place more emphasis on learning moral behavior and others who believe that moral reasoning may be based more on emotional factors than on ideas about justice and fairness.
- Delinquent teens are usually found to be far behind their peers in both role-taking and moral reasoning. Other factors, such as parenting style, may be equally important in delinquency.

Social Relationships

- Adolescents have two, apparently contradictory, tasks in their relationships with their parents; to establish autonomy from them and to maintain a sense of relatedness with them.
- Friendships become far more significant in adolescence than they have been at any earlier period, and perhaps than they will be at any time later in life.

- The structure of peer groups changes during the teenaged years, and the social system of crowds becomes increasingly differentiated.
- Perhaps the most profound change in social relationships is the shift toward the inclusion of heterosexual relationships that prepare teens for assuming a full adult sexual identity. Teens who are homosexual or who are unsure about their sexual orientation face many obstacles in the formation of an identity.

AS YOU READ . . . LEARNING OBJECTIVES

After completing Chapter 12, you should be able to answer the following questions:
12.1   What happens during Erikson's identity versus role confusion stage?
12.2   How does Marcia explain identity development?
12.3   In what ways does self-understanding in adolescence differ from that in childhood?
12.4   How does self-esteem change across the teenage years?
12.5   What are the gender role concepts of adolescents?
12.6   How do minority, biracial, and immigrant teens develop a sense of ethnic identity?
12.7   What are the features of moral reasoning at each of Kohlberg's stages?
12.8   What are some important causes and effects in the development of moral reasoning?
12.9   How does Kohlberg's theory been criticized?
12.10   What are the moral reasoning abilities and other characteristics of delinquents?
12.11   What are the features of adolescents' relationships with their parents?
12.12   What are the characteristics of adolescents' friendships?
12.13   How do peer groups change over the teen years?
12.14   How does interest in romantic relationships emerge among heterosexual and homosexual teens?

AS YOU READ . . . TERM IDENTIFICATION

Clique (p. 360)
Conventional morality (p. 351)
Crowd (p. 360)
Delinquency (p. 356)
Ethnic identity (p. 347)
Foreclosure (p. 342)
Gender role identity (p. 346)
Identity (p. 341)

Identity achievement (p. 342)
Identity crisis (p. 341)
Identity diffusion (p. 342)
Identity versus role confusion (p. 341)
Moratorium (p. 342)
Postconventional morality (p. 352)
Preconventional morality (p. 351)
Role-taking (p. 353)

AS YOU READ . . . GUIDED STUDY QUESTIONS

THEORIES OF SOCIAL AND PERSONALITY DEVELOPMENT

Psychoanalytic Perspectives (pp. 341-342)

12.1 **What happens during Erikson's identity versus role confusion stage?**

1.　Define the following terms:
　　a.　identity (p. 341)

　　c.　identity versus role confusion (p. 341)

　　d.　identity crisis (p. 341)

2.　For Freud, what is the primary developmental task of the genital stage?

3.　According to Erikson, what is the central crisis of adolescence?

4.　Explain why Erikson states that an identity crisis is inevitable during adolescence.

5.　According to Erikson, what is the function of the peer group?

Marcia's Theory of Identity Achievement (pp. 342-343)

12.2 **How does Marcia explain identity development?**

6.　Define the following terms:
　　a.　identity achievement (p. 342)

　　b.　moratorium (p 342)

　　c.　foreclosure (p. 342)

　　d.　identity diffusion (p. 342)

7.   What are the two key parts of adolescent identity formation? Give examples of each.

Key Part	Example

8.   What is the relationship between identity formation and the development of logical thinking?

9.   How do extreme stressors affect identity achievement?

Research Report: The Effects of Teenaged Employment (P. 345)

10.   The more hours adolescents work, the more likely they were to experience negative consequences. List the negative effects.

11.   How does the kind of work teenagers do as well as how many hours they spend on the job affect them?

AFTER YOU READ . . . PRACTICE TEST #1
THEORIES OF SOCIAL AND PERSONALITY DEVELOPMENT

Indicate whether each of the following statements is true or false.

_____
1.
According to Freud, The primary developmental task of the latency stage is to channel the libido into a healthy sexual relationship.

_____
2.
In Erikson's model, the central crisis of adolescence is identity versus role confusion.

_____
3.
According to Erikson, the teenaged group forms a base of security form which the young person can move toward an integrated view of herself, including her patterns of beliefs, occupational goals, and relationships.

_____
4.
In Marcia's theory, identity achievement is the status of a person who has been through a crisis and reached a commitment to ideological or occupational goals.

_____
5.
In Marcia's theory, foreclosure is the status of a person who is in a crisis but who has made no commitment.

_____
6.
The quest for personal identity is complete at the end of adolescence.

_____
7.
Teens facing extreme stressors, such as life-threatening illness, seem to be most optimally adjusted when they adopt the status of foreclosure.

_____
8.
Culture is not related to adolescent identity development.

SELF-CONCEPT

Self-Understanding (pp. 344-345)

12.3   In what ways does self-understanding in adolescence differ from that in childhood?

12.   Compare the school-aged child's self-understanding with that of the adolescent.

13.   Give examples of how an adolescent's self-concept becomes differentiated as she comes to see herself somewhat differently in each of several roles.

14.   Give examples of how the adolescents' academic self-concepts seem to come both from internal comparisons of their performance to a self-generated ideal and from external comparisons to peer performance.

15.   Give examples of how social self-concepts predict behavior.

16.   Compare how girls and boys construct various components of self-concept differently.

Self-Esteem (pp. 345-346)

12.4   How does self-esteem change across the teenage years?

17.   What is the overall trend of self-esteem during the years of adolescence?

18.   Describe the four groups based on the stability of their self-esteem rating across adolescence.

Group	*Description*
High Self-Esteem throughout Teens	
Steady Increase in Self-Esteem	
Consistently Low Self-Esteem	
Steady Decline in Self-Esteem	

Gender Roles (p. 346-347)

12.5   What are the gender role concepts of adolescents?

19.   Define gender role identity (p. 346).

20.   List and describe the four basic sex-role types.

Sex-Role Type	Description

Ethnic Identity (pp. 347-349)

12.6   How do minority, biracial, and immigrant teens develop a sense of ethnic identity?

21.   Define ethnic identity (p. 347).

22.   Describe the task facing minority teenagers in creating two identities.

23.   According to Jean Phinney, describe the stages in the development of a complete ethnic identity by completing the following table.

Stage	Example
Unexamined Ethnic Identity	
Ethnic Identity Search	
Resolution of the Conflicts & Contradictions	

24.   Give examples of a "bicultural orientation."

25. List and describe four factors that interact with a biracial adolescent's personality to shape her ethnic identity.

Factor	Description

26. How is the search of personal identity affected by ethnicity and culture?

The Real World: Role Models in Life and in the Media (p. 349)

27. Summarize the research on role models of African-American boys.

AFTER YOU READ . . . PRACTICE TEST #2
SELF-CONCEPT AND PERSONALITY

1. **In adolescence, self-definition _____.**
   a. becomes more abstract
   b. becomes more concrete
   c. continues to be concrete, as in middle childhood
   d. becomes more focused on external characteristics

2. **Adolescents' academic self-concepts come from _____.**
   a. internal comparisons only
   b. external comparisons only
   c. neither internal or external comparisons
   d. both from internal and external comparisons

3. **An androgynous individual is likely to _____.**
   a. be homosexual
   b. have more feminine than masculine personality traits
   c. have both masculine and feminine personality traits
   d. have neither masculine nor feminine personality traits

4. **Each of the following is a group based on the stability of self-esteem rates across adolescence EXCEPT _____.**
   a. self-esteem increases steadily
   b. self-esteem is consistently low
   c. self-esteem decreases dramatically
   d. self-esteem is consistently high

5. **Cross-cultural research suggests that adoption of an androgynous or masculine orientation by a girls can lead to _____.**
   a. higher self-esteem
   b. lower self-esteem
   c. lower academic achievement
   d. increased likelihood of homosexuality

6. **The first stage in Jean Phinney's model of ethnic identity is _____.**
   a. unexamined ethnic identity
   b. ethnic moratorium
   c. ethnic identity search
   d. identity resolution

MORAL DEVELOPMENT

Kohlberg's Theory of Moral Reasoning (pp. 349-353)

12.7   *What are the features of moral reasoning at each of Kohlberg's stages?*

28.   Define the following terms:
   a.   preconventional morality (p. 351)

   b.   conventional morality (p. 351)

   c.   postconventional morality (p. 351)

29.   Describe Kohlberg's research method.

30.   What is the relationship between age and the stages?

Age	Stage
Children	
Adults	

31.   List and describe the three levels and six stages of Kohlberg's theory by completing the following table:

Level	Stages	Description

Causes and Consequences of Moral Development (pp. 353-354)

12.8   What are some important causes and effects in the development of moral reasoning?

32.   Define role-taking (p. 353).

33.   Describe how cognitive development affects Kohlberg's stages and chronological age.

34.   Explain why role-taking is related to cognitive development and Kohlberg's stages.

35.   How is the social environment involved in the development of moral reasoning?

36.   How do parenting style and family climate relate to the levels of moral reasoning?

37.   Give examples of how teenagers' levels of moral reasoning appear to be positively correlated with prosocial behavior and negatively related to antisocial behavior.

Criticisms of Kohlberg's Theory (pp. 354-355)

12.9   How does Kohlberg's theory been criticized?

38.   Give an example of the aspects of moral reasoning found in non-Western cultures that do not fit in well with Kohlberg's approach.

39.   How does Nancy Eisenberg use empathy to connect moral reasoning and moral emotions?

40.   Explain Carol Gilligan's claim that justice and care are involved in moral reasoning.

41.   What are the sex differences in moral reasoning, according to Gilligan?

42.   To explain inconsistencies between reasoning and behavior, learning theorists suggest that moral reasoning is situational rather then developmental. List two examples of research that learning theorists give to support this assertion.

    ▪

    ▪

Moral Development and Antisocial Behavior (pp. 355-357)

12.10   What are the moral reasoning abilities and other characteristics of delinquents?

43.　　Define delinquency (p. 356).

44.　　Give an example of how delinquents seem to be behind their peers in moral reasoning because of deficits in role-taking skills.

45.　　List and describe the two sub-varieties of delinquents.

Sub-Variety	Definition	Description of Developmental Pathway

No Easy Answers: Preventing Youth Violence (p. 357)

46.　　What percentage of all violent crimes in the U.S. is committed by individuals under age 18?

47.　　Describe the Fast Track Project, including the effects among children in the experimental group.

AFTER YOU READ . . . PRACTICE TEST #3
MORAL DEVELOPMENT

Match the letter of the term in the right column with its description in the left column.

_____ 1. The ability to took at a situation from another person's perspective.

_____ 2. Stage 6 of Kohlberg's theory that involves balancing equally valid, but conflicting, moral principles against one another to determine which should be given precedence with respect to a specific moral issue.

_____ 3. Stage 3 of Kohlberg's theory; sometimes called the good boy/nice girl stage

_____ 4. The ability to identify with others' emotions.

_____ 5. Stage 4 of Kohlberg's theory; sometimes called the law-and-order orientation.

_____ 6. Deliberately breaking laws that are believed to be immoral.

_____ 7. Stage 2 of Kohlberg's theory; sometimes called naïve hedonism stage.

_____ 8. Antisocial behavior that includes law-breaking.

a. civil disobedience
b. conventional morality
c. delinquency
d. empathy
e. individualism, instrumental purpose, and exchange
f. mutual interpersonal expectations, relationships, and interpersonal conformity
g. preconventional morality
h. punishment and obedience orientation
i. role-taking
j. social contract orientation
k. social system and conscience
l. universal ethical principles orientation

SOCIAL RELATIONSHIPS

Relationships with Parents (pp. 357-359)

12.11 What are the features of adolescents' relationships with their parents?

48. Describe the two, apparently contradictory, tasks teenagers have in their relationships with their parents.

▪

▪

49. Give examples of research on teenagers' emotional attachment to their parents.

50. What is the relationship between teens who remain closely attached to their parents and their academic success, the likelihood of antisocial behavior, and the likelihood of drug use in later adolescence and early adulthood?

51. Give examples of why the authoritative parenting style is associated with more positive outcomes during adolescence.

52.   How does family structure affect teenagers?

Friendships (pp. 359-360)

12.12 What are the characteristics of adolescents' friendships?

53.   Give examples of how the similarity of psychological characteristics and attitudes take on new significance in adolescence.

54.   Give examples of how adolescent friendships are more stable than are those of younger children.

Peers Groups (pp. 360-361)

12.13 How do peer groups change over the teen years?

55.   Define the following terms:
       a.   clique (p. 360)

       b.   crowd (p. 360)

56.   Trace the pattern of peer group conformity across adolescence.

57.   Describe how the structure of the peer group changes over the years of adolescence.

58.   Give examples of how the term crowd is used to refer to the reputation-based group with which a young person is identified, either by choice or by peer designation.

59.   Give examples of an identity prototype.

Romantic Relationships (pp. 361-362)

12.14 How does interest in romantic relationships emerge among heterosexual and homosexual teens?

60.   What is the most profound change in social relationships in adolescence?

61.   Why is the sense of being in love an important factor in adolescent dating patterns?

62.   How do romantic relationships emerge somewhat differently in the lives of homosexual teens?

AFTER YOU READ . . . PRACTICE TEST #4
SOCIAL RELATIONSHIPS

Fill in the blanks with the best answers.

1.   Teenagers have two, apparently contradictory, tasks in their relationships with their parents: to

_____ and to _____ .

2.   Teenagers' underlying emotional attachment to their parents _____ on average.

3.   Teenager's sense of well-being or happiness is more strongly correlated with the quality of her

attachment to _____ than with the quality of her relationships with _____ .

4.   Teens who remain closely attached to their parents are .most likely to be _____

successful and to enjoy good _____

5.   Despite the importance of family relationships to adolescents, it is an undeniable fact that

_____ become far more significant in adolescence than they have been at any

earlier period.

6.   Teens' friendships are increasingly _____, in the sense that adolescent friends share
more and more of their inner feelings and secrets and are more knowledgeable about each other's
feelings.

7.   A _____ is four to six young people who appear to be strongly attached to another.

8.   The word crowd refers to the _____ group with which a young person is
identified, either by choice or by peer designation.

9.   The sense of _____ is an important factor in adolescent dating patterns.

10.   Homosexual teenagers become aware of same-sex attraction at around age _____ or _____ .

AFTER YOU READ . . . CRITICAL REFLECTION EXERCISE

Sense of Self

Utilizing information from the text, provide detailed answers to the following questions:

1. You are a teacher at an inner city school. You firmly believe that one of the most important things you can provide for youth is a sense of self-worth and purpose. Develop a program that you could use to help adolescents develop a positive image of themselves. Why did you design the program this way? What impact(s) will this program have on these youth as they mature into adulthood?

2. What does self-concept look like? Draw a diagram or picture that illustrates self-concept and how it develops. It does not matter what you draw as long as you could explain to someone else how the drawing illustrates the major factors that determine self-concept and feelings of self-worth. Write out an explanation of how your drawing illustrates these factors.

3. Choose any characteristic of your self. Consider how this characteristic has developed in the fashion that it has. Are you pleased with this development? Why or why not? If you are not pleased, what would you do to change it? Why would you change it?

AFTER YOU READ . . . COMPREHENSIVE PRACTICE TEST
MULTIPLE CHOICE QUESTIONS

1. **A period during which an adolescent is troubled by his lack of identity is called the _____.**
    a.   identity crisis
    b.   identity shift
    c.   identity commitment
    d.   identity status

2. **According to Marcia, a _____ is a period of decision-making when old values and old choices are reexamined.**
    a.   conviction
    b.   crisis
    c.   curiosity-seeking experience
    d.   commitment

3. **Adolescent moratorium means that the adolescent _____.**
    a.   is in a stage of rigid identity acceptance
    b.   stops seeking self-related feedback
    c.   adopts an identity that is unhealthy
    d.   is in a state of crisis

4. **In comparison to younger children, the adolescent's self-concept may be described as _____.**
    a.   centering more on ideology than in childhood
    b.   less differentiated than in childhood
    c.   centering more on external characteristics than in childhood
    d.   centering more on physical characteristics than in childhood

5. **Self-esteem levels during adolescence _____.**
    a.   go down dramatically for girls but up for boys
    b.   stay relatively the same as in childhood
    c.   go up steadily for both boys and girls
    d.   go up for girls but down for boys

6. **Gender-related aspects of the psychological self are referred to as _____.**
    a.   gender characteristics
    b.   gender-role identity
    c.   the genital stage
    d.   sexually-active behavior

7. **The _____ is typically triggered by some experience that makes ethnicity relevant.**
    a.   ethnic identity search stage
    b.   unexamined ethnic identity stage
    c.   bicultural orientation stage
    d.   ethnic identity achievement stage

8. **Each of the following is a factor that interacts with a biracial adolescent's personality to shape her ethnic identity EXCEPT _____.**
    a. family variables
    b. hazing and emotional trauma
    c. neighborhood variables
    d. gender

9. **Which of the following illustrates Stage 4 moral development, according to Kohlberg's theory?**
    a. Moral actions are defined by expectations from a significant group.
    b. Moral actions are defined by a larger social group, such as society.
    c. Moral actions are defined by whether or not the outcome is positive or negative.
    d. Moral actions are defined by universal ethical principles.

10. **The term _____ is used to refer to the ability to look at a situation from another person's perspective.**
    a. role-taking
    b. sympathy
    c. empathy
    d. civil disobedience

11. **According to Gilligan, the two distinct moral orientations involved in moral reasoning are _____.**
    a. justice and empathy
    b. justice and care
    c. honesty and sincerity
    d. right and wrong

12. **Delinquency is defined as _____.**
    a. disobedience
    b. intentional law-breaking
    c. age-appropriate activities
    d. mischief

13. **Teenagers must establish autonomy from their parents and _____.**
    a. prove to the their parents that they can do things on their own
    b. maintain their sense of relatedness with their parents
    c. sever their attachment bonds for the transition into adulthood
    d. display the differences between themselves and their peers

14. **What is a clique?**
    a. groups of ten to 12 persons who really are not attached to each other
    b. four to six young people strongly attached to one another
    c. a group of adolescents together because there is power in numbers
    d. a street gang that terrorizes the neighborhood

15. **Labeling others and oneself as belonging to one or more groups is called _____.**
    a. establishing prejudice
    b. stereotyping
    c. identity prototype
    d. reputation-based group

TRUE-FALSE QUESTIONS

Indicate whether each of the following statements is true or false.

_____
1. According to Erikson, identity is an understanding of one's unique characteristics and how they are manifested across ages, situations, and social roles.

_____
2. According to Marcia, a young person who is not in the midst of a crisis and has not made a commitment is in the foreclosure status.

_____
3. The adolescent's self-concept becomes more differentiated as she comes to see herself somewhat differently in each of several roles: as a student, with friends, with parents, and in romantic relationships.

_____
4. Androgynous individuals see themselves as having both masculine and feminine traits.

_____
5. The most common types of moral reasoning among adolescents are stage 2 and stage 3.

_____
6. There are at least two important sub-varieties of delinquents, distinguished by the age at which the delinquent behavior begins.

_____
7. Teens who remain closely attached to their parents are most likely to be academically unsuccessfully.

_____
8. Like friendships, peer groups are very unstable in adolescence.

ESSAY QUESTIONS

1. James Marcia describes four identity statuses, and states that they are based on the notion of crisis and commitment. Describe each status noting the role of or lack of crisis and commitment for each.

2. Discuss the three stages in the formation of an ethnic identity proposed by Jean Phinney. Give examples of each.

3. Describe the developmental pathway for early-onset delinquency.

WHEN YOU HAVE FINISHED . . . PUZZLE IT OUT

Across

3. Level of moral reasoning in which judgments are based on authorities outside the self
7. A combination of cliques which includes both males and females
9. In Freud's theory, the period during which people reach psychosexual maturity
10. Identity status in which the young person is not in the midst of a crisis and has not made a commitment
11. Four to sex young people who appear to be strongly attached to one another
12. An understanding of one's own unique characteristics
13. Level of moral reasoning in which judgments are based on the integration of individual rights and the needs of society
14. Individuals who see themselves as having both masculine and feminine personality traits

Down

1. The ability to identify with others' emotions
2. Identity status in which a crisis is in progress, but no commitment has yet been made
4. Level of moral reasoning in which judgments are based on rules or norms of a group
5. Identity status in which a person has been through a crisis and has reached commitment
6. Identity status in which the person has made a commitment without have gone through a crisis
8. Antisocial behavior that includes law-breaking

Created by Puzzlemaker at DiscoverySchool.com

WHEN YOU HAVE FINISHED . . . RESEARCH PROJECT

Student Project 23: Who Am I?

The purpose of this project is to replicate, on a small scale, the research by Montemayor and Eisen (1977). For the project you will need to find three or four teenagers, preferably one or two who are in early adolescence (12 to 14) and several who are near the end of high school (16 to 18). Obtain the appropriate informed consent from each of these youngsters, following whatever guidelines your instructor specifies.

Procedure

For each student, prepare a sheet of paper with 20 numbered spaces on it. At the top, write the instructions: *In the spaces below, write 20 different answers to the question, "Who am I?"* Each subject should be interviewed alone. Hand the teenager the sheet, and ask him or her to fill out all 20 blanks, each time giving one answer to the "Who am I" question.

Analysis and Report

Analyze the answers your subjects give using the categories of physical appearance and ideology (or any other categories you may identify). Do your subjects' answers match the pattern reported in the text? Are there any other differences in the responses given by your younger and older subjects?

Reference

Montemayor, R., & Eisen, M. (1977). The development of self-conceptions from childhood to adolescence. *Developmental psychology*, *13*, 314-319.

CHAPTER 12 ANSWER KEY

Practice Test #1 Theories of Social and Personality Development

1. F   2. T   3. T   4. T   5. F   6. F   7. T   8. F

Practice Test #2 Self-Concept

1. a   2. d   3. c   4. c   5. b   6. a

Practice Test #3 Moral Development

1. i   2. l   3. f   4. d   5. k   6. a   7. e   8. c

Practice Test #4 Social Relationships

1.   establish autonomy from them; maintain a sense of relatedness with them
2.   remains strong
3.   her parents; peers
4.   academically; peer relations
5.   peer relationships
6.   intimate
7.   clique
8.   reputation-based
9.   being in love
10.   11; 12

Comprehensive Practice Test

Multiple Choice Questions

1. a   2. b   3. d   4. a   5. c   6. b   7. a   8. d   9. b   10. a
11. b   12. b   13. b   14. b   15. c

True-False Questions

1. T   2. F   3. T   4. T   5. T   6. T   7. F   8. F

Essay Questions

1.
- Identity achievement: The person has been through a crisis and has reached a commitment to ideological, occupational, or other goals.
- Moratorium: A crisis is in progress, but no commitment has yet been made.
- Foreclosure: The person has made a commitment without having gone through a crisis. No reassessment of old positions has been made. Instead, the young person has simply accepted a parentally or culturally defined commitment.
- Identity diffusion: The young person is not in the midst o f crisis (although there may have been one in the past) and has not made a commitment. Diffusion may this represent either an early stage in the process (before a crisis) or a failure to reach a commitment after a crisis.

2.
- Unexamined ethnic identity: Includes the negative images and stereotypes common in the wider culture.
- Ethnic identity search: Typically triggered by some experience that makes ethnicity relevant. The young person begins to compare his own ethnic group with others, to try to arrive at his own judgments.
- Resolution of the conflicts and contradictions: Often a difficult process. Some may take on the values of the dominant culture, and risk being ostracized by their friends. Some create two identities. Some wholeheartedly choose their own ethnic group's patterns and values.

3.
- Directed by factors inside the child, such as temperament and personality.
- In early life, they throw temper tantrums and defy parents. They may also develop insecure attachments.
- Once the defiance appears, if the parents are not up to the task of controlling the child, the child's behavior worsens. He may display overt aggression toward others, who then reject him, which aggravates the problem.
- The seriously aggressive child is pushed in the direction of other children with similar problems, who then become the child's only supportive peer group.
- In adolescence, they may exhibit serious disturbances in thinking. Most have friends who are also delinquent teens. The situation is reinforced by frequent rejection by non-delinquent peers.
- Parents have histories of antisocial behavior.
- Cluster of other problem behaviors, such as drug and alcohol use, truancy or dropping out of school, and early and risky sexual behavior.

Puzzle It Out

Across
3. Preconventional
7. Crowd
9. Genital
10. Diffusion
11. Clique
12. Identity
13. Postconventional
14. Androgynous

Down
1. Empathy
2. Moratorium
4. Conventional
5. Achievement
6. Foreclosure
8. Delinquency

POLICY QUESTION III

HAS TEST-BASED REFORM IMPROVED SCHOOLS IN THE UNITED STATES?

Learning Objective: Summarize the issues involved in test-based school reform (pp. 346-347).

1. Define the test-based school reform movement.

2. Briefly trace the history of test-based school reform.

3. What is meant by the term "standards"?

4. Complete the table to describe the criticisms of test-based school reform from each of the following perspectives:

Perspective	Description of Criticism
Teaching the Test	
Textbook Quality	
Quality of the Tests	
Claims of Cultural Bias	

5. Give examples of the positive impact of test-based reform.

6. Give examples of the negative impact of test-based reform.

7. You should be able to learn more about test-based school reform in your state by doing the following:
   a. Talk to public school teachers and administrators about your state's testing program. How has No child Left Behind affected their schools?
   b. Check your state education agency's Web site for information on standards and testing.
   c. Locate newspaper articles that report on what your governor and state legislators think about test-based reform. Do they support a national test?
   d. Find links to parent organizations in your state that oppose test-based reform at http://www.fairtest.org/parents.html.
   e. Visit http://nces.ed.gov/nationsreportcard/about/statehistorypublic.asp to learn about your state's history of participation in the NAEB.

PHYSICAL AND COGNITIVE DEVELOPMENT IN EARLY ADULTHOOD

BEFORE YOU READ . . . CHAPTER SUMMARY

Young adulthood, the period from 20 to 40, is the time in life when individuals' developmental pathways begin to diverge significantly.

Physical Functioning

- Primary aging is caused by basic biological forces. Secondary aging is the result of illness and lifestyle choices.
- There is a major growth spurt in the brain across the late teens and early twenties. Some neuroscientists believe that there is another significant spurt in the mid to late twenties.
- The body's other systems, such as the heart and lungs, the reproductive system, and the immune system, are at their peak level of functioning during early adulthood.

Health and Wellness

- Individual differences in health habits and personality variables begin to affect physical functioning in these years.
- Sexually transmitted diseases are one of the major health concerns of the early adult years.
- Intimate partner abuse is another health risk of early adulthood; women are at greater risk than are men. Many young adults, especially women, are also victimized by sexual violence.
- Mental health problems are more prevalent in early adulthood than in later periods, perhaps because young adults' expectations in intimate relationships and in other areas of life are often in conflict with their actual experiences.
- Physical dependence on drugs occurs when changes in the brain make it necessary to take a drug in order to avoid withdrawal symptoms. Psychological dependence is the craving that some substance abusers have for the effects of the drugs on which they are dependent.

Cognitive Changes

- Young adults more often exhibit formal operational thinking than do adolescents, and many psychologists believe there are even more advanced levels of thought than Piaget's final stage of cognitive development.
- Longitudinal studies show that IQ scores change little across early and middle adulthood. Likewise, memory skills are fairly stable in young and middle-aged adults.

Post-Secondary Education

- Young adults who attend college experience greater economic success in later years and display more advanced cognitive skills than those who do not go do college.
- Traditional students, those who go to college full-time directly after high school, are more likely to attain degrees than those who possess many "nontraditional" factors such as having children prior to entering post-secondary education.
- Modifications help many students with disabilities succeed in college.

- Women are more successful in college than men, but still tend to avoid traditionally male fields of study such as mathematics and engineering.
- Members of many minority groups are less likely to drop out of college than whites; however, many African-American students who leave college report that experiences with overt racism in the college environment influenced their decision.

AS YOU READ . . . LEARNING OBJECTIVES

After completing Chapter 13, you should be able to answer the following questions:

13.1   What is the difference between primary and secondary aging?
13.2   What changes in the brain take place in early adulthood?
13.3   How do other body systems change during these years?
13.4   What habits and personal factors are associated with good health?
13.5   What are some of the viral and bacterial STDs that afflict young adults?
13.6   What are the causes and effects of intimate partner abuse?
13.7   Which mental disorders occur most frequently in young adulthood?
13.8   What is the difference between physical and psychological substance dependence?
13.9   What types of postformal thought have developmentalists proposed?
13.10   How do the concepts of crystallized and fluid intelligence help to explain age-related changes in IQ scores?
13.11   What are some of the ways in which college attendance affects individual development?
13.12   How do traditional and nontraditional post-secondary students differ?
13.13   What does research suggest about the experiences of college students with disabilities?
13.14   How is the college experience different for men and women?
13.15   How does ethnicity affect the college experiences of minority students?

AS YOU READ . . . TERM IDENTIFICATION

Crystallized intelligence (p. 393)
Dialectical thought (p. 39`)
Fluid intelligence (p. 393)
Intimate partner abuse (p. 382)
Limbic system (p. 374)
Locus of control (p. 380)
Maximum oxygen uptake (VO_2 max) (p. 376)
Nontraditional post-secondary student (p. 394)
Pelvic inflammatory disease (p. 381)
Personality disorder (p. 387)
Phobia (p. 387)

Postformal thought (p. 391)
Post-secondary education (p. 393)
Primary aging (senescence) (p. 372)
Reflexive judgment (p. 391)
Relativism (p. 391)
Schizophrenia (p. 388)
Secondary aging (p. 372)
Sexual violence (p. 385)
Substance abuse (p. 389)
Traditional post-secondary student (p. 384)

AS YOU READ . . . GUIDED STUDY QUESTIONS

PHYSICAL FUNCTIONING

Primary and Secondary Aging (pp. 372-373)

13.1   *What is the difference between primary and secondary aging?*
1.   Define the following terms, and give examples of each to distinguish between them:
a.   primary aging (senescence) (p. 372)

b.   secondary aging (p. 372)

2.   Give examples of how social class differences in health may be due to secondary aging.

The Brain and Nervous System (pp. 373-374)

13.2   *What changes in the brain take place in early adulthood?*
3.   What is the limbic system? (p. 374).

4.   List and describe the two spurts in brain growth in early adulthood.

5.   What is meant by response inhibition? How is the limbic system involved?

6.   Give examples of bodily functions that undergo the gradual loss of speed as a result of very gradual changes at the neuronal level.

Research Report: Gender Differences in the Brain Youth (p. 374)

7.   Distinguish between the following, and give examples of how they may cause sex differences in the adult brain:

Type of Tissue	*Examples of Sex Differences*
Gray Matter	
White Matter	

Other Body Systems (pp. 374-378)

13.3   How do other body systems change during these years?

8.   Define maximum oxygen uptake (VO_2 max) (p. 376).

9.   Compare young adults in their 20s and 30s to middle-aged or older adults on physical measures.

10.   List the bodily functions that show a gradual decline in physical functioning through the years of adulthood (from Table 13.2).

11.   Give examples of how VO_2 max changes as a person ages:

12.   Give examples of changes in strength and speed with age.

13.   Compare women's and men's reproductive capacity.

14.   List the two key organs in the immune system, and explain how they are involved in immune system functioning.

15.   Distinguish between B cells and T cells.

No Easy Answers: Assisted Reproductive Technology (p. 377)

16.   How do physicians use infertility drugs?

17.   Distinguish between artificial insemination and in vitro fertilization.

Artificial Insemination	*In Vitro Fertilization*

18.   List the risks of vitro fertilization.

AFTER YOU READ . . . PRACTICE TEST #1
PHYSICAL FUNCTIONING

Fill in the blanks with the best answers.

1. The basic, underlying inevitable aging process is called _____. In contrast. _____ is the product of environmental influences.

2. Regardless of income level, _____ may prevent or even reverse the effects of aging.

3. Just as is true in childhood and adolescence, a _____ probably supports brain development.

4. Neuropsychologists hypothesize that the _____ that emerge in the middle of the early adulthood period seem to depend on changes in the brain.

5. The most common measure of overall aerobic fitness is _____, which reflects the ability of the body to take in and transport oxygen to various body organs.

6. The collective effect of changes in muscles and cardiovascular fitness in early adulthood is _____.

7. The end point of reproductive aging for women involves a _____ of the capacity for reproduction.

8. The two key organs in the immune system are the _____ and the _____.

9. _____ fight against external threats by producing antibodies against such disease organisms as viruses or bacteria; _____ defend against essentially internal threats, such as transplanted tissue, cancer cells, and viruses that live within the body's cells.

10. The functioning of the immune system is highly responsive to _____ and _____.

HEALTH AND WELLNESS

Health Habits and Personal Factors (pp. 378-381)

13.4 What habits and personal factors are associated with good health?

19.   Define locus of control (p. 380).

20.   List the seven good health habits that researchers identified from the Alameda County Study. Indicate which two were unrelated to mortality.
-
-
-
-
-
-
-

21.   Give examples of the benefits of social support when an individual is under high stress.

22.   Complete the following table. Describe each of the following terms, identify the researcher associated with each, and explain how it is related to a sense of control in a person's life.

Term	Theorist	Relationship to a Sense of Control
Self-Efficacy		
Locus of Control		
Optimism/Pessimism		

The Real World: Smoking Cessation (p. 380)

23.   Why is it difficult to quit smoking?

24.   Why is the timing of a smoker's efforts to quit important?

Sexually Transmitted Diseases (pp. 381-382)

13.5   What are some of the viral and bacterial STDs that afflict young adults?

25.   Define pelvic inflammatory disease (p. 381).

26.   Complete the following tables with information about sexually transmitted diseases.

Bacterial STD	Description of Effects

Viral STD	Description of Effects

27.   What is the key to STD prevention?

Intimate Partner Abuse (pp. 482-386)

13.6   What are the causes and effects of intimate partner abuse?

28.   Define the following terms:
        a.   intimate partner abuse (p. 382)

        b.   sexual violence (p. 385)

29.   Briefly summarize the prevalence of intimate partner abuse in the United States.

30.   Give examples of how each of the following can contribute to the rates of intimate partner abuse:

Cause	Example
Cultural Attitudes	
Gender-Role Prescriptions	

31.   List the characteristics of intimate partner abusers and victims

Abusers	Victims

32.   List the effects of abuse on women.

33.   How does witnessing abuse influence children's development?

34.   List ways to prevent intimate partner abuse.

35.   Describe the psychological effects of being a victim of sexual violence.

36.   What is date rape, and what are two causes of it?

37.   How can sexual violence be prevented?

Mental Health Problems (pp. 386-388)

13.7   Which mental disorders occur most frequently in young adulthood?

38.   Define the following terms:
        a.   phobia (p. 387)

        b.   personality disorder (p. 387)

c.   schizophrenia (p. 388)

39.   List the possible causes and consequences of mental disorders in young adulthood.

Causes	Consequences

40.   What are the most common mental disorders?

41.   Give examples of how phobias are learned, as well as how they can be unlearned.

Learned	Unlearned

42.   Explain why the rates of depression are higher in early adulthood than in either adolescence or middle age.

43.   List two criteria for diagnosing personality disorders.
■

■

44.   Distinguish between delusions and hallucinations.

Delusions	Hallucinations

Substance Use and Abuse (pp. 388-390)

13.8   What is the difference between physical and psychological substance dependence?

45.   Define substance abuse (p. 389).

46.   What is binge drinking?

47.   List four factors that influence the addictive potential of a drug.
        ▪

        ▪

        ▪

        ▪

48.   Distinguish between physical drug dependence and psychological dependence.

Physical Drug Dependence	*Psychological Drug Dependence*

AFTER YOU READ . . . PRACTICE TEST #2
HEALTH AND WELLNESS

1. **Each of the following is one of the seven good health habits EXCEPT _____.**
   a.   not smoking
   b.   skipping breakfast
   c.   getting physical exercise
   d.   getting regular sleep

2. **The social network index reflected an objective measure of each of the following EXCEPT _____.**
   a.   membership at an exercise facility
   b.   number of contacts with friends and relatives
   c.   marital status
   d.   church and group membership

3. **The _____ believes that setbacks are temporary and usually caused by circumstances.**
   a.   helpless person
   b.   pessimist
   c.   optimist
   d.   person with low self-efficacy

4. **_____ STDs are those that are caused by microorganisms that can be eradicated through the use of antibiotic medications.**
   a.   Sensitive
   b.   Contagious
   c.   Viral
   d.   Bacteria

5. **The primary symptom of _____ is the presence of growths in the genitals.**
   a.   genital warts
   b.   genital herpes
   c.   syphilis
   d.   gonorrhea

6. **Each of the following is a method of transmission of HIV EXCEPT _____.**
   a.   sexual intercourse with a person with HIV
   b.   sharing needles with an intravenous drug user with HIV
   c.   drinking after a person with HIV
   d.   a blood transfusion from someone with HIV

7. **The term _____ refers only to incidents of abuse involving individuals who live in the same household.**
   a.   partner abuser
   b.   domestic abuse
   c.   intimate partner abuse
   d.   sexual abuse

8.   **Each of the following is a characteristic of an abuser EXCEPT _____.**
   a.   sudden mood swings
   b.   a need for dependency in the partner
   c.   a tendency toward irrational jealousy
   d.   a slow temper

COGNITIVE CHANGES

Formal Operations and Beyond (pp. 390-392)

13.9   *What types of postformal thought have developmentalists proposed?*

49.   Define the following terms:
a.   postformal thought (p. 391)

b.   relativism (p. 391)

c.   dialectical thought (p. 391)

d.   reflective judgment (p. 391)

50.   Describe three concepts of new structures of stages in thinking that occur in adulthood.

Theorist	Concept	Description
Gisela Labouvie-Vief	Contextual Validity	
Michael Basseches	Dialectical Thought	
Patricia King & Karen Kitchener	Reflective Judgment	

Intelligence (pp. 392-393)

13.10   *How do the concepts of crystallized and fluid intelligence help to explain age-related changes in IQ scores?*

51.   Define the following terms:
a.   crystallized intelligence (p. 393)

b.   fluid intelligence (p. 393)

52.   Give examples of how IQ scores remain stable across middle childhood, adolescence, and early adulthood. Include the results of Werner Schaie's Seattle Longitudinal Study in your examples.

AFTER YOU READ . . . PRACTICE TEST #3
COGNITIVE CHANGES

Fill in the blanks with the best answers.

1. Like most aspects of physical functioning, _____ are at their peek in early adulthood. The intellectual peak lasts longer than originally thought and the rate of decline is quite slow.

2. Kohlberg and Perry emphasized the shift toward _____, the idea that some propositions cannot be adequately described as either true or false.

3. Adults learn how to solve the problems associated with the particular social roles they occupy, or the particular jobs they hold. In the process, the trade the deductive thoroughness of formal operations for _____.

4. _____ is a form of thought involving recognition and acceptance of paradox and uncertainty.

5. Patricia King and Karen Kitchener have proposed that _____, the capacity to identify the underlying assumptions of differing perspectives on controversial issues, is an important feature of postformal thought.

6. Examination of intelligence in early adulthood suggests that both _____ and _____ characterize this component of cognitive functioning.

7. There is good support for the temptingly optimistic view that intellectual ability _____ _____ through most of adulthood.

8. _____ depends heavily on education and experience; _____, in contrast, involves more "basic" abilities—it is the aspect of intelligence that depends more on the efficient functioning of the central nervous system and less on specific experience.

POST-SECONDARY EDUCATION

Developmental Impact (pp. 393-395)

13.11 What are some of the ways in which college attendance affects individual development?

53. Define post-secondary education (p. 393).

54. Describe economic impact of post-secondary education.

55.   How does post-secondary education provide socialization opportunities?

Traditional and Nontraditional Students (pp. 394-395)

13.12 How do traditional and nontraditional post-secondary students differ?

56.   Define the following terms:
       a.   traditional post-secondary students (p. 394)

       b.   non-traditional post-secondary students (p. 394)

57.   List the seven criteria used to classify students as nontraditional post-secondary students.
■

■

■

■

■

■

■

58.   Explain the classification of nontraditional as minimally, moderately, or highly nontraditional.

59.   Give examples to describe the differences in support for nontraditional students in four-year
       institutions and two-year institutions.

Students with Disabilities (pp. 395-396)

**13.13 What does research suggest about the experiences of college students with
disabilities?**

60.   Describe how the Americans with Disabilities Act (1990) affected college students in the United
       States.

Gender and the College Experience (p. 396)

13.14 How is the college experience different for men and women?

61. List differences in the attitudes and behaviors of men and women that significantly affect the likelihood of graduation.

Race and the College Experience (pp 396-397)

13.15 How does ethnicity affect the college experiences of minority students?

62. How do economic pressures impact the college graduation rates of minority students?.

63. Give an example of support for each of the following groups of students.

Group	Example
Hispanic Americans	
African Americans	
Native Americans	

AFTER YOU READ . . . PRACTICE TEST #4
POST-SECONDARY EDUCATION

Indicate whether each of the following statements is true or false.

_____
1.
People who succeed in completing a college degree have no income advantage over those who have only some college.

_____
2.
During their years of college enrollment, students' academic and vocational aspirations rise.

_____
3.
The more nontraditional factors a student possesses, the less likely he is to graduate from college.

_____
4.
Women have slightly higher graduation rates then men at all degree levels and in both traditional and nontraditional post-secondary groups.

_____
5.
College women are more likely to cheat than men.

_____
6.
Studies indicate that African American students who attend historically Black institutions show more gains in both cognitive and social competence than their peers who attend predominately White colleges.

AFTER YOU READ . . . CRITICAL REFLECTION EXERCISES

Crystallized Intelligence and Fluid Intelligence

Give three examples of crystallized intelligence and three examples of fluid intelligence. What profession do you intend to pursue and which of these intelligences will you rely on more in that profession? Why?

Social Stress

Describe the concept of social stress. Why is this type of stress so potentially damaging? Discuss three things a person could do to minimize the negative effects of social stress.

AFTER YOU READ . . . COMPREHENSIVE PRACTICE TEST
MULTIPLE CHOICE QUESTIONS

1. **Age-related changes that are due to environmental influences, poor health habits, or disease are called _____.**
   a. primary aging
   b. auxiliary aging
   c. secondary aging
   d. maturation

2. **The part of the brain that regulates emotional responses is the _____.**
   a. pituitary gland
   b. thymus
   c. limbic system
   d. gray matter

3. **When VO$_2$ max is measured in a person at rest, it _____.**
   a. begins to decline systematically at about age 35
   b. exhibits only minimal decrements associated with age
   c. increases gradually starting at age 40
   d. declines for women and goes up for men as a function of aging

4. **The belief in one's capacity to cause an intended event to occur or to perform a task is called _____.**
   a. hardiness
   b. pessimism
   c. helplessness
   d. self-efficacy

5. **An individual's set of beliefs about the causes of event is called _____.**
   a. pessimism
   b. relativism
   c. locus of control
   d. contextual validity

6. **In contrast to other types of disease, most _____ is(are) more common among 15-to 24-year-olds than in any other age group.**
   a. sexually transmitted diseases
   b. colds and the flu
   c. coronary heart disease
   d. osteoporosis

7. **Undiagnosed chlamydia increases the risk of _____, which can cause infertility.**
   a. malaria
   b. pelvic inflammatory disease
   c. cancer
   d. schizophrenia

8. **Physical acts or other behaviors intended to intimidate or harm an intimate partner is called _____.**
   a. pessimism
   b. intimate partner abuse
   c. helplessness
   d. depression

9. **An irrational fear of an object, a person, a place, or a situation is called _____.**
   a. schizophrenia
   b. a panic attack
   c. a phobia
   d. depression

10. **A person with _____ is suspicious of others' behavior and is emotionally guarded and highly sensitive to minor violations of personal space or perceived rights.**
    a. paranoid personality disorder
    b. antisocial personality disorder
    c. borderline personality disorder
    d. histrionic personality disorder

11. **Dialectical thought deals with _____.**
    a. fact
    b. declarative memories
    c. uncertainty
    d. how and why we develop accents in our speaking

12. **Which of the following is an example of fluid intelligence?**
    a. a reaction time test
    b. technical job skills
    c. knowledge about your culture
    d. the ability to read

13. **Any formal educational experience that follows high school is called _____.**
    a. formal operational thinking
    b. dialectical learning
    c. post-secondary education
    d. the virtual college

14. **Each of the following is one of the factors used to classify nontraditional post-secondary students EXCEPT _____.**
    a. delay in entering college for more than one year after high school
    b. are enrolled full-time
    c. are employed while enrolled in college
    d. are single parents

15. **Which of the following statements is true regarding gender and the college experience?**
    a. Women are more likely to be accepted into honors programs.
    b. Men display a greater number of study strategies than women.
    c. Men are more likely to be admitted to selective institutions.
    d. Women are more likely to pursue difficult majors.

TRUE-FALSE QUESTIONS

Indicate whether each of the following statements is true or false.

_____
1.

No matter what age an individual is, new synapses are forming, myelinization is occurring, and old connections are dying off.

_____
2.

Men's reproductive capacity declines at the same rate as women's

_____
3.

Adults with adequate social support have lower risk of disease, death, and depression than do adults with weaker social networks or less supportive networks.

_____
4.

The most prevalent of the bacterial STDs is chlamydia.

_____
5.

Formal operational thinking is more characteristics of adolescents than adults.

_____
6.

IQ scores remain quite stable across middle childhood, adolescence, and early adulthood.

_____
7.

College graduates earn more than non-graduates.

_____
8.

The most common modification for a disability is a large-print version of the exams.

ESSAY QUESTIONS

1. Give examples of how secondary aging is related to social class.

2. Behavioral change is the key to STD prevention. How could you convince young adults to modify their behavior to prevent acquiring a sexually transmitted disease such as HIV/AIDS?

3. Discuss the characteristics of women who are victims of abuse. How might social support and a sense of control assist her?

WHEN YOU HAVE FINISHED . . .PUZZLE IT OUT

Across

2. Intelligence that depends heavily on education and experience
4. A bacterial STD that is very resistant to antibiotics
8. An irrational fear of an object, a person, a place, or a situation
9. Post-secondary student who attend college gull-time immediately after graduating from high school
11. Thought involving recognition and acceptance of paradox and uncertainty
12. System of the brain that regulates emotional responses
13. Age-related physical changes that have a biological basis and are inevitable
14. Age-related changes that are due to environmental influences, poor health habits, or disease

Down

1. Intelligence that involves "basic" abilities
3. A serious mental disorder characterized by delusions and hallucinations
5. A bacterial STD that can lead to serious mental disorders and death if not treated in the early stages
6. STD that is a bacterial infection three times more common to women than men
7. Post-secondary student who either attends college part-time or delays enrollment after high school graduation
10. The failure to conceive after twelve consecutive months of unprotected intercourse

Created by Puzzlemaker at DiscoverySchool.com

WHEN YOU HAVE FINISHED . . .AT-HOME PROJECT

Student Project 24: Estimating Your Own Longevity

Given the importance of health habits in longevity (the length of expected life), you may be interested in estimating your own longevity, based on your own habits and other factors that we know affect the length of life. Respond to each of the following items honestly and sum the various negative and positive factors. The average 20-year-old male in the United States can expect to live to age 72.8; the average 20-year-old female can expect to live to age 79.4, so add or subtract your total number from this expectation to find your estimated length of life. (Remember, please, that this will provide only a very rough estimate. I am not offering a guarantee here that you will live as long or as short a time as the formula suggests.)

Health Habits

1.   *Weight*: Using the following table, determine the number of years to subtract (if any):

	10% to 30% heavier than standard weight tables		30% or more above standard weight tables	
	Women	Men	Women	Men
Age 20-29	-5	-10	-6.5	-13
Age 30-49	-4	-4	-5	-6
Age 50 +	-2	-2	-4	-4

2.   *Diet*: If your diet is truly low in fat and sugar, and you never eat to the point past fullness, +1

3.   *Smoking*: If you smoke less than a pack a day, -2; between 1 and 2 packs a day, -7; more than 2 packs a day, -12.

4.   *Drinking*: Heavy drinkers, -8; moderate drinkers, +2; light or abstainer, +1 1/2.

5.   *Exercise*: If you do some aerobic exercise for 20 to 30 minutes at least 3 times a week, + 3.

6.   *Sleep*: If you sleep more than 10 or less than 7 hours a night, -2

Health History

1.   If you have any chronic health condition, such as high blood pressure, diabetes, cancer, or ulcers, or are frequently ill, -5.

2.   If your mother was older than 35 or younger than 18 at your birth, -1.

3.   If you are the oldest child in your family. +1.

4.   If you have an annual physical examine, +2.

5.   Women only: If you have no children (or plan to have none), -1/2.

Heredity

1.   For each of your grandparents who has lived past age 80, +1. (If your grandparents have not yet reached this age, simply ignore the item).

2.   For each grandparent who have lived past 70, but not 80, +1/2.

3.   If your mother lived past 80, +4.

4.   If your father lived past 80, +2.

5.   For each sibling, parent, or grandparent who died of heart disease before age 50, -4.

6.   For each sibling, parent, or grandparent who died of heart disease between age 50 and 60, -2
7.   Women only: For each mother or sister who died of breast cancer before age 60, -1.

Social Class, Personality, and Other Characteristics

1.   If your intelligence is superior, +2.

2.   If you have only an eighth grade education or less, -2
      If you have completed high school but no further, +1
      If you have completed 1 to 3 years of college, +2
      If you have 4 or more years of college, +3

3.   If your occupation is professional, technical, or managerial, +1; if it is unskilled, -4.

4.   If your income is above average for your education and occupation, +1; if it is below average, -1.

5.   If your job is sedentary, -2; if it is physically active, +2.

6.   If you have lived in urban areas most of your life, -1; if you have lived mostly in a rural area, +1.

7.   If you are married and living with your spouse, +1.

8.   If you are separated or divorced, -4 if you are a women, -9 if you are a man.

9.   If you are widowed, -4 if you are a women, -7 if you are a man.

10.   Women: If you have never been married. -1 for each decade unmarried past the age of 25.

11.   Men: if you have never married and are living with your family, -1 for each decade unmarried past age 25; if you live alone, -2 for each decade unmarried past age 25.

12.   If you have at least two close confidants, +1.

13.   If your personality is noticeably hostile and aggressive, and you regularly feel under time pressure, subtract between 2 and 5 years, depending on how well the description fits.

14.   If you easy-going, relaxed, and calm, and adapt easily to changing circumstances, add between 1 and 3 years, depending on how well the description fits.

15.   If you have a lot of fun in life and are basically happy, +2.

16.   If you have had at least one period of a year or more in your life when you were depressed, very tense, very worried, or guilty, subtract between 1 and 3, depending on how severe the depression was.

17.   If you live in a high crime neighborhood, or take physical risk regularly, -2.

18.   If you generally avoid risk and wear seatbelts regularly, +1.

When you have calculated the score, think about the result. How many of the factors that affect longevity do you have control over? Make a list of specific steps you could take today that might increase your longevity.

Reference

Adapted from D. S. Woodruff-Pak (1988), *Psychology and aging*. Englewood Cliffs, NJ: Prentice-Hall, pp. 145-154.

CHAPTER 13 ANSWER KEY

Practice Test #1 Physical Functioning

1. primary aging; secondary aging
2. changes in behavior
3. challenging environment
4. cognitive skills
5. maximum oxygen uptake (VO_2 max)
6. a general loss of strength and speed with age
7. total loss
8. thymus gland; bone marrow
9. B cells; T cells
10. psychological stress; depression

Practice Test #2 Health and Wellness

1. b   2. a   3. c   4. d   5. a   6. c   7. b   8. d

Practice Test #3 Cognitive Changes

1. intellectual processes
2. relativism
3. contextual validity
4. dialectical thought
5. reflective judgment
6. continuity; change
7. remains essentially stable
8. crystallized intelligence; fluid intelligence

Practice Test #4 Post-Secondary Education

1. F   2. T   3. T   4. T   5. F   6. T

Comprehensive Practice Test

Multiple Choice Questions

1. c   2. c   3. b   4. d   5. c   6. a   7. b   8. b   9. c   10. a
11. c   12. a   13. c   14. b   15. c

True-False Questions

1. T   2. F   3. T   4. T   5. F   6. T   7. T   8. F

Essay Questions
1.
- Differences among young adults across social class are fairly small, but increase with age.
- Better-educated adults and those with higher incomes have longer life expectancies and better health than do those with less education or lower incomes.
- Social class differences in health result from income-related variations in both social environments and individual behavior. Doctors in low-income neighborhoods tend to have less training and less access to hospitals equipped with advanced diagnostic and treatment facilities.
- The same factors that contribute to economic differences are also related to health habits. Among individuals who drop out of high school, physical activity rates decline significantly during the late teens and remain low in adulthood. Physical activity is a predictor of cardiovascular health, and educational level is associated with income.

- The emotions underlying individuals' perceptions of their social class may be more important than their actual economic status. People who are unhappy with their economic situation are more likely to be sick than those who are relatively satisfied.

2.
- Answers will vary, but should include sexual behavior (i.e., abstinence, monogamy, condom use, HIV testing, etc.), bodily fluids, intravenous needles, etc.

3.
- Characteristics of women who are victims of abuse: likely to have been abused as children, young, lack of education and/or work experience, young women may be caring for infants and young children for whom they do not have access to day care.
- A person's perception of the adequacy of her social contacts and emotional support is more strongly related to physical and emotional health than are the actual number of such contacts.
- Self-efficacy is the belief in one's capacity to cause in intended event to occur or to perform a task. It is affected by one's experiences with mastering tasks and overcoming obstacles.
- Optimists believes that setbacks are temporary and usually caused by circumstances.
- Those with a more helpless attitude or a low sense of self-efficacy are more likely to become depressed or physically ill.

Puzzle It Out

Across
2. Crystallized
4. Gonorrhea
8. Phobia
9. Traditional
11. Dialectical
12. Limbic
13. Primary
14. Secondary

Down
1. Fluid
3. Schizophrenia
5. Syphilis
6. Gonorrhea
7. Nontraditional
10. Infertility

CHAPTER 14

SOCIAL AND PERSONALITY DEVELOPMENT IN EARLY ADULTHOOD

BEFORE YOU READ . . . CHAPTER SUMMARY

In early adulthood, individuals turn away from the preoccupation with self that is characteristic of social relationships in adolescence. For most, the formation of an intimate relationship with a long-term partner is a theme that dominates this period of development.

Theories of Social and Personality Development

- Erikson proposed that the crisis of intimacy versus isolation is the defining theme of early adulthood.
- Levinson's theory suggests that adult development is characterized by alternating periods of stability and instability, such as the young adult's moving away from home. Through these periods of instability, adults redefine what Levinson calls their life structures.
- The parts of the brain that are involved in decision making and self-control mature between the late teens and early twenties. Emerging adults develop in five domains.

Intimate Relationships

- Evolutionary theories of mate selection suggest that women are more interested in long-term relationships and are more selective than are men in choosing partners because their investment in parenting is greater. Social role theory emphasizes factors such as gender roles, similarity, and economic exchange in explaining sex differences in mating.
- Attachment, love, and personality contribute to marital success. Marriage has many health benefits; divorce increases the likelihood of depression.
- Numerous factors contribute to the relationship between premarital cohabitation and divorce.
- Factors that contribute to relationship satisfaction are similar across homosexual and heterosexual couples. Monogamy is not as important to gay male couples as it is to lesbian or heterosexual couples.
- Singles rely on family and friends for intimacy. After many years of singlehood, single adults tend to incorporate "singleness" into their sense of identity.

Parenthood and Other Relationships

- The transition to parenthood is stressful and is made more so by perceived inequities in the division of labor between mother and father and by several other factors.
- Young adults' social networks are important sources of support. These networks include friends as well as an intimate partner and other family members.

The Role of Worker

- Career choice is influenced by family history, intelligence, resources, personality, gender and other variables.
- Job satisfaction rises during early adulthood.
- The quality of work-life movement includes on-site child care, telecommuting, flextime, and job sharing. These innovations help employees achieve a balance between work and non-work roles.

- Women's patterns of work are less continuous because many take time out from their careers to bear and raise children. Women with more continuous work histories are more economically successful. In dual-earner families, women often carry a heavier load of responsibility for child-care and household tasks.

AS YOU READ . . . LEARNING OBJECTIVES

After completing Chapter 14, you should be able to answer the following questions:
14.1 What did Erikson mean when he described early adulthood as a crisis of intimacy versus isolation?
14.2 What is a life structure, and how does it change?
14.3 What are the characteristics of emerging adulthood?
14.4 What types of research do evolutionary and social role theorists cite to support their theories of mate selection?
14.5 How do marriage and divorce affect the lives of young children?
14.6 What factors contribute to the relationship between premarital cohabitation and divorce?
14.7 In what ways are gay and lesbian couples similar to and different from heterosexual couples?
14.8 How do singles accomplish Erikson's psychosocial developmental task of intimacy?
14.9 What happens during the transition to parenthood?
14.10 How are family and friends important to young adults?
14.11 What factors influence an individual's occupational choices?
14.12 How do career goals and job satisfaction change over time?
14.13 What are some of the innovations that are associated with the quality of work-life movement?
14.14 In what way do women's work patterns differ from those of men?

AS YOU READ . . . TERM IDENTIFICATION

Assortative mating (homogamy) (p. 429)
Avoidant couples (p. 413)
Career development (p. 423)
Emerging adulthood (p. 407)
Hostile/detached couples (p. 413)
Hostile/engaged couples (p. 413)
Intimacy (p. 405)
Intimacy versus isolation (p. 405)

Kin-keeper (p. 420)
Life structure (p. 406)
Parental investment theory (p. 408)
Quality of work life (QWL) (p. 424)
Social role theory (p. 408)
Validating couples (p. 412)
Volatile couples (p. 412)
Work-life balance (p. 424)

AS YOU READ . . . GUIDED STUDY QUESTIONS

THEORIES OF SOCIAL AND PERSONALITY DEVELOPMENT

Erikson's Stages of Intimacy versus Isolation (p. 405-406)

14.1   What did Erikson mean when he described early adulthood as a crisis of intimacy versus isolation?

1.   Define the following terms:

    a.   intimacy versus isolation (p. 405)

    b.   intimacy (p. 405)

2.   According to Erikson, what does the successful resolution of intimacy versus isolation depend upon? Why?

Levinson's Life Structures (p. 406)

14.2   What is a life structure, and how does it change?

3.   Define life structure (p. 406).

4.   How does a life structure changes over the course of adulthood?

5.   List and describe the three phases of each life structure. Give an example to support the definitions.

Phase	Description

Emerging Adulthood (p. 407)

14.3   What are the characteristics of emerging adulthood?

6.   Define emerging adulthood (p. 407).

7.   Give examples of how neuroimaging studies provide support for the notion that emerging adulthood is a unique period of life.

8.   List the five domains of emerging adulthood.
-
-
-
-
-

9.   Describe the challenge that emerging adults face in the work and romantic domains.

Domain	Description
Work	
Romantic	

AFTER YOU READ . . . PRACTICE TEST #1
THEORIES OF SOCIAL AND PERSONALITY DEVELOPMENT

Match the letter of the term in the right column with its description in the left column.

_____ 1. Erikson's central crisis of early adulthood.

_____ 2. The underlying pattern or design of a person's life at a given time, which includes all the roles, relationships, and behavior patterns

_____ 3. The capacity to engage in a supportive, affectionate relationship without losing one's own sense of self

_____ 4. The period from the late teens to early twenties when individuals explore options prior to committing to adult roles.

_____ 5. Phase of Levinson's theory that is the period of adjustment.

_____ 6. Phase of Levinson's theory in which adults become more competent at meeting the new challenges through reassessment and reorganization of the life structure.

a. Emerging adulthood
b. Culmination
c. Evolutionary
d. Intimacy
e. Intimacy versus isolation
f. Life structures
g. Mid-era
h. Novice

INTIMATE RELATIONSHIPS

Theories of Mate Selection (pp. 408-409)

14.4   What types of research do evolutionary and social role theorists cite to support their theories of mate selection?

10.   Define the following terms:
   a.   parental investment theory (p. 408)

   b.   social role theory (p. 408)

   c.   assortative mating (homogamy) (p. 408)

11.   Give examples of how each of the following theories explains mate selection.

Theory	*Example*
Evolutionary Theory	
Parental Investment Theory	
Social Role Theory	
Assortative Mating (Homogamy) Theory	

Marriage (pp. 409-414)

14.5   How do marriage and divorce affect the lives of young children?

12.   Define the following terms:
   a.   validating couples (p. 412)

   b.   volatile couples (p. 412)

   c.   avoidant couples (p. 413)

   d.   hostile/engaged couples (p. 413)

e.　　　hostile/detached couples (p. 413)

13.　　List the benefits for married adults.

14.　　Give an example of each of the following influences on marital success.

Factor	Example
Personal Characteristics	
Attachment to Family of Origin	
Emotional Affection	
Management of Conflict	

15.　　List and describe the three components of Robert Sternberg's theory of love.

Component	Description

16.　　List and describe seven subvarieties of love of Sternberg's theory.

Phase	Description

17. Describe the three types of stable or enduring marriages and two types of unsuccessful marriages by completing the following tables:

Type of Stable or Enduring Marriage	Description
Validating Couples	
Volatile Couples	
Avoidant Couples	

Type of Unsuccessful Marriage	Description
Hostile/Engaged Couples	
Hostile/Detached Couples	

18. Describe the possible negative stressors of divorce.

19. Explain how the economic effects of divorce may be worse for women than for men.

20. How might divorce affect the sequence and timing of family roles?

No Easy Answers: Avoiding Bridal Stress Disorder (p. 410)

21. Explain how to balance problem-focused coping and emotional-focused coping by giving examples of each.

22. What is marriage insurance?

Research Report: Sex Differences in the Impact of Marriage (p. 412)

23. Arrange the following list in order with "1" being greatest health and longest life., and "4" being the lest healthy with the shortest life.

_____ Unmarried men
_____ Unmarried women
_____ Married men
_____ Married women

24. Give examples of how the levels of cortisol explain the quality of a person's marriage, including the sex differences.

Cohabiting Heterosexual Couples (pp. 414-415)

14.6 What factors contribute to the relationship between premarital cohabitation and divorce?

25. Describe the following explanations of the relationship between premarital cohabitation and divorce.

Explanation	Description
Couples are less homogamous	
Lumping all cohabitating couples into a single category	
Previous cohabitation and premarital sexual experience	
Firm intentions to marry or not	

26. The critical variable at work in the cohabitation-divorce relationship is the fact that a large proportion of cohabitants have been in prior cohabiting or sexual relationships. Explain why.

Gay and Lesbian Couples (pp. 415-416)

14.7 In what ways are gay and lesbian couples similar to and different from heterosexual couples?

27. List the similarities and differences between satisfaction and stability of heterosexual and homosexual relationships.

Similarities	Differences

Singlehood (p. 416)

14.8   How do singles accomplish Erikson's psychosocial developmental task of intimacy?

28.   Why does the impact of singlehood on an adult's life often depend on the reason for his or her relationship status?

29.   How does singleness affect a person's relationship with family and friends?

30.   Trace the development of singleness as a positive component of the individual's identity.

AFTER YOU READ . . . PRACTICE TEST #2
INTIMATE RELATIONSHIPS

1. _____ is the idea that sex differences in mate preferences and mating behavior are adaptations to gender roles.
   a. Evolutionary theory
   b. Social role theory
   c. Parental investment theory
   d. Homogamy

2. Assortative mating theory is _____.
   a. sociobiologists' term for the tendency to mate with someone who has traits similar to one's own
   b. the theory that sex differences in mate preferences and mating behavior are based on the different amounts of time and effort men and women must invest in child-rearing
   c. the explanation of behavior that focuses on survival value
   d. the idea that sex differences in mate preferences and mating behavior are adaptations to gender roles

3. Each of the following is a benefit of marriage EXCEPT _____.
   a. increased happiness
   b. greater health
   c. lower rates of psychiatric problems
   d. lower income

4. Each of the following is an influence in the quality of the marriage relationship EXCEPT _____.
   a. emotional affection
   b. socio-economic status
   c. the personality characteristics of the partners
   d. the security of each partner's attachment to his or her family of origin

5. What is companionate love?
   a. love that is long lasting, but is non-emotional
   b. love that is without passion
   c. love that will definitely evolve into romantic love
   d. very similar to empty love

6. Which of the following marriage represents volatile couples?
   a. The couple has no humor or affection.
   b. The couple agrees to disagree.
   c. The couple does not listen to each other well during arguments.
   d. The couple expresses mutual respect for each other.

7. Each of the following is associated with recent separation or divorce EXCEPT _____.
   a. less likely to become depressed
   b. more automobile accidents
   c. more likely to commit suicide
   d. lose more days at work because of illness

8. **One critical variable at work in the cohabitation-divorce relationship is _____**
   a. the individuals' relationship with their family of origin
   b. the individual' religions beliefs
   c. the fact that a large proportion of cohabitants have been in prior cohabiting or sexual relationships
   d. the fact that cohabitants are homogamous

9. **Similarities between homosexual and heterosexual couples include each of the following EXCEPT _____.**
   a. attachment quality
   b. neuroticism in one or both partners
   c. both partners are committed to the relationship
   d. closeness to their families of origin

10.. **A single person's self-affirmation _____.**
   a. may increase the likelihood of depression
   b. may protect singles from some of the negative health consequences associated with singlehood
   c. may decrease the likelihood of individual autonomy
   d. may decrease the likelihood for personal growth

PARENTHOOD AND OTHER RELATIONSHIPS

Parenthood (pp. 416-419)

14.9   What happens during the transition to parenthood?

31.   Summarize the statistics about the desire to become a parent.

32.   Describe the transition experience for new parents.

33.   What is postpartum depression (PPD)?

34   List the characteristics of women who are likely to develop postpartum depression. What is the best predictor of postpartum depression?

35.   What is the positive impact of the transition to parenthood?

36.   List the variables that may affect marital satisfaction as a result of the transition to parenthood.

37.   How does childlessness affect the shape of an adult's life?

Social Networks (pp. 419-420)

14.10   How are family and friends important to young adults?

38.   Define kin-keeper (p. 420).

39.   Summarize young adults' relationships with their parents.

40.   How does proximity affect a young adult's contact with his or her family?

41.   Give examples of how cultural differences impact young adults' involvement with their families.

42. Describe the sex differences in both the number and quality of friendships in the social networks of young adults.

Women	Men

43. Give examples of the behavior of a person who is a kin-keeper.

AFTER YOU READ . . . PRACTICE TEST #3
PARENTHOOD AND OTHER RELATIONSHIPS

Fill in the blanks with the best answers.

1.   Despite the opportunistic attitude toward mating that evolutionary theory ascribes to men, the percentage of _____ who feel strongly that they want to become parents and who view parenting as a life-enriching experience is actually greater than the percentage of _____ who feel this way.

2.   The best predictor of postpartum depression is _____ during pregnancy.

3.   Despite its inherent stressfulness, the transition to parenthood is associated with _____ behavior change.

4.   Marital satisfaction tends to _____ after the birth of a child.

5.   The amount and kind of contact an adult has with kin is strongly influenced by _____.

6.   Beyond the basic requirement of similarity, close friendships seem to rest on _____ and _____.

7.   Adult women friends _____; adult men friends _____.

8.   Women most often fill the role of _____, a role which includes responsibility for maintaining family and friendship relationships.

THE ROLE OF THE WORKER

Choosing an Occupation (pp. 4121-422)

14.11 What factors influence an individual's occupational choices?

44.   Give examples of how families influence a young person's choice of job or career in each of the following areas by completing the table:

Area of Influence	Examples
Education	
Value System	
Urging College	

45.   Describe the stereotypical differences between "women's jobs" and "men's jobs."

Men's Jobs	Women's Jobs

46.   List the six personality types, according to John Holland. Describe the personality of each, and identify the work preferences of each by completing the following table:

Type	Description of Personality	Work Preference
Realistic		
Investigative		
Artistic		
Social		
Enterprising		
Conventional		

Career Development (pp. 423-424)

14.12 How do career goals and job satisfaction change over time?

47.   Define career development (p. 423)

48.   Describe the four stages of career development, according to Donald Super).

Stage	Age Range	Description
Growth Stage		
Exploratory Stage		
Establishment (Stabilization) Stage		
Maintenance Stage		

49.   What are the variables that contribute to job satisfaction in young adults?

The Quality of Work-Life Movement (pp. 424-425)

14.13 What are some of the innovations that are associated with the quality of work-life movement?

50.   Define the following terms:
    a.   work-life balance (p. 424)

    b.   quality of work-life (QWL) movement (p. 424)

51.   Describe the following innovations to increase QWL:

Innovation	Description
Telecommuting	
Flextime	
Job Sharing	

Women's Work Patterns (pp. 425-426)

14.14   In what way do women's work patterns differ from those of men?

52.   Describe women's work patterns.

53.   How does the division of work and family responsibilities among couples affect a women's work?

The Real World: Strategies for Coping with Conflict between Work and Family Life (p. 426)

54.   Describe strategies for coping with the conflict between work and family life.

Strategy	*Description*
Cognitive Restructuring	
Redefining Family Roles	
Time Management Class	

AFTER YOU READ . . . PRACTICE TEST #4
THE ROLE OF THE WORKER

Indicate whether each of the following statements is true or false.

_____ 1. Satisfying work seems to be an important ingredient in mental health and life satisfaction of men but not for women.

_____ 2. Typically, young people tend to choose occupations at the same general social class level as those of their parents.

_____ 3. Stereotypically male jobs are concentrated in service occupations and are typically lower in status and lower-paid.

_____ 4. John Holland's hypothesis is that each of us tends to choose, and be most successful at, an occupation that matches our personality.

_____ 5. Career development is the process of adapting to the workplace, managing career transitions, and pursuing personal goals through employment.

_____ 6. According to Donald Super, the first stage of work sequence is the establishment stage.

_____ 7. Young adults engaged in careers for which they prepared in high school or college have higher levels of satisfaction.

_____ 8. Work-life balance is the interactive influences among employees' work and non-work roles.

_____ 9. Job sharing is a QWL innovation which involves allowing employees to create their own work schedules.

_____ 10. The great majority of women move in and out of the work force at least once.

AFTER YOU READ . . . CRITICAL REFLECTION EXERCISES

Relationships in Early Adulthood

Utilizing the information in the text, provide detailed responses to the following questions:

1. If the divorce rate is higher in the United States than in most other industrialized countries, what might cause this? Discuss at least three factors that may contribute to cultural differences in the divorce rate.

2. Discuss the importance of the following quote, "to develop in a healthy fashion in young adulthood, one must risk what is so difficult to acquire in adolescence."

3. If you are married, name and discuss three things you can do to maximize the success of your marriage. If you are not currently married, name and discuss three things that you can do with a potential partner prior to getting married to increase the likelihood that an eventual marriage will succeed.

Parenting an Adolescent

You are the parent of a fourteen-year-old. Based on the information in the text, discuss at least three things that you could do to enhance the likelihood that your adolescent will make a smooth and successful transition into young adulthood.

AFTER YOU READ . . . COMPREHENSIVE PRACTICE TEST
MULTIPLE CHOICE QUESTIONS

1. **For Erikson, the central crisis of early adulthood is _____.**
    a.   industry versus inferiority
    b.   identity versus role confusion
    c.   intimacy versus isolation
    d.   integrity versus despair

2. **The ability to fuse your identity with someone else's without fear that you are going to lose something yourself, is the definition of _____.**
    a.   selflessness
    b.   intimacy
    c.   generativity
    d.   role confusion

3. **All the roles an individual occupies, all his or her relationships, and the conflicts and balance that exist among them are called _____.**
    a.   a life structure
    b.   intimacy
    c.   homogamy
    d.   a kin-keeper

4. **On average, what are women concerned with in a potential mate?**
    a.   economic prospects
    b.   education level
    c.   physical attractiveness
    d.   personality similarity

5. **The theory that contrasts men's and women's differing amounts of investment in rearing children is called _____.**
    a.   mate-switching
    b.   the parental investment theory
    c.   assortative mating
    d.   social role theory

6. **Sternberg suggests that love has the following three key components:**
    a.   intimacy, passion, and commitment
    b.   sincerity, consistency, and convenience
    c.   significance, maintenance, and playfulness
    d.   lust, compatibility, and persistence

7. **Which of the following groups generally experience an improvement in their economic status after a divorce?**
    a.   men
    b.   women
    c.   both men and women
    d.   neither men nor women

8. **Cohabiting couples differ more often than married couples in each of the following ways EXCEPT _____.**
    a. religious beliefs
    b. educational levels
    c. socio-economic status
    d. age

9. **Which of the following statements about homosexual relationships is true?**
    a. Homosexual couples report being less satisfied than heterosexual couples.
    b. Homosexual couples tend to be more monogamous than heterosexual couples.
    c. Homosexual couples are more egalitarian than heterosexual couples.
    d. Homosexual couples tend to experience more physical abuse than heterosexual couples.

10. **What is postpartum depression?**
    a. depression that starts with the realization of an unwanted pregnancy
    b. a transient depressed mood following all pregnancies
    c. a depression following pregnancy that lasts for several weeks
    d. an unusual depression that is more common in young mothers

11. **Why might the birth of a child affect marital satisfaction?**
    a. The child makes all of the effort seem so worthwhile.
    b. Spouses feel that their efforts are not being recognized.
    c. Both spouses gain so much satisfaction from the new parent role.
    d. The role of parent and the role of spouse are somewhat incompatible.

12. **According to John Holland, which of the following personality types tends to choose a career such as nursing or education?**
    a. social
    b. conventional
    c. artistic
    d. enterprising

13. **Which of the following statements about job satisfaction is true?**
    a. It stays high for men until retirement.
    b. It is lowest in early adulthood.
    c. It is highest in young adulthood.
    d. It stays high for women until retirement.

14. **Which of the following accurately describes family roles?**
    a. Men feel more conflict between the roles of spouse, worker, and parent than women.
    b. Work and family roles tend to be sequential for women.
    c. Work and family roles tend to be simultaneous for men.
    d. Women view themselves as mother and wives all day.

15. **Recasting or reframing a situation in a way that identifies the positive elements is called _____.**
    a. conflict management
    b. depression
    c. homogamy
    d. cognitive restructuring

TRUE-FALSE QUESTIONS

Indicate whether each of the following statements is true or false.

_____
1.
Successful resolution of the intimacy versus isolation stage depends on a good resolution of the identity versus role confusion crisis.

_____
2.
Cross-culturally studies conducted over a period of several decades suggest that men prefer physically attractive, younger women, while women look for men whose socio-economic status is higher than their own, who offer earning potential and stability.

_____
3.
After a couple has been married for eight years, the probability that they will divorce increases significantly.

_____
4.
Close friends are likely to play a more prominent role in the social networks of singles than among married couples or cohabitants.

_____
5.
Childless married women are much more likely to have full-time continuous careers.

_____
6.
A family's value system has no impact on job choices of a young adult.

_____
7.
Stereotypically male jobs are more varied, more technical, and higher in both status and income than stereotypically female jobs.

_____
8.
Advocates of the quality of work-life movement suggest that when people are happier at work, they will be more productive.

ESSAY QUESTIONS

1. Select the theory of Social and Personality Development (Erikson's Psychosocial Theory, Levinson's Life Structures, Parental Investment Theory, or Social Role Theory) that you believe most accurately reflects development in young adulthood. Support your answer.

2. Discuss Sternberg's theory of romantic love. Explain why Sternberg emphasized the importance of the presence of all three elements (intimacy, passion, and commitment) in consummate love.

3. Select the personality type from John Holland's list (Table 14.1) that most closely resembles your personality type. Compare your chosen career to the personality and work preferences.

WHEN YOU HAVE FINISHED . . . PUZZLE IT OUT

Across

2. Personality type that prefers structured activities and subordinate roles
5. Couples who are called "conflict minimizers"
7. Personality type that is oriented toward thinking, organizing, and planning
10. Depression experienced by some new mothers
11. Couples who squabble a lot, disagree, and don't listen to each other when they argue
12. Theory that explains behavior by focusing on survival value
13. Also known as assortative mating

Down

1. Personality type that is people-oriented, sociable, and needs attention
2. Third phase in Levinson's life structure
3. First phase in Levinson's life structure
4. Personality type that is aggressive, masculine, and physically strong
5. Personality type that is asocial and who prefer unstructured, highly individual activity
6. Includes a feeling of intense longing for union with the other person, including sexual union
7. The capacity to engage in a supportive, affectionate relationships without losing one's own identity
8. Couples who have disagreements which rarely escalate
9. Personality type that his highly verbal and dominating

Created by Puzzlemaker at DiscoverySchool.com

WHEN YOU HAVE FINISHED . . . INVESTIGATIVE PROJECT

Student Project 25: Social Networks among Young Adults

For this project, based on the work of Antonucci and Akiyama (1987), collect some data from young adults. You should locate at least four adults, one each in the following age ranges: 20-24, 25-29, 30-34, and 35-40. It would be simpler if they were all the same gender, but that may not be practical. If you can, find eight willing subjects; try for one woman and one man in each group. (If all the students in your class complete this project, each with a minimum of four subjects, you could end up with quite a large sample, allowing you to look at sex differences and age trends.)

Procedure

You will need to obtain the appropriate informed consent from each subject, following the procedure as specified by your instructor. For each subject prepare an 8½" x 11" sheet of paper on which you have drawn a bull's-eye. In the center should be a very small circle (about the size of a dime) labeled "you." Around this circle draw three more concentric circles, spaced equally apart. This will give you three areas, each further from the center "you."

Tell your subjects that you are interested in knowing something about the people who are important in his (her) life. Present the sheet with the concentric circles on it and say:

> *The three circles should be thought of as including people who are important in your life right now, but to whom you are not equally close. The innermost circle (point to the circle immediately next to "you") includes people to whom you feel so close that it is hard to imagine life without them. Please put the names of anyone who fits that description into this innermost circle, along with some indication of how they are related to you—friend, parent, spouse, or whomever.*

When the subject has entered names in the innermost circle, point to the next circle and say:

> *Please put in this circle the names of people to whom you may not feel quite that close but who are still very important to you, and indicate your relationship to each one.*

Finally, point to the outermost circle and say:

> *Finally, put here the names of the people you haven't already mentioned but, who are close enough and important enough in your life that they should be placed in your personal network. As usual, indicate how you are related to each one.*

In addition, you will need to ask each subject a set of questions to amplify your analysis. Write the answers on the back of the subject's concentric circle sheet:

> *Are you married?*

> *How old are you?*

> *How many years of education have you completed?*

Also note the gender of the subject on the back of the sheet. Your subject's name should NOT appear anywhere on the sheet.

Analysis and Report

For each circle, count the total number of names, the number of males and females listed, and the relationship listed (family member, friend, spouse). Is there any noticeable difference in these characteristics as a function of age, gender, or education among your subjects?

Some other questions you might consider:
- Do all married subjects put their spouse in the center circle?
- How many put either or both parents in the center circle?
- Is there any married subject who put both the spouse and one or both parents in the center circle? If so, what does this say about the issue of the relative strength of a person's attachment to partner and parent?
- Is there a friend in the center circle, or do friends only begin to be listed in the second circle? Does this vary as a function of marital status? That is, do unmarried adults put more friends in the center circle?

Consider all these results in light of what is said in the text about networks and relationships in early life. What else might you want to know about your subjects to help you interpret their answers?

Reference

Antonucci, T. C., & Akiyama, H. (1987). Social networks in adult life and a preliminary examination of the convoy model. *Journal of Gerontology*, *42*, 519-527.

CHAPTER 14 ANSWER KEY

Practice Test #1 Theories of Social and Personality Development
1. e   2. f   3. d   4. a   5. h   6. g

Practice Test #2 Intimate Relationships
1. b   2. d   3. b   4. b   5. b   6. c   7. a   8. c   9. d   10. b

Practice Test #3 Parenthood and Other Relationships
1. men; women
3. positive
5. proximity
7. talk to one another; do things together

2. depression
4. decline
6. mutual openness; personal disclosure
8. kin-keeper

Practice Test #4 The Role of Worker
1. F   2. T   3. F   4. T   5. T   6. F   7. T   8. T   9. F   10. T

Comprehensive Practice Test
Multiple Choice Questions
1. c   2. b   3. a   4. a   5. b   6. a   7. a   8. d   9. c   10. c
11. d   12. a   13. b   14. d   15. d

True-False Questions
1. T   2. T   3. F   4. T   5. T   6. F   7. T   8. T

Essay Questions
1. ▪ Answers should accurately describe the basics of the theory and provide evidence in its support.

2. ▪ Intimacy: Includes feelings of closeness and connectedness.
   ▪ Passion: Includes a feeling of intense longing or union with the other person , including sexual union.
   ▪ Commitment: To a particular other, often over a long period of time.
   ▪ Consummate love requires all three to fill a partner's needs.

3. ▪ Answers will vary; they should reflect the basics of Holland's theory.

Puzzle It Out
Across
2. conventional
5. avoidant
7. investigative
10. postpartum
11. volatile
12. evolutionary
13. homogamy

Down
1. social
2. cumulative
3. novice
4. realistic
5. artistic
6. passion
7. intimacy
8. validating
9. enterprising

CHAPTER 15

PHYSICAL AND COGNITIVE DEVELOPMENT IN MIDDLE ADULTHOOD

BEFORE YOU READ . . . CHAPTER SUMMARY

In middle adulthood, the period from 40 to 60, the story of human development in the physical and cognitive domains becomes more an account of differences than a description of universals. This happens because there are so many factors—behavioral choices, poor health, and so on—that determine the developmental pathway that an individual adult follows.

Physical Changes

- In most individuals, the brain is somewhat smaller at the end of middle adulthood than at the beginning of the period. Some declines in brain function are evident. However, middle-aged adults use a variety of strategies to compensate for these declines and, as a result, often outperform younger adults on practical tasks such as driving.
- Both males and females experience changes in reproductive hormones - the *climacteric* - in these years. In women, reproductive capacity declines slightly and then ceases altogether at menopause. In men, the process is more gradual, and most continue to be capable of fathering children into late adulthood.
- At about age 30, bone mass begins to decline. The process is accelerated in women at menopause. Lifestyle choices, such as diet and exercise, influence bone loss in both men and women.
- Both visual and auditory acuity decline in most middle-aged adults. Men experience greater hearing losses than women do.

Health and Wellness

- Cardiovascular disease results from the build-up of a fatty substance in the arteries. Smoking, high blood pressure, high cholesterol, obesity, and a high-fat diet increase the likelihood that a middle-aged adult will suffer from cardiovascular disease. Men are more likely than women to have this disease.
- Some studies suggest that high-fat diets increase the risk of cancer. Smoking, obesity, and an inactive lifestyle may also contribute to this disease.
- On average, women live longer than men, but they are more likely suffer from chronic conditions such as arthritis.
- Ethnicity and socioeconomic class are linked to health in middle adulthood. African Americans, Native Americans, and Hispanic Americans experience higher rates of cardiovascular disease, cancer, and diabetes than members of other groups. Poor adults of all ethnic groups are more likely to suffer from chronic illnesses and have higher rates of death in middle age than peers who are better off economically.
- Alcoholism can develop at any age, but its effects become evident in middle age when it is associated with increased mortality.

Cognitive Functioning

- Nancy Denney's model of aging hypothesizes that exercising physical and cognitive abilities slows down the rate of decline in the middle and later adulthood years. Such exercise may also improve the level of functioning according to this model. Paul and Margaret Baltes assert that middle-aged adults balance the gains and losses associated with aging by selecting tasks on which to focus limited resources, optimizing some skills through practice, and compensating for declines.
- Research suggests that variations in health are associated with variations in cognitive functioning in middle-aged and older adults. Physical exercise clearly affects health and may also be related to cognitive functioning.
- Verbal abilities continue to grow in middle adulthood. Some memory skills decline, but middle-aged adults maintain high levels of functioning in areas of expertise.
- In adults who work in challenging professions, creative productivity appears to be at its peak in middle adulthood.

AS YOU READ . . . LEARNING OBJECTIVES

After completing Chapter 15, you should be able to answer the following questions:
15.1   What do researchers know about brain function in middle age?
15.2   How do reproductive functions change in men and women in middle age?
15.3   What is osteoporosis, and what factors are associated with it?
15.4   How do vision and hearing change in middle age?
15.5   How does cardiovascular disease develop?
15.6   What factors contribute to cancer?
15.7   What are some important differences in the health of middle-aged men and women?
15.8   How are socioeconomic status and ethnicity related to health in middle adulthood?
15.9   What are some of the consequences of alcoholism for middle-aged adults?
15.10   How do Denney's and the Balteses' models explain the relationship between health and cognitive functioning in middle age?
15.11   What has research revealed about the link between health and cognitive functioning?
15.12   How do young and middle-aged adults differ in performance on memory tests?
15.13   What does research suggest about age-related changes in creativity?

AS YOU READ . . . TERM IDENTIFICATION

Alcoholism (p. 448)
Atherosclerosis (p. 443)
Cardiovascular disease (CVD) (p. 443)
Climacteric (p. 437)
Creativity (p. 453)
Episodic memories (p. 452)
Hypertension (p. 447)
Menopause (p. 437)

Osteoporosis (p. 440)
Perimenopausal phase (p. 438)
Postmenopausal phase (p. 438)
Premenopausal phase (p. 438)
Presbycusis (p. 442)
Presbyopia (p. 442)
Selective optimization with compensation (p. 450)
Semantic memories (p. 452)

AS YOU READ . . . GUIDED STUDY QUESTIONS

PHYSICAL CHANGES

The Brain and Nervous System (pp. 436-437)

15.1   What do researchers know about brain and function in middle age?

1.   Why is there so little information about the normal, undamaged brains of middle-aged adults?

2.   Describe the information about the brains of middle-aged adults that is known.

3.   Give examples of how cognitive tasks activate a larger area of brain tissue in middle-aged adults than they do in younger adults.

4.   Give examples of how the brains of middle-aged and younger adults respond differently to sensory stimuli.

5.   How do both primary and secondary aging affect studies of the middle-aged brain?

The Reproductive System (pp. 437-440)

15.2   How do reproductive functions change in men and women in middle age?

6.   Define the following terms:
    a.   climacteric (p. 437)

    b.   menopause (p. 437)

    c.   premenopausal phase (p. 438)

    d.   perimenopausal phase (p. 438)

    e.   postmenopausal phase (p. 438)

7.   Describe the male climacteric, including the causal factor.

8.   How is the production of testosterone implicated in the incidence of erectile dysfunction?

9.   List the hormones involved in menopause.

10.   Describe the phases of menopause by completing the following table:

Phase	Description
Premenopausal Phase	
Perimenopausal Phase	
Postmenopausal Phase	

11.   Describe the results of research on the psychological effects of menopause.

12.   How does menopause affect the sexual activity of middle-aged adults?

No Easy Answers: The Pros and Cons of Hormone Therapy (p. 439)

13.   List the negative symptoms of menopause.

14.   Briefly trace the history of hormone therapy.

The Skeletal System (pp. 440-441)

15.3   What is osteoporosis, and what factors are associated with it?
15.   Define osteoporosis (p. 440).

16.   How is osteoporosis linked to the levels of estrogen and progesterone?

17.   Aside from taking hormones, list and describe three strategies to prevent osteoporosis.

Strategies	Description

Vision and Hearing (p. 441)

15.4   How do vision and hearing change in middle age?

18.   Define the following terms:
    a.   presbyopia (p. 441)

    b.   presbycusis (p. 442)

AFTER YOU READ . . . PRACTICE TEST #1
PHYSICAL CHANGES

Match the letter of the term in the right column with its description in the left column.

_____ 1.   Drug therapy to treat to symptoms of menopause.

_____ 2.   Loss of bone mass with age resulting in more brittle and porous bones.

_____ 3.   The phase of menopause during which estrogen and progesterone levels are erratic, menstrual cycles may be very irregular, and women begin to experience symptoms such as hot flashes.

_____ 4.   Normal loss of visual acuity with aging, especially the ability to focus the eyes on near objects.

_____ 5.   The term used to describe the adult period during which reproductive capacity declines or is lost.

_____ 6.   The inability to achieve or maintain an erection.

_____ 7.   The last phase of menopause; a woman has had no menstrual periods for a year or more.

_____ 8.   The cessation of monthly menstrual cycles in middle-aged women.

a. Climacteric
b. Erectile dysfunction
c. Hormone therapy
d. Menopause
e. Osteoporosis
f. Perimenopausal
g. Postmenopausal
h. Premenopausal
i. Presbycusis
j. Presbyopia

HEALTH AND WELLNESS

Cardiovascular Disease (pp. 442-445)

15.5   How does cardiovascular disease develop?

19.   Define the following terms:
   a.   cardiovascular disease (CVD) (p. 443)

   b.   atherosclerosis (p. 443)

20.   Describe the risk factors of heart disease by completing the following table:

Risk	Description of Risk for Heart Disease
Smoking	
Blood Pressure	
Weight	
Cholesterol	
Inactivity	
Diet	
Alcohol	
Heredity	

21.   State the two important points to be made about CVD.
■

■

22.   Explain how type A personality may contribute to heart disease.

23.   Describe the link between CVD and hostility.

24.   What is type D personality, and how does it affect CVD?

Cancer (p. 445)

15.6   What factors contribute to cancer?

25.   Describe the risk factors of cancer by completing the following table:

Risk	Description of Risk for Heart Disease
Smoking	
Blood Pressure	
Weight	

Risk	Description of Risk for Heart Disease
Cholesterol	
Inactivity	
Diet	
Alcohol	
Heredity	

26.   Summarize the current research on the relationship between diet and cancer.

27.   List the infections agents that are known to cause cancer.

Gender and Health (p. 446)

15.7   What are some important differences in the health of middle-aged men and women?

28.   State the paradox involving the life expectancy of women and men.

29.   Give examples of the sex differences in potentially fatal diseases such as cardiovascular disease and non-fatal diseases such as arthritis.

Socio-Economic Class, Ethnicity, and Health (pp. 446-447)

15.8   How are socioeconomic status and ethnicity related to health in middle adulthood?

30.   How is social class a significant predictor of variations in health in middle age?

31.   Describe the differences in the following diseases by completing the table:

Disease	*Ethnic Differences*
Cardiovascular Disease (CVD)	
Diabetes	
Cancer	

32.   Define hypertension (p. 447).

Alcoholism (pp. 447448

15.9   What are some of the consequences of alcoholism for middle-aged adults?

33.   Define alcoholism (p. 448).

34.   How does long-term heavy drinking affect the body?

Research Report: Is the Internet Addictive? (p.448)

35.   What is Internet Addictive Disorder, IAD, and what are the criteria for its diagnosis?

36.   What are the arguments of mental health professions who oppose the idea of Internet addiction?

AFTER YOU READ . . . PRACTICE TEST #2
HEALTH AND WELLNESS

1. **The single variable that most affects the quality of life in middle and late adulthood is _____.**
   a. employment
   b. income
   c. health
   d. an intimate partnership

2. **A set of disease processes in the heath and circulatory systems is called _____.**
   a. presbycusis
   b. cardiovascular disease
   c. atherosclerosis
   d. osteoporosis

3. **The key problem in cardiovascular disease is in the _____.**
   a. lungs
   b. arteries
   c. intestines
   d. bones

4. **Which of the following statements about risk factors for heart disease is TRUE?**
   a. The great majority of Americans have at least one of these risk factors.
   b. The only consistent controllable cause is smoking.
   c. Men are at a higher risk because they strain their hearts more than women.
   d. The risk factors are completely controllable with the right effort.

5. **Which of the following statements about gender and health is TRUE?**
   a. Men are more likely to live longer than women.
   b. Men live longer than women once they contract a disease.
   c. Women are more likely than men to die from cardiovascular disease.
   d. Women are more likely than men to suffer from nonfatal chronic ailments such as arthritis.

6. **Which of the following statements about ethnic differences in health in middle adulthood is true?**
   a. Mexican Americans have higher rates of heart disease than whites.
   b. Mexican Americans have lower rates of cancer than whites.
   c. African Americans have higher rates of cancer, but lower rates of heart disease, than whites.
   d. Native Americans have lower rates of cardiovascular disease then whites.

7. **Each of the following statements about diabetes is true EXCEPT _____.**
   a. Minority adults often have less access to regular medical care for diabetes than whites.
   b. Diabetes itself kills people.
   c. Diabetes can lead to severe complications such as cardiovascular disease, kidney failure, and blindness.
   d. Minorities have significantly higher rates of diabetes than whites.

8.   **Each of the following statements about alcoholism is true EXCEPT _____.**
   a.   Long-term use of alcohol causes damage to the digestive system.
   b.   Long-term use of alcohol causes losses in muscle strength.
   c.   Long-term use of alcohol causes a delay in the course of the phases of menopause.
   d.   Long-term use of alcohol is associated with a reduced likelihood of death from cancer.

COGNITIVE FUNCTIONING

Models of Physical and Cognitive Aging (pp. 449-450)

15.10 How do Denney's and the Balteses' models explain the relationship between health and cognitive functioning in middle age?

37.   Explain Nancy Denney's model of physical and cognitive changes in adulthood.

38.   How does Denney use the word exercise in her model?

39.   Define selective optimization with compensation (p. 450).

40.   Give examples of Paul and Margaret Balteses' theory.

Health and Cognitive Functioning (pp. 450-451)

15.11 What has research revealed about the link between health and cognitive functioning?

41.   What is the link between secondary aging and cognitive functioning?

42.   Describe the longitudinal study of physical activity of Harvard alumni.

43.   What is the connection between physical exercise and cognitive abilities in middle-adulthood?

Changes in Memory and Cognition (pp. 451-453)

15.12 How do young and middle-aged adults differ in performance on memory tests?

44.   Why do researchers often infer the memory performance of middle-aged adults?

45.   Describe the subjective experience of forgetfulness in middle age.

46.   Compare visual memory and memory for auditory stimuli in middle age with that of younger adults.

Type of Memory	Description
Visual Memory	
Auditory Memory	

47.   Define the following terms:
    a.   episodic memory (p. 452)

    b.   semantic memory (p. 452)

48   How do semantic memories and episodic memories differ in young adults and middle-aged adults?

Semantic Memory	Episodic Memory

49.   How does the phrase "use it or lost it" hold true for cognitive abilities? Give examples.

50.   How do the cumulative effects of many years of using some cognitive skills and the development of a large body of relevant information in long-term memory affect performance?

Creativity (pp. 453-454)

15.13 What does research suggest about age-related changes in creativity?

51.   Define creativity (p. 453).

52.   Describe Simonton's research on the lifetime creativity and productivity of notable scientists from the 19th century and earlier. Compare the results to the lifetime creative output of modern-day scientists.

53.   What is divergent thinking, and how does it affect creativity?

54.   Describe each of the four stages in Daniel Goleman's description of "mulling over" a problem.

Stage	Description
Preparation	
Incubation	
Illumination	
Translation	

The Real World: Working: Maintaining the Creative "Edge" in Mid-Life and Beyond (p. 454)

55.   List the two conclusions from the research on maintaining creativity and productivity in the middle and late adult years.

AFTER YOU READ . . . PRACTICE TEST #3
COGNITIVE FUNCTIONING

Indicate whether each of the following statements is true or false.

_____ 1. Nancy Denney proposed that on nearly any measure of physical or cognitive functioning, age-related changes follow a typical curve.

_____ 2. Most fluid abilities are at least moderately exercised, whereas many crystallized abilities are relatively unexercised.

_____ 3. Many of the same characteristics that are linked to increased or decreased risk of heart disease and cancer are also linked to the rate of change of the maintenance of intellectual skill in the middle years.

_____ 4. Results of the long-term Harvard study showed that the more exercise a man reported, the lower his mortality risk.

_____ 5. Physical exercise seems to have no effect on maintaining cognitive abilities in the middle adult years.

_____ 6. The subjective experience of forgetfulness clearly increases with age.

_____ 7. Both memory for visual and auditory stimuli seem to remain stable throughout adulthood.

_____ 8. Adults who engage in intellectual challenging activities show fewer losses in cognitive skills than those who do not.

_____ 9. Middle-aged adults outperform those who are younger on tasks that involve comprehending and remembering reading material.

_____ 10. The ability to apply creative thinking to complex problems may be at its peak in the middle adult years.

AFTER YOU READ . . . CRITICAL REFLECTION EXERCISE

Mid-Life Development

Utilizing information from the text, provide complete answers to the following questions:

1.   What is the Type A Behavior Pattern? Suggest three things that an individual could do to minimize the likelihood of Type A characteristics influencing his or her health.

2.   Do you believe in the concept of a "midlife crisis?" Why or why not?

3.   Discuss how identity development in the early phases of development may be related to life satisfaction in middle adulthood.

AFTER YOU READ . . . COMPREHENSIVE PRACTICE TEST
MULTIPLE CHOICE QUESTIONS

1. **Which of the following statements is true about the brain at mid-life?**
   a. There is no difference in the distribution of electrical activity in the brains of alcoholics and non-alcoholics.
   b. Cognitive tasks activate a larger area of brain tissue in middle-aged adults than they do in younger adults.
   c. In middle age, more new synapses are formed than are lost.
   d. Synaptic density continues to increase across adulthood.

2. **What reproductive event in middle adulthood is included in the term climacteric?**
   a. a gradual loss of interest in sexual activity
   b. a steady increase in the number of miscarriages
   c. the occurrence of menopause in women
   d. decreased incidence of impotence in men

3. **What seems to be the cause of the decrease in viable sperm in men across middle adulthood?**
   a. less sexual activity which results in decreased sperm production
   b. increased exposure to teratogens from the environment
   c. there is no drop in viable sperm production
   d. gradual decline in testosterone levels beginning in early adulthood

4. **What do we know about the incidence of osteoporosis in middle adulthood?**
   a. It only occurs in women.
   b. The process for women is accelerated by menopause.
   c. The process for men is linked to impotence.
   d. It is unavoidable.

5. **Presbyopia is _____.**
   a. a process by which muscle mass is lost
   b. the thickening of the lens that causes the eye muscles to have difficulty changing the shape of the lens for focusing
   c. the hardening of the arteries accompanied by a slight, but steady, decline in blood pressure during middle adulthood
   d. a sharp decline in taste sensitivity

6. **What is atherosclerosis?**
   a. a narrowing of the arteries that occurs with age
   b. clogging of the arteries with fibrous or fatty tissue
   c. a neuromuscular disorder often diagnosed in middle adulthood
   d. a normal part of aging that can be slowed but not avoided

7. **What is the second leading cause of death among adults over the age of 45?**
   a. cardiovascular disease
   b. pulmonary disorders
   c. cancer
   d. accidents

8. **Which of the following statements is true concerning gender and health?**
   a.   Men are more likely to live longer than women.
   b.   Women have fewer diseases and disabilities than men.
   c.   Men live longer once they contract a disease than women.
   d.   Women live longer, but they have more diseases and disabilities than men.

9. **What is hypertension?**
   a.   cardiovascular disease
   b.   high blood pressure
   c.   low blood sugar
   d.   elevated cardiac rate

10. **Which of the following statements about diabetes is true?**
   a.   At least three undiagnosed cases of diabetes exist for every individual who has been diagnosed with it.
   b.   More men than women have diabetes.
   c.   Minority adults who have been diagnosed with diabetes are more likely than their white counterparts to develop complications.
   d.   Diabetes itself frequently kills people.

11. **Which of the following statements describes Nancy Denney's model of physical and cognitive aging?**
   a.   Denney uses the word exercise to refer to physical exercise.
   b.   Unexercised abilities generally have a lower peak of performance; exercised abilities generally have a higher peak.
   c.   Only crystallized intelligence is affected by exercise, not fluid intelligence.
   d.   Skills that are not exercised by age 30 can never be improved.

12. **Each of the following is part of Paul and Margaret Baltes' research on health and cognitive functioning EXCEPT _____.**
   a.   exercise
   b.   compensation
   c.   selection
   d.   optimization

13. **Which of the following statements accurately reflects the results of the longitudinal study of the physical activity of Harvard alumni?**
   a.   The more exercise a man reported in his 30s, 40s, and 50s, the lower his mortality risk over the next 25 years.
   b.   Physical activity and cognitive functioning are not related.
   c.   Physical activity and cognitive functioning are negatively correlated.
   d.   Cardiovascular disease is linked to the presence of lead in drinking water.

14. **At about what age might we expect to see a decline in performance on more complex memory tasks, such as remembering lists of words and passages of text?**
   a.   at about age 35
   b.   not until age 45
   c.   after about age 55
   d.   at about age 65

15. **Each of the following is a stage in Daniel Goleman's research on "mulling over" a problem EXCEPT _____.**
   a. translation
   b. incubation
   c. divergence
   d. illumination

TRUE-FALSE QUESTIONS

Indicate whether each of the following statements is true or false.

_____
1.
Cognitive tasks activate a larger area of brain tissue in middle-aged adults than they do in younger adults.

_____
2.
During the perimenopausal phase, estrogen levels decrease and women experience more extreme variations in the timing of their menstrual cycles.

_____
3.
The more high-risk health behaviors or characteristics you have, the higher your risk of heart disease.

_____
4.
There is little doubt that several types of cancers are caused by infectious agents.

_____
5.
The main cause for variations in cancer rates is family history of cancer.

_____
6.
In Nancy Denney's model, any skill that is not fully exercised cannot be improved.

_____
7.
Physical exercise seems to help maintain cognitive abilities in the middle adult years, very likely because it helps to maintain cardiovascular fitness.

_____
8.
A person who uses divergent thinking can provide multiple solutions to problems that have no clear answer.

ESSAY QUESTIONS

1. Using Table 15.2 as a reference, design a plan to reduce your health risks for heart disease and cancer.

2. How would you encourage a middle-aged adult relative to "use it or lose it" to maintain her or his cognitive abilities in middle age?

3. Discuss the relationship between creativity and productivity in middle adulthood.

WHEN YOU HAVE FINISHED . . . PUZZLE IT OUT

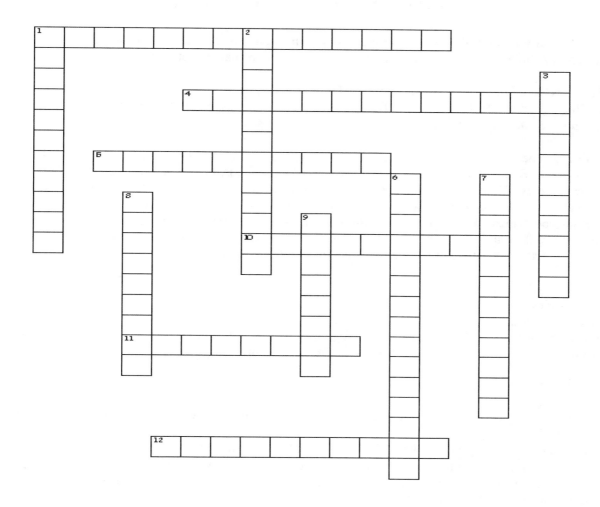

Across

1. Phase during which menstrual cycles may be very irregular and women experience hot flashes
4. Phase during which estrogen levels fall somewhat and menstrual periods are less regular
5. Physical and psychological dependence on alcohol
10. The inability to achieve or maintain an erection; also called erectile dysfunction
11. Memories of general knowledge
12. Normal loss of visual acuity with aging

Down

1. Normal loss of hearing with aging
2. Loss of bone mass with age resulting in more brittle and porous bones
3. The adult period during which reproductive capacity declines or is lost
6. Narrowing of the arteries caused by deposits of plaque
7. Elevated blood pressure
8. The cessation of monthly menstrual cycles in middle-aged women
9. Memories of personal events

WHEN YOU HAVE FINISHED . . . AT-HOME PROJECT

Student Project 26: Assessing Your Own Diet

Since both dietary fat and fiber intake are increasingly implicated as potentially casual factors in cancer, heart disease, or both, it may be useful and informative for you to analyze your own diet.

For five days, write down everything you eat. Do not change your normal eating pattern just to make yourself look good and feel less guilty. If you normally eat Twinkies, go ahead and eat them, but write it down—and keep the wrapper so that you can do a food analysis later.

You will also need some source of detailed information about the total calories, fat content, and fiber content of food. Some of this is now listed on most packaged foods, but for non-packaged foods, you'll need other sources. Your public library may have appropriate sources; some cookbooks offer good lists. (In that category, an excellent resource is a book called *Laurel's Kitchen*, which lists a great deal of information about many kinds of foods. But since it is a vegetarian cookbook, it will not give you information about meat, fish, or poultry.) Other possible sources would be the American Cancer Society, or the County Extension office in your area, which may have pamphlets or brochures.

For your food list for each of the five days, calculate the following:
- total calories
- total grams of fat
- percentage of total calories that is fat. Each gram of fat is nine calories. so simply multiply the total fat grams by nine, then divide that amount by the total calories to give the percent of calories that is fat
- number of grams of fiber

Average these figures over the five days, and then compare the averages with the recommendations from leading public health groups:
- You should be getting no more than 30% of your total calories from fat.
- You should have a minimum of 20 and a maximum of 35 grams of fiber per day. Some experts recommend levels of fat considerably lower than 30%, but 30 is the number that is presently recommended by both the American Heart Association and the American Cancer Society.

How does your diet measure up to these standards? If you do not meet either or both of them, what changes would you need to make in your diet to reach these goals? If your fat levels are too high, can you identify the foods in your normal diet that are raising the percentages? You may be surprised.

CHAPTER 14 ANSWER KEY

Practice Test #1 Physical Changes

1. c   2. e   3. f   4. j   5. a   6. b   7. g   8. d

Practice Test #2 Health and Wellness

1. c   2. b   3. b   4. a   5. d   6. a   7. b   8. d

Practice Test #3 Cognitive Functioning

1. T   2. F   3. T   4. T   5. F   6. T   7. F   8. T   9. T   10. T

Comprehensive Practice Test

Multiple Choice Questions

1. b   2. c   3. d   4. b   5. b   6. a   7. c   8. d   9. c   10. b
11. b   12. a   13. a   14. c   15. c

True-False Questions

1. T   2. T   3. T   4. T   5. F   6. F   7. T   8. T

Essay Questions

1. ▪ Answers will vary, but could include changes in diet, increase in exercise, reduction of alcohol intake or quitting smoking.

2. ▪ Most adults maintain or even gain skill on any task that they practice often or that is based on specific learning, Engaging in intellectually challenging activities reduces the likelihood of loss of cognitive skills. Answers will vary, but should include reference to engaging in intellectually challenging activities.

3. ▪ In every scientific discipline represented, the thinkers produced their best work at about age 40, on average. Researchers proposed that the reason people tend to do their best work at about 40 is not that the mind works better at that age, but that productivity is at its highest at that time. Chance alone suggests that the best work will come during the time when the most work is being done.

Puzzle It Out

Across
1. Perimenopausal
4. Premenopausal
5. Alcoholism
10. Impotence
11. Semantic
12. Presbyopia

Down
1. Presbycusis
2. Osteoporosis
3. Climacteric
6. Atherosclerosis
7. Hypertension
8. Menopause
9. Episodic

CHAPTER 16

SOCIAL AND PERSONALITY DEVELOPMENT IN MIDDLE ADULTHOOD

BEFORE YOU READ . . . CHAPTER SUMMARY

In Western culture, middle-aged adults are viewed as highly competent and capable of assuming important family and occupational roles. Consequently, in most families, the middle-aged cohort provides some degree of both material and emotional support for both younger and older family members. Still, most middle-aged adults feel much less constricted by social roles than in earlier periods, and, for most, these roles shift considerably between the ages of 40 and 60.

Theories of Social and Personality Development

- For Erikson, the primary task of middle adulthood is the development of generativity through mentoring younger individuals. Vaillant proposed two additional stages to Erikson's theory: career consolidation and keeper of the meaning.
- There is little empirical support for the popular notion of a "mid-life" crisis, as described by Levinson. The life events approach focuses on normative and non-normative event and how adults respond to them. The stresses of the events of middle age are often complicated by role conflict.

Changes in Relationships and Personality

- Marital conflicts decline in middle age leading to higher levels of relationship satisfaction.
- Middle-aged adults are "sandwiched" between younger and older cohorts. They provide assistance and advice both up and down the generational chain.
- Most adults become grandparents sometime in the middle adult years. For most, the role is a very rewarding one.
- A small proportion of middle-aged adults become primary caregivers for their elderly parents. Many report feeling burdened and depressed by the experience. Women are more likely to become primary caretakers for elders than are men.
- The number of friendships an individual adult has declines in middle age, perhaps narrowing the social network to include only those friends to whom an adult feels particularly close.
- The Big Five personality traits are stable across middle adulthood. However, some middle-aged adults exhibit "mellowing" of negative traits such as neuroticism.

Mid-Life Career Issues

- Job satisfaction peaks in middle age, however work takes on a less important role in an adult's overall sense of well-being during these years.
- Most middle-aged adults continue to be highly productive in their careers.
- Anxiety and depression sometimes accompany both involuntary and voluntary mid-life career changes.
- Preparation for retirement includes financial planning as well as a decline in the number of hours a middle-aged adult works each week.

AS YOU READ . . . LEARNING OBJECTIVES

After completing Chapter 16, students should be able to answer the following:
16.1   How do the views of Erikson and Vaillant differ with regard to generativity?
16.2   How do proponents of the midlife crisis and the life events perspective approach middle age differently?
16.3   What contributes to the "mellowing" of partnerships in middle adulthood?
16.4   What is the family role of middle-aged adults with respect to older and younger generations?
16.5   How does the grandparent role affect middle-aged adults?
16.6   How might caregiver burden affect a middle-aged adult's life?
16.7   How do social networks change during middle adulthood?
16.8   What is the evidence for continuity and change in personality throughout adulthood?
16.9   What factors influence work satisfaction in middle adulthood?
16.10   What strategies do middle-aged workers use to maintain job performance at a satisfactory level?
16.11   What are the factors that contribute to career transitions in mid-life?
16.12   How do Baby Boomers differ from previous cohorts with respect to preparation for retirement?

AS YOU READ . . . TERM IDENTIFICATION

Burnout (p. 471)
Caregiver burden (p. 469)
Companionate relationships (p. 468)
Generativity (p. 462)

Involved relationships (p. 468)
Life events approach (p. 463)
Remote relationships (p. 468)
Role conflict (p. 464)

AS YOU READ . . . GUIDED STUDY QUESTIONS

THEORIES OF SOCIAL AND PERSONALITY DEVELOPMENT

Erikson's Generativity versus Stagnation Stage (p. 462-363)

16.1   How do the views of Erikson and Vaillant differ with regard to generativity?
1.   Define generativity (p. 462).

2.   Give examples of ways that generativity can be expressed, in addition to bearing and rearing one's own children.

3.   Describe Erikson's view of those who do not express generativity.

4.   Describe George Vaillant's findings about career consolidation.

5.   Describe Vaillant's findings about the keeper of the meaning stage.

Mid-Life Crisis: Fact or Fiction? (p. 463-464)

16.2   How do proponents of the midlife crisis and the life events perspective approach middle age differently?

6.   Define the following terms:
   a.   life events approach (p. 463)

   b.   role conflict (p. 464)

7.   According to Levinson, list the difficult tasks a person must confront at mid-life.

8.   Give examples of the unique stresses of the middle adulthood period that are part of the life events approach.

9.   Give examples of role conflict and role strain.

Term	Example
Role Conflict	
Role Strain	

AFTER YOU READ . . . PRACTICE TEST #1
THEORIES OF SOCIAL AND PERSONALITY DEVELOPMENT

Indicate whether each of the following statements is true or false.

_____
1.
According to Erikson, middle-aged adults' developmental task is to acquire a sense of generativity.

_____
2.
According to Erikson, middle-aged adults who fail to develop generativity often suffer from a "pervading sense of stagnation and personal impoverishment" as if they were their own one and only child."

_____
3.
According to Levinson, each person must confront a constellation of difficult tasks at mid-life: accepting one's own mortality, recognizing new physical limitations and health risks, and adapting to major changes in most roles.

_____
4.
The outcome of the keeper of meaning stage is the creation of a new social network for which the middle-aged adult's primary work serves as a hub.

_____
5.
The life events approach focuses on normative and non-normative events and how middle-aged adults respond to them.

_____
6.
Role strain is a situation in which two or more roles are at lest partially incompatible.

CHANGES IN RELATIONSHIPS AND PERSONALITY

Partnerships (pp. 464-465)

16.3   What contributes to the "mellowing" of partnerships in middle adulthood?

10.   Why do marital stability and marital satisfaction, on average, increase in middle adulthood?

11.   What is skilled diplomacy, and how is it helpful in solving problems in a partnership?

Children and Parents (pp. 465-467)

16.4   What is the family role of middle-aged with respect to older and younger generations?

12.   What is meant by mid-life squeeze and the sandwich generation? Give examples of how they affect middle-aged adults:

Research Report: The Empty Nest and the Revolving Door (p. 466)

13.   What is meant by the terms "empty nest" and "revolving door?"

Empty Nest	Revolving Door

14.   How the "boomerang kids" affect the lives of their middle-aged parents?

Grandparenting (pp. 467-469)

Objective 16.8: Describe the impact of grandparenting on middle-aged adults.

15.   Define the following terms:
    a.   remote relationships (p. 468)

    b.   companionate relationships (p. 468)

    c.   involved relationships (p. 468)

16.   Describe the gender differences in the styles of grandparenting in the United States.

Sons	Daughters

The Real World: Me, a Mother-in-Law? (p. 468)

17.   Why is the role of mother-in-law perceived negatively? Give examples of how the stereotype may be somewhat accurate in some societies.

18.   List five recommendations to help middle-aged women adjust to the mother-in-law role and to forestall conflict.
   ▪

   ▪

   ▪

   ▪

   ▪

Caring for Aging Parents (pp. 469-470)

16.6   How might caregiver burden affect a middle-aged adult's life?

19.   Define caregiver burden (p. 469).

20.   Why are parents symbolically important to middle-aged adults?

No Easy Answers: Who Cares for Aging Parents? (p. 470)

21.   Within a group of siblings, which are most likely to take on the task of caregiver of an aging parent? How does the gender of the frail elder affect who becomes the caregiver?

22.   Describe how daughters and sons typically are involved in the caregiver role?

Friends (p. 469-470)

16.7   How do social networks change during middle adulthood?

23.   What does research suggest about the total number of friendships of middle-aged adults? What does research suggest about the quality of the friendships of middle-aged adults?

Continuity and Change in Personality (pp. 470-471)

16.8   *What is the evidence for continuity and change in personality throughout adulthood?*

24.   How do personality traits change across adulthood?

25.   How is personality related to an adults' capacity for managing stress?

AFTER YOU READ . . . PRACTICE TEST #2
CHANGES IN RELATIONSHIPS AND PERSONALITY

1. **Each of the following is a reason for improvements in marital satisfaction EXCEPT _____.**
    a.   conflicts over child-rearing decline
    b.   the number of non-shared friends increases
    c.   increased sense of control
    d.   relationship stability is maintained through skilled diplomacy

2. **An approach to solving problems that involves confrontation about an issue followed by attempts to restore harmony is called _____.**
    a.   determined goal accomplishment
    b.   tenacious goal pursuit
    c.   flexible goal adjustment
    d.   skilled diplomacy

3. **Divorce in middle age is typically _____.**
    a.   less traumatic for middle-aged women than for younger women
    b.   more traumatic for middle-aged women than for younger women
    c.   more traumatic for middle-aged men than women
    d.   not traumatic for middle-aged adults

4. **Middle-aged adults are sometimes called the _____.**
    a.   sandwich generation
    b.   companionate generation
    c.   friendship generation
    d.   remote generation

5. **Middle-aged adults give and receive help of various kinds from _____.**
    a.   no one
    b.   only aging parents
    c.   only adult children
    d.   both adult children and aging parents

6. **The least common type of grandparenting in the U. S. is _____.**
    a.   involved relationships
    b.   remote relationships
    c.   friendship relationships
    d.   companionate relationships

7. **Each of the following is an effect of caregiver burden EXCEPT _____.**
    a.   Caregivers are more likely to be depressed than those in comparison groups.
    b.   Those who are for frail elders are more often ill themselves than those in comparison groups.
    c.   Caregivers are healthier than those in comparison groups.
    d.   Caregivers have lower marital satisfaction than those in comparison groups.

8. Each of the following statements about friendship in middle adulthood is true EXCEPT _____.

a. The total number of friendships is lower than in young adulthood.
b. Mid-life friendships are as intimate and close as those at earlier stages.
c. Friendship depends less on frequent contact than on a sense the friends are there to provide support as needed.
d. The number of friendships increases throughout adulthood.

MID-LIFE CAREER ISSUES

Work Satisfaction (pp. 471-472)

16.9 What factors influence work satisfaction in middle adulthood?

26.   Define burnout (p. 471).

27.   List the two paradoxes that characterize work in mid-life.
■

■

28.   Give examples of burnout.

29.   List reasons for increases in work satisfaction during middle age.

30.   List the sources of work dissatisfaction in middle age for men and women.

31.   List some reasons why both men and women in mid-life have a greater sense of control over their work lives than younger adults do.

Job Performance (pp. 472-473)

16.10 What factors influence work satisfaction in middle adulthood?

32.   Briefly summarize the subprocesses of "selective optimization with compensation."

Subprocess	*Description*

33.   What is the relationship between increasing age and the use of selection, optimization, and compensation?

Unemployment and Career Transitions (pp. 473-475)

16.11 What are the factors that contribute to career transitions in mid-life?

34.   Why might career transitions be more difficult in middle age than earlier in adulthood?

35.   Describe involuntary career changers.

36.   Describe the effects of job loss on changes in family relationships and loss of self-esteem..

37.   Which of the Big Five personality dimensions contribute to mental health during involuntary career transitions?

38.   How do a person's coping skills affect an involuntary career change?

39.   What suggestions do counselors offer to assist a person who is an involuntary career changer?

40.   Describe voluntary career changers.

41.   How do voluntary career changers differ from involuntary career changers? How are they similar?

Similarities	*Differences*

Preparing for Retirement (p. 475)

16.12 How do Baby Boomers differ from previous cohorts with respect to preparation for retirement?

42.   Describe several ways that the Baby Boom cohort's retirement plans may differ dramatically from their parents' plans.

Baby Boomers	*Baby Boomer's Parents*

43.   Describe each of the distinct approaches to Baby Boomer's approaches to non-work pursuits during retirement.

Approach	Description
Wealth Builders	
Anxious Idealists	
Empowered Trailblazers	
Stretched and Stressed	
Leisure Lifers	

AFTER YOU READ . . . PRACTICE TEST #3
MID-LIFE CAREER ISSUES

Indicate whether each of the following statements is true or false.

_____ 1. Work satisfaction is at its peak in middle adulthood, despite the fact that most adults receive few work promotions.

_____ 2. Work-related burnout is much more likely during middle adulthood than in early adulthood.

_____ 3. Men and women cite the same sources of work satisfaction in middle age.

_____ 4. The link between the use of selection, optimization, and compensation and the quality of work performance gets stronger with increasing age.

_____ 5. Career transitions are much easier in middle-age than earlier in adulthood.

_____ 6. Involuntary career changers are people who are in transition for external reasons.

_____ 7. The effects of job loss include changes in family relationships and self-esteem.

_____ 8. The effects of unemployment are unaffected by social support.

_____ 9. Wealth builders plan to spend their spare time in retirement finding new ways to make money.

_____ 10. Leisure lifers intend to spend most of their time in retirement doing volunteer work.

AFTER YOU READ . . . CRITICAL REFLECTION EXERCISES

Mid-Life Transitions

Utilizing information from the text, provide complete responses to the following issues. Whenever possible, cite specific information from the readings to support your responses.

1. What are three major life transitions that may be experienced during middle adulthood? Be sure to discuss the positive and negative effects of these life transitions. What advice would you give someone about how he or she can respond successfully to these life transitions?

Generativity versus Stagnation

2.   Discuss the concepts of generativity versus stagnation. What effects might divorce have on these life crises?

3.   How would you define mentoring? What kind of a program could you develop to utilize the knowledge and experience of those in late middle adulthood? Be sure that the program you develop utilizes Erikson's concepts of generativity versus stagnation and integrity versus despair. Why would you design the program in these ways?

AFTER YOU READ . . . COMPREHENSIVE PRACTICE TEST
MULTIPLE CHOICE QUESTIONS

1. **Which of the following individuals is exhibiting generativity? The person who _____.**
    a. believes that having children is important for one's identity
    b. is doing volunteer work training youth
    c. has come to terms with what she has done with her life
    d. feels that his life has had little meaning

2. **Each of the following is a factor in the life events approach EXCEPT _____.**
    a. Many of the stresses of mid-life last for some time.
    b. A mid-life crisis is common for most middle-aged adults.
    c. The physical changes in middle adulthood are a backdrop for the major event.
    d. Most mid-life adults face major shifts in the nature of parent-child relationships.

3. **Any situation in which two or more roles are at least partially incompatible is called _____.**
    a. role status
    b. role strain
    c. role conflict
    d. role incompatibility

4. **During mid-life _____.**
    a. marital satisfaction tends to increase
    b. depression begins to increase gradually
    c. role overload begins to set in
    d. self-esteem increases but boredom also sets in

5. **Middle-aged adults are sometimes referred to as the sandwich generation because _____.**
    a. financial burdens of retirement begin to push in on these persons
    b. these individuals are squeezed for help from both children and their own parents
    c. time begins to seem like it is passing faster than ever before
    d. the changes in role status cause these persons to feel less needed

6. **The empty nest _____.**
    a. is simply the time at which the grown children leave the home and then return
    b. is usually a time of stress because the children have moved and roles have changed
    c. is a very stressful time for some women when their children leave home
    d. involves the loss of role identity because of retirement

7. **Which of the following statements about the revolving door is TRUE?**
    a. Stress decreases for parents and their adult children when they share a home.
    b. Few parents are satisfied with their arrangements with their live-in adult children.
    c. Few parents with adult resident children manage to work out a good system for handling potential stresses.
    d. Some parents enjoy social support from their resident children.

8. **Which type of grandparenting is the most common in the U.S.?**
    a. remote relationships
    b. companionate relationships
    c. involved relationships
    d. friendship relationships

9. **What effect does caring for an ill elderly parent have on the middle-aged adult?**
    a. It tends to increase some aspects of depression and to lower marital satisfaction.
    b. It tends to give the individual a sense of direction and purpose.
    c. It creates a sense of conflict and hostility.
    d. It creates a jaded sense of futility about the future.

10. **What happens to friendships in middle adulthood?**
    a. They become more numerous, but less satisfying.
    b. They become more same-sexed again, just like in childhood.
    c. The total number remains the same, but the degree of intimacy is lessened.
    d. The total number of friendships is lower.

11. **Which of the following statements is TRUE about the continuity and change of personality?**
    a. Masculinity and femininity are correlated with self-esteem in adults of all ages.
    b. Neuroticism declines as adults age.
    c. Personality consistently changes with age.
    d. Traits are gained across adulthood, but traits are not lost.

12. **Job satisfaction is _____.**
    a. only minimally linked to self-esteem
    b. typically at its peak in middle adulthood
    c. at a plateau in young adulthood, and decreases after that
    d. closely related to marital satisfaction in middle adulthood

13. **What is optimization?**
    a. pragmatic strategies for overcoming specific obstacles
    b. increases in job skills as a function of age
    c. deliberate practice of crucial abilities
    d. seeking jobs that most closely match our abilities

14. **Voluntary career changers _____.**
    a. are people who are in transition because of external reasons
    b. leave one career to pursue another for a variety of internal reasons
    c. are young adults in the trial stage of employment
    d. are older adults who retire

15. **Which of the following is a difference between Baby Boomers and their parents?**
    a. Baby Boomers expect to die in their mid-70s or later; their parents expect to die long after age 80.
    b. Baby Boomers saved for their retirement funds; their parents borrowed for their retirement investments.
    c. Baby Boomers put their nest eggs into the stock market; their parents put their funds for retirement in very safe investments.
    d. Baby Boomers expect to retire in their mid-60s; their parents expect to retire before age 60.

TRUE-FALSE QUESTIONS

Indicate whether each of the following statements is true or false.

_____
1.
Studies support Erikson's belief that generativity is related to mental health among middle-aged adults.

_____
2.
According to Levinson, accepting one's own mortality is one of the difficult tasks that middle-aged adults must face.

_____
3.
Skilled diplomacy is practiced more often by husbands than by wives, but it appears to be an effective technique for marital problem-solving no matter which spouse uses it.

_____
4.
Grandparents seem to be an especially important source of stability in the lives of children of divorced parents.

_____
5.
Among all ethnic groups, the role of grandfather is likely to be both broader and more intimate than that of grandmother.

_____
6.
The role of major caregiver for aging parents has little impact on a middle-aged adult's overall life satisfaction.

_____
7.
The indirect effects of job loss include changes in family relationships and loss of self-esteem.

_____
8.
The notion of retirement is relatively new and tends to be exclusive to industrialized cultures.

ESSAY QUESTIONS

1.   Discuss the issues involved in achieving generativity rather than stagnation in middle adulthood.

2.   Describe how caring for aging parents impacts overall life satisfaction.

3.   Discuss the indirect and direct relationship between job loss and emotional or physical distress.

WHEN YOU HAVE FINISHED . . . PUZZLE IT OUT

Across

5. Workers narrow their range of activities
6. Situation in which two or more roles are at least partially incompatible
9. Relationship in which grandparents are directly involved in everyday care of grandchildren
10. Experienced when a person's own qualities or skills do not measure up to the demands of some role
11. A behavior pattern in which middle-aged adults remain committed to goals that are difficult

Down

1. The content of a social position—the behaviors and characteristics expected of a person filling that position.
2. Workers deliberately "exercise" crucial abilities
3. A sense that one is making a valuable contribution to society
4. Relationship in which grandparents do not see their grandchildren often
6. Workers adopt pragmatic strategies for overcoming specific obstacles
7. A behavior pattern in which middle-aged adults adjust goals to enhance the likelihood of success
8. Relationship in which grandparents have frequent contact and warm interactions with grandchildren
10. Interlocking positions in a social system

Created by Puzzlemaker at DiscoverySchool.com

WHEN YOU HAVE FINISHED . . . RESEARCH PROJECT

Student Project 27: Social Networks among Middle-Aged Adults

It would be extremely interesting to repeat Project 16, except this time with middle-aged subjects. You should locate at least six adults between the ages of 40 and 65. They could be all men, all women, or three of each, and should cover the age range as much as possible. Obtain the appropriate informed consent from each, and follow the identical procedure as for Project 16. If a group of students in your class all complete this project, you will have a fascinating cross-sectional study.

If you have completed both Projects 16 and 17, compare the responses of the two age groups. Do your middle-aged subjects include fewer people in their three circles? Do they list fewer friends? Are their friends more likely to be in the first or second circle, rather than in the outermost circle? Any differences you can detect?

CHAPTER 16 ANSWER KEY

Practice Test #1 Theories of Social and Personality Development

1. T   2. T   3. T   4. F   5. T   6. F

Practice Test #2 Changes in Relationships and Personality

1. b   2. d   3. a   4. a   5. d   6. a   7. c   8. d

Practice Test #3 Mid-Life Career Issues

1. T   2. F   3. T   4. T   5. F   6. T   7. T   8. F   9. T   10. F

Comprehensive Practice Test

Multiple Choice Questions

1. b   2. b   3. c   4. a   5. b   6. c   7. d   8. b   9. a   10. d
11. b   12. b   13. c   14. b   15. c

True-False Questions

1. T   2. T   3. F   4. T   5. F   6. F   7. T   8. T

Essay Questions

1. ▪ Acquiring generativity involves an interest in establishing and guiding the next generation. It is expressed not only in bearing or rearing one's own children, but through teaching, serving as mentor, or taking on leadership roles in various civic, religious, or charitable organizations.
   ▪ The optimum expression of generativity requires turning outward from a preoccupation with self.
   ▪ Expressions of generativity appear to be normal middle-aged experiences that are relatively independent of ethnicity and economic factors.

2. ▪ Most adult children give more assistance to their parents than they did before, but also continue to see them regularly for ceremonial and celebratory occasions and to feel affection as well as filial responsibility.
   ▪ Within a group of siblings, the one most likely to take on the task of caregiving is the one who has no children still at home, is not working, not married, and lives closest to the aging parent. It is most often a daughter or a daughter-in-law.
   ▪ Caregivers are more depressed and have lower marital satisfaction. Those who care for frail elders are more often ill themselves or have some reduced efficiency of immune system functioning.

3. ▪ Direct: The financial strain of job loss contributes to heightened levels of anxiety and depression.
   ▪ Indirect: Include changes in family relationships and loss of self-esteem; marital relationships deteriorate rapidly after one or the other spouse has been laid off; the number of hostile or negative interactions increases, and the number of warm and supportive interactions declines; separation and divorce become much more common.

Puzzle It Out

Across

5. Selection
6. Conflict
9. Involved
10. Strain
11. Tenacious

Down

1. Role
2. Optimization
3. Generativity
4. Remote
6. Compensation
7. Flexible
8. Companionate
10. Statuses

POLICY QUESTION IV

WHAT TYPE OF COUPLES SHOULD BE SANCTIONED BY SOCIETY?

Learning Objective: Summarize the issues about the types of couples sanctioned by society (pp. 455-456).

1.   How did the sexual revolution of the 1960s and 1970s affect society's view of marriage?

2.   Distinguish between a registered domestic partnership and a civil union.

3.   State the case of the right-to-marry movement.

4.   State the case against the right-to-marry movement.

5.   Policies about the legal status of couples are different in every state. What are the relevant policies in your area? Student research could include answering the following questions:

   a.   How have policymakers in your area responded to the same-sex marriage movement? (go to http://www.stateline.org and http://www.gay-civil-unions.com to find out.) How much support does the movement have in your states' legislature and among the citizens of your state?

   b.   What do your classmates and friends think about the idea of covenant marriage?

   c.   Find our whether your city and/or state has a domestic partnership law. If so, does the law guarantee employer benefits such as health insurance coverage to domestic partners?

   d.   Interview a marriage therapist. What does this professional think about the effects of legal status on partners' commitment to one another, the quality of their relationship, and their development as individuals?

PHYSICAL AND COGNITIVE DEVELOPMENT IN LATE ADULTHOOD

BEFORE YOU READ . . . CHAPTER SUMMARY

Most older adults experience some degree of physical and cognitive decline. Thus, the experience of aging often involves learning to offset weaknesses, such as increasing forgetfulness, with strengths, such as practicality and inventiveness.

Variability in Late Adulthood

- The elderly are often classified as young-old (60-75), old-old (75-85), and oldest-old (85+). The oldest-old are the fastest-growing group of elderly. There are significant individual differences in aging among all three groups. Heredity, overall health, current and prior health habits (especially exercise) contribute to variability among the elderly. Regularly used skills decline more slowly than those that are used less frequently.
- Most elders view their health status positively. With increasing age, the proportion of elders whose health interferes with activities of living rises. Chronic diseases, such as arthritis and hypertension, afflict many older adults.

Physical Changes

- Neurons are less dense in the elderly than in younger adults, resulting in slower reaction times to a variety of stimuli.
- Changes in vision and hearing affect the lives of most elderly adults. The senses of smell and touch become less sensitive in the later years.
- Aging theorists suggest that there may be genetic limits on the human lifespan. Further, the cumulative effects of cell malfunctions may be responsible for primary aging.
- Behavior changes that result from physical changes include general slowing, changing patterns of eating and sleeping, and an increased number of falls. Most older adults continue to be sexually active, although the frequency of sexual activity decreases in late adulthood.

Mental Health

- Dementia becomes steadily more common in the late adult years. The most common type of dementia is Alzheimer's Disease. Its causes are not yet known.
- Mild forms of depression rise somewhat in the later years, but serious clinical depression is rare. African-American elders are less likely to be depressed than peers in other groups.

Cognitive Changes

- Cognitive changes result from the general slowing of the nervous system and perhaps from a loss of short-term memory capacity.
- Wisdom and creativity may be important aspects of cognitive functioning in old age.

AS YOU READ . . . LEARNING OBJECTIVES

After completing Chapter 17, you should be able to answer the following questions:

17.1   What factors contribute to life expectancy and longevity?

17.2   What variables contribute to individual differences in health among older adults?

17.3   How does the brain change in late adulthood?

17.4   What changes happen in the sensory organs?

17.5   How do theorists explain biological aging?

17.6   What are the behavioral effects of changes in the various body systems of older adults?

17.7   What is Alzheimer's disease, and how does it differ from other dementias?

17.8   What does research suggest about depression among older adults?

17.9   What kinds of memory differences distinguish older and younger adults?

17.10 What do theory and research on wisdom and creativity reveal about cognitive functioning in late adulthood?

AS YOU READ . . . TERM IDENTIFICATION

Activities of daily living (ADLs) (p. 487)

Alzheimer's disease (p. 496)

Cross-linking (p. 493)

Dementia (p. 496)

Frail elderly (p. 488)

Free radicals (p. 493)

Gerontology (p. 485)

Hayflick limit (p. 493)

Instrumental activities of daily living (IADLs) (p. 487)

Multi-infarct dementia (p. 498)

Programmed senescence theory (p. 493)

Satiety (p. 495)

Synaptic plasticity (p. 490)

Telomere (p. 493)

Terminal drop hypothesis (p. 493)

Tinnitus (p. 491)

Wisdom (p. 505)

AS YOU READ . . . GUIDED STUDY QUESTIONS

VARIABILITY IN LATE ADULTHOOD

Life Expectancy and Longevity (p. 485)

17.1   What factors contribute to life expectancy and longevity?

1.   Define gerontology (p. 485).

2.   Give examples of how life expectancy increases as adults get older.

3.   Distinguish among each of the following sub groups of elders by completing the following table:

Subgroup	Ages	Description
Young Old		

Subgroup	Ages	Description
Old Old		
Oldest Old		

4.   Trace the growth of the number of centenarians in the United States, from the beginning of the 20th century to the middle of the 21st century.

No Easy Answers: The Coming Demographic Crisis (p. 486)

5.   Why will there be a worldwide demographic crisis in the near future?

6.   What are the two options with respect to the pension plans in the U.S.?   State the pros and cons of each.

Health (pp. 486-489)

17.2   What variables contribute to the individual differences in health among older adults?

7.   Define the following terms:
        a.   activities of daily living (ADLs) (p. 487)

        b.   instrumental activities of daily living (IADLs) (p. 487)

        c.   frail elderly (p. 488)

8.   How do the majority of older adults regard their health?

9.   How does their optimistic view of their health protect older adults against the long-term effects of serious health threats such as strokes?

10.   How do gerontologists define disability?

11.   Give examples ADLs and IADLs to distinguish between the terms.

Term	Examples
Activities of Daily Living (ADLs	
Instrumental Activities of Daily Living (IADLs)	

12.   How do chronic health conditions such as hypertension and arthritis affect functioning in later adulthood?

13.   Summarize the racial and ethnic differences in late adulthood.

14.   What evidence exists to support the idea that longevity is inherited?

15.   Why is physical exercise said to be the most crucial health habit?

16.   How might calorie restriction and alternate day fasting moderate the effects of physical aging?

AFTER YOU READ . . . PRACTICE TEST #1
VARIATIONS IN LATE ADULTHOOD

Match the letter of the term in the right column with its description in the left column.

_____ 1.   Also known as high blood pressure.

_____ 2.   A person in his or her 80s.

_____ 3.   Self-help tasks such as bathing, dressing, and using the toilet.

_____ 4.   Elders aged 60-75.

_____ 5.   The expected lifespan of a species.

_____ 6.   The scientific study of aging.

_____ 7.   Older adults whose physical and/or mental impairments are so extensive that they cannot care for themselves.

_____ 8.   A method of moderating one's eating habits for decreasing calories.

a. Activities of daily living (ADLs)
b. alternative day fasting
c. arthritis
d. calorie restriction
e. Centenarian
f. Frail elderly
g. Gerontology
h. hypertension
i. Instrumental activities of daily living (IADLs)
j. Life expectancy
k. Octogenarian
l. Oldest old
m. Old old
n. Young old

PHYSICAL CHANGES

The Brain and Nervous System (pp. 490)

17.3   How does the brain change in late adulthood?

17.   Define synaptic plasticity (p. 490), and describe how it is related to dendritic loss.

18.   List and describe the four main changes in the brain during the adult years.

Change	Description

19.   How does education relate to dendritic density?

The Senses (pp. 490-492)

17.4   What changes happen in the sensory organs?

20.   Define tinnitus (p. 491)

21.   List and describe three problems with vision in late adulthood, in addition to presbyopia.

Vision Problem	Description

22.   Distinguish among the following terms:

Term	Description
Cataracts	
Glaucoma	
Macular Degeneration	

23.   State the gender difference in auditory problems of the elderly. How is the difference related to the work environment?

24.   Describe the components of hearing difficulties in late adulthood by completing the following table:

Change	Description
Loss of ability to hear high-frequency sounds	
Difficulties with word discrimination	
Problems hearing under noisy conditions	
Tinnitus	

25.   Describe the changes in the sense of taste associated with aging.

26.   How does the sense of smell change in old age?

27.   What sex difference accompanies the change in the sense of smell? What is the environmental component that accompanies it?

28.   What changes in the sense of touch can occur in old age?

Theories of Biological Aging (pp. 492-494)

17.5   How do theorists explain biological aging?

29.   Define the following terms:
        a.   Hayflick limit (p. 493)

        b.   telomere (p. 493)

        c.   programmed senescence theory (p. 493)

        d.   cross-linking (p. 493)

        e.   free radicals (p. 493)

        f.   terminal drop hypothesis (p. 494)

30.   Describe each of the following theories of biological aging:

Theory	*Description*
Hayflick Limit	
Programmed Senescence Theory	
Cross-Linking	
Free Radicals	
Terminal Drop Hypothesis	

31.   Distinguish between oxygen free radicals and antioxidants. Include how they impact health.

Oxygen Free Radicals	Antioxidants

Behavioral Effects of Physical Changes (pp. 494-496)

17.6   What are the behavioral effects of changes in the various body systems of older adults?

32.   What is the biggest single behavioral effect of age-related physical changes?

33.   List three factors that explain the general slowing down in late adulthood, and explain how general slowing down affects functioning in late adulthood.

Factor	Description

34.   How do age-related physical changes impact complex motor activity, such as driving?

35.   How do changes in temperature sensitivity affect an older adult's health?

36.   Describe the changes in sleeping patterns in late adulthood, and how it affects functioning.

37.   Define satiety (p. 495), and explain how it is involved in functioning in late adulthood.

38.   How do each of the following affect functioning in late adulthood?

Factor	Effect
Stamina	
Dexterity	
Balance	

39.   How is sexual activity affected by the cumulative physical changes of aging?

AFTER YOU READ . . . PRACTICE TEST #2
PHYSICAL CHANGES

1. **Which of the following is NOT a major brain change during the adult years?**
   a. a change in dendritic density
   b. increase in brain weight
   c. slower synaptic speed
   d. loss of gray matter

2. **The redundancy in the nervous system that ensures that it is always possible for a nerve impulse to move from cell to cell is called _____.**
   a. brain weight
   b. dendritic density
   c. pruning
   d. synaptic plasticity

3. **Which of the following tends to happen to vision as we age?**
   a. increased blood flow to the eyes resulting in blurred peripheral vision
   b. an expanded field of vision, though with less lens focus
   c. an enlarged blind spot
   d. an increase in the density of the optic nerve

4. **From which of the following would a man be more likely to suffer than a woman in late adulthood?**
   a. auditory problems
   b. cataracts
   c. Alzheimer's disease
   d. depression

5. **Each of the following is a component of hearing difficulties in the elderly EXCEPT _____.**
   a. hearing under noisy conditions
   b. difficulties with word discriminations
   c. the ability to hear high-frequency sounds
   d. the ability to hear low-frequency sounds

6. **Which of the following appears to be true about the sense of taste?**
   a. Older adults prefer salty foods because of a decline in taste discrimination.
   b. The ability to taste the four basic flavors does not decline over the years.
   c. Taste receptors are never replaced once they are lost.
   d. The sense of taste declines or increases depending on life experiences.

7. **_____ occurs when undesirable chemical bonds form between proteins or fats.**
   a. The formation of free radicals
   b. The production of antioxidants
   c. Cross-linking
   d. Senescence

8.   _____ inhibit the formation of free radicals or promote chemical processes that help the body defend against them.
   a.   Antioxidants
   b.   Collagens
   c.   Senescence
   d.   Satiety

9.   The hypothesis that mental and physical functioning decline drastically only in the few years immediately preceding death is called the _____.
   a.   repair of genetic material hypothesis
   b.   terminal drop hypotheses
   c.   programmed senescence hypothesis
   d.   satiety hypothesis

10.   Older adults _____.
   a.   become "night people" instead of "morning people"
   b.   wake up less frequently than younger adults, but they don't sleep as deeply
   c.   take more naps because they need more sleep than younger adults
   d.   show decreases in rapid eye movement (REM) sleep

MENTAL HEALTH

Alzheimer's Disease and Other Dementias (pp. 496-498)

17.7 **What is Alzheimer's disease, and how does it differ from the other dementias?**

40. Define the following terms:
    a. dementia (p. 496)

    b. Alzheimer's disease (p. 496)

    c. multi-infarct dementia (p. 498)

41. Trace the symptoms of Alzheimer's as the disease progresses.

Stage	Description
Early Stage	
Loss of memory for Recent Events	
Late Stage	

42. How is Alzheimer's disease definitively diagnosed?

43. What are neurofibrillary tangles?

44. Describe the most common gene implicated in Alzheimer's disease.

45. How is multi-infarct dementia different from Alzheimer's disease?

Multi-Infarct Dementia	Alzheimer's Disease

46.   List 12 other causes of dementia.

1.	2.	3.
4.	5.	6.
7.	8.	9.
10.	11.	12.

47.   What are the group differences in the rates of dementias?

Research Report: Mild Cognitive Impairment and Alzheimer's Disease (p. 497)

48.   Distinguish between mild cognitive impairment (MCI) and age-associated cognitive decline (AACD).

Mild Cognitive Impairment (MCI)	*Age-Associated Cognitive Decline (AACD)*

Depression (pp. 499-502)

17.8   What does research suggest about depression among older adults?

49.   How does the definition of depression impact the estimates of its prevalence?

50.   List five risk factors for depression.
-
-
-
-
-

51.   Why is health status the strongest predictor of depression?

52.   How does gender affect the rate of depression?

53.   How do poverty and education affect the risk of depression?

Poverty	Education

54.   What factors impact the ethnic differences in depression? What cultural differences may impact the low incidence of depression among African-Americans?

55.   List the factors that predict suicide at all ages.

56.   Describe the therapies for depression in older adults. Why is the appropriate use of antidepressant medications among the elderly critical?

57.   Give examples of how each of the following can help prevent depression in older adults by completing the following table:

Factor	Example
Social Involvement	
Support of Spiritual Needs	

The Real World: Computers in Rehabilitation Programs (p. 500)

58.   List several ways that computers are used in the treatment of various neurological disorders affecting the elderly.

AFTER YOU READ . . . PRACTICE TEST #3
MENTAL HEALTH

Indicate whether each of the following statements is true or false.

_____   Dementia is the leading cause of institutionalization of the elderly in the U.S.
1.

_____   The early stages of Alzheimer's disease usually become evident very rapidly.
2.

_____   At autopsy, the brains of Alzheimer's victims are far more likely to contain extensive
3.   neurofibrilary tangles than the brains of individuals with other kinds of dementia.

_____   Dementia can be caused by depression, cardiovascular disease, and alcohol abuse.
4.

_____   The risk factors for depression among the elderly include inadequate social support,
5.   inadequate income, and emotional loss.

_____   The more disabling conditions older adults have, the fewer depressive symptoms they
6.   have.

_____   Elderly white men are less likely to commit suicide than any other group in the U.S.
7.

_____   Social involvement may be important in preventing depression in the elderly.
8.

COGNITIVE CHANGES

Memory (pp. 502-505)

17.9   *What kinds of memory differences distinguish older and younger adults?*

59.   What are the basic rules that apply to memory processes among both older and younger adults?

60.   How is short-term memory affected in late adulthood?

61.   Distinguish between retrospective memory and prospective memory, and compare the ability of older adults with younger adults to use each.

Retrospective Memory	*Prospective Memory*

62.   How can strategy learning improve memory?

63.   Describe how everyday memory is impacted in late adulthood.

64.   What is source memory?

65.   Summarize Timothy Salthouse's research on the slower reaction times in older adults.

Wisdom and Creativity (pp. 505-506)

17.10   *What do theory and research on wisdom and creativity reveal about cognitive functioning in late adulthood?*

66.   Define wisdom. (p. 505)

67.   List Paul Baltes' five criteria that are central to wisdom as it relates to solving practical life
       problems.

   ▪

   ▪

   ▪

   ▪

   ▪

68.   Describe Baltes' findings about wisdom in later adulthood.

69.   Describe Gene Cohen's four-stage theory of mid-to late-life creativity by completing the
       following table:

Age	Stage	Description
50s		
60s		
70s		
80s		

AFTER YOU READ . . . PRACTICE TEST #4
COGNITIVE CHANGES

Fill in the blanks with the best answers.

1. The same basic rules apply to memory processes among both older and younger adults: recognition is easier than _____, tasks that require speed are _____, and metamemory skills are _____.

2. Older adults typically perform more poorly than younger adults on tasks involving _____ (recalling something in the past); older adults' performance on _____ (those that require individuals to remember to do something on the future) depends on the type of task involved.

3. Remembering where they heard something is an example of _____.

4. Virtually all experts agree with Salthouse that loss of _____ is a key aspect of the process of memory decline.

5. _____ reflects understanding of "universal truths" or basic laws or patterns.

6. Baltes' five criteria of wisdom are _____, _____, _____, _____, and _____.

7. The speed of accessing _____ remains constant across adulthood, unlike speed of information processing in other domains.

8. Cohen's four stages are _____, _____, _____, and _____.

AFTER YOU READ . . . CRITICAL REFLECTION EXERCISE

Longevity

Utilizing information from the text, provide complete responses to the following issues. Whenever possible, cite specific information from the readings to support your responses.

1.   Name and discuss three things that you do that you think will INCREASE your chances of living a longer life. Why do you do these things? (i.e., were they taught to you by your parents? Did you learn them on your own?). How, specifically, do you think they will affect your longevity?

2.   Name and discuss three things that you do that you think will DECREASE your chances of living a longer life. Why do you do these things?(or where did these things come from - like genetics?) How, specifically, do you think they will affect your longevity?

3.   What four pieces of advice would you give a person on how to slow the effects of aging? What are these effects and what specific things can be done to slow them?

4.   Imagine that you are being hired by a Senior Citizen Living Community to develop an activity program for the adults. Describe two activities that you would develop and explain why you would develop them the way you have. What specific goals do you have for each of these activities? How would you explain these goals to the individuals living in the community?

AFTER YOU READ . . . COMPREHENSIVE PRACTICE TEST
MULTIPLE-CHOICE QUESTIONS

1. **The scientific study of aging is called _____.**
    a.   senescence
    b.   the Hayflick limit
    c.   life expectancy
    d.   gerontology

2. **Which of the following appears to be true about physical exercise?**
    a.   it is more important in young adulthood than any other age
    b.   it may be more important in older adulthood than other ages
    c.   even with moderate exercising, genetics influences overall health more
    d.   men benefit more from physical exercise than women

3. **What happens to dendritic density with aging?**
    a.   it continues to thicken
    b.   more redundant neural pathways are added
    c.   it begins to thin as dendrites are lost and not replaced
    d.   the loss of density is equally distributed throughout the brain

4. **An example of synaptic plasticity is _____.**
    a.   expansion of dendritic tangling that leads to disorders such as Alzheimer's disease
    b.   the elimination of redundant neural pathways
    c.   the brain's ability to recall information memorized years ago
    d.   the brain's ability to find the shortest routes between two neurons

5. **What is tinnitus?**
    a.   a tendon problem associated with overexertion
    b.   a recurring nasal problem that results in snoring
    c.   a persistent ringing in the ears
    d.   a gradual decline in taste sensitivity as a result of smoking

6. **Which of the following is consistent with the Hayflick limit?**
    a.   the maximum number of times a cell can divide before degenerating
    b.   understanding that human beings have a set maximum age limit
    c.   life expectancy is limited more by environment than by genetics
    d.   cognitive changes lead to physical changes which lead to death

7. **The view that age-related declines are the result of species-specific genes for aging is called _____.**
    a.   life expectancy
    b.   cross-linking
    c.   terminal drop hypothesis
    d.   programmed senescence theory

8.   **What is a free radical?**
        a.   an outspoken political deviant
        b.   a derivative of beta carotene
        c.   a molecule or atom that possesses an unpaired electron
        d.   a toxin or carcinogen that floats in the body causing damage

9.   **Which of the following statements about automobile accidents is true?**
        a.   Older adults have more accidents than younger drivers because they drive too fast.
        b.   Older adults have fewer accidents than any other age group.
        c.   Older adults have more accidents than younger drivers, but they are usually not fatal.
        d.   Older adults have more accidents per mile than younger drivers, but fewer total accidents.

10.   **What is the definition of dementia?**
        a.   a sudden loss of memory
        b.   a distortion of place or time
        c.   a neurological disorder involving problems with memory and thinking
        d.   senility-induced paranoia

11.   **Each of the following is a motor function that is associated with physical changes in later adulthood EXCEPT _____.**
        a.   satiety
        b.   balance
        c.   stamina
        d.   dexterity

12.   **Dementia caused by a series of small strokes is called _____.**
        a.   Alzheimer's disease
        b.   multi-infarct dementia
        c.   Parkinson's disease
        d.   presenile disease

13.   **Which of the following group of elders has the highest rate of suicide completion in the U.S.?**
        a.   African-American men
        b.   Asian-American men
        c.   white-American men
        d.   Hispanic-American men

14.   **Each of the following is one of Paul Baltes' criteria of wisdom EXCEPT _____.**
        a.   understanding relevance of context
        b.   semantic knowledge
        c.   factual knowledge
        d.   procedural knowledge

15.   **Which of the following represents the correct order of phases in Gene Cohen's theory of mid- to late life creativity?**
        a.   reevaluation phase, liberation phase, summing-up phase, encore phase
        b.   liberation phase, reevaluation phase, encore phase, summing-up phase
        c.   reevaluation phase, summing up phase, encore phase, liberation phase
        d.   summing-up phase, liberation phase, encore phase, reevaluation phase

TRUE-FALSE QUESTIONS

Indicate whether each of the following statements is true or false.

_____
1.   The "young old" are the fastest growing segment of the population in the United States.

_____
2.   The sense of smell clearly deteriorates in old age.

_____
3.   A telomere is a string of repetitive DNA at the tip of each chromosome that appears to serve as a kind of timekeeping mechanism.

_____
4.   The terminal drop hypothesis states that mental and physical functioning decline drastically in the ten years preceding death.

_____
5.   The most common gene implicated in Alzheimer's disease is on chromosome 21.

_____
6.   Depressed women outnumber depressed men two to one among the elderly.

_____
7.   Task-specific knowledge seems to make a difference in the everyday memory among the elderly.

_____
8.   Baltes' research on wisdom found that intelligence and professional experience, rather than age, are correlated with responses to the dilemma task.

ESSAY QUESTIONS

1.   Discuss the finding that older adults who continue to challenge themselves with complex mental activities can delay, or even reverse, the normal decline in brain mass that is part of primary aging.

2.   Discuss the factors involved in the general slowing down in late adulthood.

3.   Is wisdom more likely to be found in middle-aged and older adults? Defend your answer with examples.

WHEN YOU HAVE FINISHED . . . PUZZLE IT OUT

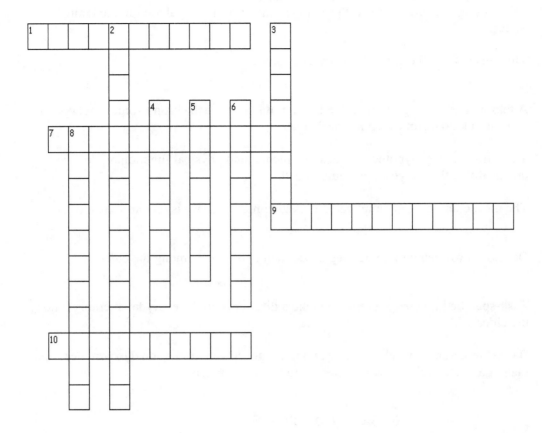

Across
1. The scientific study of aging
7. A person in his or her 80s
9. Foods that inhibit the formation of free radicals
10. A limitation in an individual's ability to perform certain roles and tasks

Down
2. Tangles found in the brains of individuals with Alzheimer's disease
3. Neurological disorders involving problems with memory and thinking
4. String of DNA at the tip of each chromosome that serves as a timekeeping mechanism
5. The feeling of fullness that follows a meal
6. Persistent ringing in the ears
8. A person over 100 years of age

Created by Puzzlemaker at DiscoverySchool.com

WHEN YOU HAVE FINISHED . . . RESEARCH PROJECT

Student Project 28: Facts on Aging Quiz

Procedure

For this project locate at least six adults, of any age below 65. Each of your subjects must, naturally, provide written permission for participation in this project, following procedures specified by your instructor.

Tell each subject that you are interested in knowing how much people of different ages know about aging and the aged in United States. Ask each one to answer the 25 items, the Facts On Aging Quiz. (If your subject wishes to know the correct answers afterward, the scoring is easy: alternating pairs are true or false. 1 & 2 are true, 3 & 4 are false, 5 & 6 are true, etc., and item 25 is true. Item 21 was true in 1981, when this was originally written; it was not true in 1992 when it was revised.) After each subject has completed the items, mark on the back of each sheet the subject's gender and age. Do NOT put the subject's name anywhere on the sheet.

Analysis and Report

Determine the average number of correct answers for your subjects. Were there differences in knowledge as a function of either age or gender of the subjects? Also analyze each item: Were there more incorrect answers to some items than others? Does it seem important to correct some of the misconceptions?

References

Duerson, M. C., Thomas, J. W., Chang, J., & Stevens, C. B. (1992). Medical students' knowledge and misconceptions about aging: Responses to Palmore's facts on aging quizzes. *The Gerontologist, 32,* 171-4.

Palmore, E. B. (1981). The fact on aging quiz: Part two. *The Gerontologist, 21,* 431-7.

Palmore, E. B. (1992). Knowledge about aging: What we know and need to know. *The Gerontologist, 32,* 149-150.

Facts on Aging Quiz

Please mark each item either "T" for True or "F" for False.

_____ 1. A person's height tends to decline in old age.
_____ 2. More older persons (over 65) have chronic illnesses that limit their activity than do younger persons.
_____ 3. Older persons have more acute (short-term) illnesses than persons under 65.
_____ 4. Older persons have more injuries in the home than do persons under 65.
_____ 5. Older workers have less absenteeism than do younger workers.
_____ 6. The life expectancy of blacks at age 65 is about the same as whites.
_____ 7. The life expectancy of men at age 65 is about the same as women.
_____ 8. Medicare pays over half of the medical expenses for the aged.
_____ 9. Social Security benefits automatically increase with inflation.
_____ 10. Supplementary Security Income guarantees a minimum income for needy aged.
_____ 11. The aged do not get their proportionate share (about 11%) of the nation's income.
_____ 12 The aged have higher rates of criminal victimization than persons under 65.
_____ 13. The aged are more fearful of crime than are persons under 65.
_____ 14. The aged are the most law abiding of all adult groups according to official statistics.
_____ 15. There are two widows for each widower among the aged.
_____ 16. More of the aged vote than any other age group.
_____ 17. There are proportionately more older persons in public office than in the total population.
_____ 18. The proportion of blacks among the aged is growing.
_____ 19. Participation in voluntary organizations (churches and clubs) tends to decline among the healthy aged.
_____ 20. The majority of aged live alone.
_____ 21. About 3% more of the aged have incomes below the official poverty level than does the rest of the population.
_____ 22. The rate of poverty among aged blacks is about 3 times as high as among aged whites.
_____ 23. Older persons who reduce their activity tend to be happier than those who remain active.
_____ 24. When the last child leaves the home, the majority of parents have serious problems adjusting to their "empty-nest."
_____ 25. The proportion of widowed persons is decreasing among the aged.

WHEN YOU HAVE FINISHED . . . RESEARCH PROJECT

Student Project 29: Definitions of Wisdom

For this project, you will need to locate two adults in each of the three broad age ranges of adulthood defined in the text: early adulthood, middle adulthood, and late adulthood.

Procedure

After obtaining suitable informed consent, following whatever procedure your instructor specifies, ask each subject the following four basic questions, with suitable probes:

1.   What is your definition of wisdom? (If the individual gives you a very brief answer, or one you do not understand, probe by asking him or her to tell you more about it. If that still doesn't elicit anything useful, ask "How would a wise person behave that would be different from the way a non-wise person would act?)

2.   Do you know people who are wise, according to your definition? How old are they? What gender? (Ask the subject to describe the wise individual(s), and say how they display their wisdom.)

3.   Do you think that wisdom is something that only comes with old age, or can a young person or a middle-aged person be wise?

4.   How do you think a person gets to be wise?

Analysis and Report

Compare the answers given by your six subjects in whatever way makes sense to you. Are there common themes in their definitions of wisdom, or in their ideas about origins of wisdom? What are the ages and genders of those named as wise?

If a number of students in your class complete this project, you can combine data, which will give you a cross-sectional comparison.

CHAPTER 17 ANSWER KEY

Practice Test #1 Variability in Late Adulthood

1. h   2. k   3. a   4. n   5. j   6. g   7. f   8. d

Practice Test #2 Physical Changes

1. b   2. d   3. c   4. a   5. d   6. b   7. c   8. a   9. b   10. d

Practice Test #3 Mental Health

1. T   2. F   3. T   4. T   5. T   6. F   7. F   8. T

Practice Test #4 Cognitive Changes

1. recall; more difficult; important to memory functions
2. retrospective memory; prospective memory tasks
3. source memory
4. speed
5. Wisdom
6. factual knowledge, procedural knowledge, understanding relevance of context, understanding relevance of values, recognition that it is impossible to know in advance how any decision will ultimately affect one's life
7. wisdom-related knowledge
8. reevaluation phase, liberation phase, summing-up phase, encore phase

Comprehensive Practice Test

Multiple Choice Questions

1. d   2. b   3. c   4. d   5. c   6. a   7. d   8. c   9. d   10. c
11. a   12. b   13. c   14. b   15. a

True-False Questions

1. F   2. T   3. T   4. F   5. F   6. T   7. T   8. T

Essay Questions

1. ▪ Answers should include notion of "use it or lose it" as well as self-selection, social class, education, and physical health.

2. ▪ Answers should include dendritic loss, arthritic changes in the joints, loss of elasticity in the muscles, changes in vision and hearing.

3. ▪ Answers will vary, but should include a definition of wisdom and examples to support the answer.

Puzzle It Out

Across
1. gerontology
7. octogenarian
9. antioxidants
10. disability

Down
2. neurofibrillary
3. dementia
4. telomere
5. satiety
6. tinnitus
8. centenarian

CHAPTER 18

SOCIAL AND PERSONALITY DEVELOPMENT IN LATE ADULTHOOD

BEFORE YOU READ . . . CHAPTER SUMMARY

Maintaining a sense of personal uniqueness can be especially challenging for older adults, who are often stereotyped by others as sick, disabled, or incompetent. Moreover, changes in social roles and relationships are just as important as the physical changes of late adulthood. Thus, late adulthood is perhaps the most socially and personally challenging period of life.

Theories of Social and Personality Development

- Erikson's ego integrity stage has been influential in studies of social and personality functioning in older adults; however, research does not support his view that ego integrity is essential to mental health in old age.
- Most older adults are not disengaged from the social world and seem to benefit from social involvement as much as those who are younger.

Individual Differences

- The successful aging paradigm emphasizes the degree of control individuals have over how they experience the aging process. Critics claim that emphasis on successful aging causes disabled elders to appear to be incompetent.
- Religious coping, defined both in social and psychological terms, appears to be important to health and well-being in late adulthood.

Social Relationships

- Most unmarried elders live alone, and the majority prefer this living arrangement.
- Older adults who are married exhibit high levels of relationship satisfaction. Many elderly spouses are primary caretakers for a spouse who is ill or disabled. The positive effects of marriage seem to be greater for men than for women, as is true at younger ages.
- Most older adults see their adult children regularly and enjoy satisfying relationships with them. Sibling relationships may be more positive than at younger ages. Contact with friends appears to be an important component of life satisfaction among the elderly.
- Women have larger social networks than men. Across ethnicities, African Americans have larger networks than members of other groups.

Career Issues in Late Life

- In most Western developed countries, adults retire in their early 60s. The timing of retirement is affected by an individual's health, economic circumstances, family responsibilities, and job satisfaction. Most of the elderly have adequate incomes, despite declines at retirement. Women and minorities are more likely to be poor in old age.
- Some elders choose not to retire and continue to be productive in their occupations. Research suggests that older adults can learn new job skills just as well as younger adults, although they do so at a slower pace.

AS YOU READ . . . LEARNING OBJECTIVES

After completing Chapter 18, you should be able to answer the following questions:

18.1   What does research say about Erikson's stage of ego integrity versus despair?
18.2   What are the main ideas of activity, disengagement, and continuity theory?
18.3   How is successful aging manifested in the lives of older adults?
18.4   How does religious coping influence physical and mental health in late adulthood?
18.5   What are the living arrangements of most elderly people in the United States and in other industrialized countries?
18.6   How do intimate partnerships contribute to development in late adulthood?
18.7   What is the significance of family relationships and friendships for older adults?
18.8   What are some gender and ethnic differences in older adults' social networks?
18.9   What factors contribute to the decision to retire?
18.10   How does retirement affect income, health, attitudes, emotions, mobility, and social relationships?
18.11   What does research suggest about the decision not to retire?

AS YOU READ . . . TERM IDENTIFICATION

Activity theory (p. 514)
Aging in place (p. 520)
Amenity move (p. 532)
Compensatory (kinship) migration (p. 532)
Continuity theory (p. 515)
Disengagement theory (p. 515)
Ego integrity (p. 513)

Institutional migration (p. 532)
Life review (p. 514)
Religious coping (p. 518)
Reminiscence (p. 514)
Successful aging (p. 516)
Volunteerism (p. 517)

AS YOU READ . . . GUIDED STUDY QUESTIONS

THEORIES OF SOCIAL AND PERSONALITY DEVELOPMENT

Erikson's Stage of Ego Integrity versus Despair (pp. 513-514)

18.1   What does research say about Erikson's stage of ego integrity versus despair?

1.   Define the following terms:
    a.   ego integrity (p. 513)

    b.   reminiscence (p. 514)

    c.   life review (p. 514)

2.   Why is reminiscence important?

3.   Describe how reminiscence is a healthy part of achieving ego integrity.

4.   How is a life review related to ego integrity versus despair?

Other Theories of Late-Life Psychological Functioning (pp. 514-515)

18.2   What are the main ideas of activity, disengagement, and continuity theory?

5.   Define the following terms, so as to distinguish between them:
      a.   activity theory (p. 514)

      b.   disengagement theory (p. 515)

      c.   continuity theory (p. 515)

6.   How does the Baltes' ideas about selection, optimization, and compensation theory relate to the elderly?

7.   List the main ideas of each of the theories listed below.

Theory	*Main Ideas*
Activity Theory	
Disengagement Theory	
Continuity Theory	

AFTER YOU READ . . . PRACTICE TEST #1
THEORIES OF SOCIAL AND PERSONALITY DEVELOPMENT

Indicate whether each of the following statements is true or false.

_____
1. To achieve ego integrity, the older adult must come to terms with who she is and has been, how her life was lived, the choices that she made, the opportunities gained and lost.

_____
2. Young adults reminisce less often than middle-aged or older adults.

_____
3. A life review results in both positive and negative emotional outcomes.

_____
4. According to the Baltes, as adults get older, they maintain high levels of performance by focusing on their weaknesses.

_____
5. More social involvement in late adulthood is linked to better outcomes, even among elders who suffer from disabilities.

_____
6. According to continuity theory, the primary means by which elders adjust to aging is by engaging in the same kinds of activities that interested and challenged them in their earlier years.

INDIVIDUAL DIFFERENCES

The Successful Aging Paradigm (pp. 516-518)

18.3   How is successful aging manifested in the lives of older adults?

8.   Define the following terms:
   a.   successful aging (p. 516)

   b.   volunteerism (p. 517)

9.   List and describe the five components of successful aging (Table 18.1). Give examples of each.

Component	Description	Example

10.   What is the difference between a paradigm and a theory?

11.   List the factors that predict health and physical functioning across the lifespan.

12.   How is cognitive functioning linked to education?

13.   Define and give examples of cognitive adventurousness.

Definition	*Examples*

14.   Give examples of why older adults giving support (not just receiving it) is important to successful aging.

15.   Explain how volunteerism is beneficial to older adults.

16.   What is life satisfaction?

17.   Why is a person's perception of her own situation more important than objective measures of life satisfaction?

18.   List the criticisms of the successful aging paradigm.

Religious Coping (pp. 518-520)

18.4   How does religions coping influence physical and mental health in late adulthood?

19.   Define religious coping. (p. 518).

20.   List the benefits of religious coping found among African Americans.

21.   What are the sex differences in religious coping?

22.   Give an example of the positive benefit of religious coping.

23.   List the benefits of attendance at religious services to the elderly.

24.   Describe the alternative explanations of religious coping.

AFTER YOU READ . . . PRACTICE TEST #2
INDIVIDUAL DIFFERENCES

Fill in the blank with the best answers.

1. In recent years, one of the dominant themes in gerontology literature has been the concept of

    _____.

2. Life-long health habits contribute to successful aging, but individual's responses to the

    _____ also matter.

3. In addition to education, the complexity of the _____ older adults are willing to take on influences their cognitive functioning.

4. _____ is a willingness to learn new things, and is a component of successful aging.

5. Social engagement contributes to successful aging because it provides opportunities for older

    adults to _____.

6. _____, performing unpaid work for altruistic reasons, has been linked to successful aging.

7. _____, or a sense of personal well-being, is also an important component of successful aging.

8. Psychologists use the term _____ to refer to the tendency to turn to religious beliefs and institutions in times of stress or trouble.

SOCIAL RELATIONSHIPS

Living Arrangements (pp. 520-523)

14.5   What are the living arrangements of most elderly people in the United Sates and in other industrialized counties?

25.   Define aging in place (p. 520).

26.   What modifications might be made to facilitate an elder aging in place?

27.   List and describe factors that influence an older adult's decision to live with an adult child.

Factor	Description

28.   List and describe four residential options for older adults.

Option	Description

Research Report: Filial Piety (p. 522)

29.   What is filial piety?

30.   List factors involved in the motivation of Westerners to provide care for their elders.

No Easy Answer: Deciding on Nursing Home Care (p. 523)

31.   What factors influence the decision to more an elder to a nursing home?

32.   List six criteria for evaluating a long-term care facility.
   ▪

   ▪

   ▪

   ▪

   ▪

   ▪

Partnership (pp. 524-525)

18.6   How do intimate partnerships contribute to development in late adulthood?
33.   Describe marital satisfaction in the late adult years.

34.   List the advantages of being married in late adulthood.

The Real World: Elder Abuse (p. 524)

35.   What are some types of elder abuse in addition to physical abuse?

36.   List the characteristics of a likely victim of abuse.

Family Relationships and Friendships (pp. 526-527)

18.7   What is the significance of family relationships and friendships for older adults?

37.   Describe the contacts older adults have with adult children

38.   Identify the effects of older adults' relationships with adult children.

39.   Describe the changes in the relationships of older adults with their grandchildren and with their siblings.

40.   Why are friends important to older adults? What impact do friends have on the lives of the elderly?

Gender and Ethnic Differences in Social Networks (p. 527-528)

18.8   What are some gender and ethnic differences in older adults' social networks?

41.   Compare the social networks of women and men in late adulthood.

42.   What is meant by the term "fictive kin?"

43.   Describe the ethnic differences in social networks of older adults.

AFTER YOU READ . . . PRACTICE TEST #3
SOCIAL RELATIONSHIPS

1. **Making modifications to a non-institutional living environment to accommodate an older adult's needs is called _____.**
   a. a continuing-care retirement community
   b. an independent living community
   c. an assisted living facility
   d. aging in place

2. **Each of the following is a factor influencing an older adult's decision to live with an adult child EXCEPT _____.**
   a. ethnicity
   b. health
   c. characteristics of the elder
   d. income

3. **An apartment complex or housing development in which all the residents are over a certain age, typically 55 or 60, is called _____.**
   a. an assisted living facility
   b. an independent living community
   c. a continuing-care retirement community
   d. a skilled nursing facility

4. **Which of the following types of residential options provides the most flexibility and social continuity?**
   a. a continuing-care retirement community
   b. an assisted living facility
   c. a skilled nursing facility
   d. a n independent living community

5. **Which of the following words best applies to long-term marriages in late adulthood?**
   a. passionate
   b. committed
   c. intense
   d. romantic

6. **Which of the following statements about elders' contact with adult children is TRUE?**
   a. Most elders see their children out of a sense of obligation or duty.
   b. Most older adults see their children as rarely as once a month or less.
   c. Most older adults describe their relationship with their adult children in positive terms.
   d. Most elders receive very little aid from their adult children.

7. **Each of the following statements about elders' friendships is true EXCEPT _____.**
   a. Friendships gain importance in their lives as elders age.
   b. Contact with friends has a significant impact on overall satisfaction.
   c. Friends can provide the same sense of generational solidarity that siblings may provide.
   d. The number of friendships increases dramatically after age 65.

CAREER ISSUES IN LATE LIFE

Timing of and Reasons for Retirement (pp. 528-529)

18.9   What factors contribute to the decision to retire?

44.   How does each of the following factors affect a person's decision to retire?

Factor	Affect of Decision to Retire
Age	
Poor Health	
Family Composition	

Factor	Affect of Decision to Retire
Work Influence	
Gender	

Effects of Retirement (pp. 529-533)

19.10   How does retirement affect income, health, attitudes, emotions, mobility, and social relationships?

45.   Define each of the following terms:
    a.   amenity move (p. 532)
    b.   compensatory (kinship) move (p. 532)

    c.   institutional migration (p. 532)

46.   How is income affected by retirement?

47.   Identify the factors that influence the poverty rates among the elderly.

48.   How does retirement affect the health and overall life satisfaction of older adults?

49.   What is the best predictor of life satisfaction in late adulthood?

50.   Describe each of the three types of moves that older adults make.

Type of Move	Description
Amenity Move	
Compensatory (Kinship) Move	
Institutional Migration	

Choosing Not to Retire (pp. 533-534)

18.11   What does research suggest about the decision not to retire?

51.   Describe the two categories of men who are most likely not to retire.

52.   List the factors that predict learning success in older and younger adults.

53.   How are supervisors likely to rate older adults with respect to job functioning?

AFTER YOU READ . . . PRACTICE TEST #4
CAREER ISSUES IN LATE LIFE

Indicate whether each of the following statements is true or false.

_____ 1. The normal age of retirement is 65.

_____ 2. Poor health lowers the average age of retirement by one to three years.

_____ 3. Persons who are still supporting minor children retire earlier than do those in the post-parental stage.

_____ 4. Those who like their work and are highly committed to it retire later than do those who are less gratified by their work.

_____ 5. Extensive pre-retirement planning seems to be more important to men than women.

_____ 6. Overall, retirement seem to have positive effects on the lives of older adults.

_____ 7. Over the past several decades, poverty rates among the elderly have increased substantially.

_____ 8. Those who respond least well to retirement are those who had the least control over the decision.

_____ 9. Amenity moves usually occur early, kinship or compensatory migration is likely to occur in middle to late old age, and institutional migration clearly occurs late in life.

_____ 10. Supervisors typically give older adults higher ratings than younger adults.

AFTER YOU READ ... CRITICAL REFLECTION EXERCISE

Elderly Adults

Utilizing information from the text, provide complete responses to the following issues. Whenever possible, cite specific information from the readings to support your responses.

1.   Think about where your life has gone.
   - Discuss three things that you think will lead to feelings of integrity for you as you age. Why will these lead to feelings of integrity? Is there anything you would do to change these things? If so, how?
   - Discuss three things that you think might interfere with your developing feelings of integrity as you age. Why will these interfere with developing feelings of integrity? Is there anything you would do to change these things? If so, how?

2.   Imagine that you have a six-year-old child. She is asking you questions about why Grandma cannot do the things that other adults can do. How would you answer her questions? Suggest at least three things you would tell her.

3.   You are working as a nurse and are approached by a family member of one of your patients. This person's father has just been diagnosed with Alzheimer's but he does not know anything about the disease. Describe the suspected brain changes that may lead to Alzheimer's. What advice would you give this person about what effect these cognitive deficits will have on his father? What advice would you give this man on what can be done to help the family adjust to these cognitive changes?

AFTER YOU READ . . . COMPREHENSIVE PRACTICE TEST
MULTIPLE-CHOICE QUESTIONS

1.   **Reflecting on past experiences is called _____.**
      a.   senility
      b.   senescence
      c.   reminiscence
      d.   a waste of time

2.   **Which of the following is NOT part of the disengagement theory?**
      a.   shrinkage of life space
      b.   grandiose reminiscence
      c.   increased individuality
      d.   acceptance of old age changes

3.   **Which of the following is NOT one of the components of successful aging?**
      a.   retention of cognitive abilities
      b.   good physical health
      c.   continuing engagement in social and productive activities
      d.   financial independence

4.   **Psychologists use the term _____ to refer to the tendency to turn to religious beliefs and institutions in times of stress or trouble.**
      a.   faith-based aid
      b.   divine power
      c.   religious coping
      d.   religious involvement

5.   **A tendency to focus on the aspects of life that transcend one's physical existence is called _____.**
      a.   reminiscence
      b.   aging in place
      c.   successful aging
      d.   spirituality

6.   **The idea that children have a duty to care for their aging parents is known as _____.**
      a.   aging in place
      b.   filial piety
      c.   assisted living
      d.   an amenity move

7.   **Marital satisfaction in late adulthood _____.**
      a.   increases for elder women, but decreases for elder men
      b.   tends to drop as health becomes problematic
      c.   is higher than when children were still at home
      d.   drops initially, but then plateaus

8.   **Each of the following statements about family relationships is true EXCEPT _____.**
    a.   Most elders rarely see their adult children.
    b.   Family relationships represent an important component of most elders' overall life satisfaction.
    c.   Three-quarters of elders live within an hours' travel of at least one on their children.
    d.   Most of the time, when older adults need help that cannot be provided by a spouse, it is provided by other family members, principally children.

9.   **Contact with friends in older adulthood _____.**
    a.   can decrease life satisfaction as the elders mourn the "good old days"
    b.   can actually increase depression because these adults watch each other's health deteriorate
    c.   is less important than contact with family in influencing life satisfaction
    d.   has a positive impact on self-esteem and overall life satisfaction

10.   **Each of the following statements about gender differences in social networks is true EXCEPT _____.**
    a.   Men's social networks are just as important to them and provide them with the same kinds of emotional support as women's networks do.
    b.   Older men's networks tend to be smaller than those of older women.
    c.   Older women's networks tend to be closer than those of older men.
    d.   Women and men in late adulthood appear to form different kinds of social networks, with men's friendships involving less disclosure and less intimacy than women's

11.   **Which of the following phrases accurately portrays the transition from work to retirement?**
    a.   Most elders demonstrate a remarkable capacity for adaptation.
    b.   It is the beginning of the long downward slide into death.
    c.   Women make this transition with much less difficulty than men.
    d.   The age of the retiree impacts how positive the transition is.

12.   **What is happening to the retirement age of individuals?**
    a.   The average age has been declining in recent years throughout the industrialized world.
    b.   The age is increasing slowly in most countries.
    c.   The age is dropping slowly in the U.S., but increasing slowly in others.
    d.   The age is dropping rapidly for men, but increasing slowly for women in the U.S.

13.   **Which of the following statements about retirement is true?**
    a.   Women typically retire much earlier than men.
    b.   Extensive pre-retirement planning is typically more important to men than to women.
    c.   Health was the most important predictor of quality of life in retirement for men, but not for women.
    d.   Retirement benefits, health, or job characteristics typically predict when women will retire.

14.   **What effect does retirement have on health?**
    a.   It has a strong positive effect.
    b.   It has a slight negative effect on blood pressure and heart rate.
    c.   It has no negative effects on health.
    d.   It depends on gender and physical condition at the time of retirement.

15. **Which of the following persons is most likely to continue working past the typical retirement age?**
    a. a man who is highly educated and healthy
    b. a woman who is highly educated and healthy
    c. a man who is in poor health
    d. a woman with a limited education and poor retirement benefits

TRUE-FALSE QUESTIONS

Indicate whether each of the following statements is true or false.

_____
1. To achieve ego integrity, the elder must come to terms with who she is and has been, how her life has been lived, the choices that she made, and the opportunities gained and lost.

_____
2. The perspective typically referred to as disengagement theory, argues that the psychologically and physically healthiest response to old age is to maintain the greatest possible activity and involvement in the greatest possible number of roles.

_____
3. Volunteerism, performing unpaid work for altruistic reasons, has been linked to successful aging.

_____
4. Men make more use of religious coping than women.

_____
5. Family relationships become more harmonious as adults get older.

_____
6. In late adulthood, contact between grandchildren and grandparents declines as the grandchildren become adults themselves.

_____
7. Persons who like their work and are highly committed to it retire earlier than do those who are less gratified by their work.

_____
8. What predicts life satisfaction in late adulthood is not whether a person has retired, but whether he was satisfied with life in earlier adulthood.

ESSAY QUESTIONS

1. According to Erikson, what must a person do throughout adulthood to increase the likelihood that she or he experiences ego integrity rather than despair in late adulthood?

2. Discuss the five components of successful aging, and give examples of each.

3. Discuss the advantages that married older adults have over unmarried elders.

WHEN YOU HAVE FINISHED ... PUZZLE IT OUT

Across
2. Reflecting on past experiences
7. Performing unpaid work for altruistic reasons
8. Migration of older adults to a nursing home
9. Cognitive willingness to learn new things
10. Migration of older adults to a location near family and friends
11. Theory that it is normal and healthy for older adults to try to remain active

Down
1. Living facility for older adults who need help with one or two ADLs
3. Nursing facility for older adults who require help with three or four ADLs
4. Living community in which all residents are over a certain age
5. Theory that it is normal and healthy for older adults to scale down their social lives
6. Move in late life away from kin to a location that has some desirable feature

Created by Puzzlemaker at DiscoverySchool.com

WHEN YOU HAVE FINISHED . . . INVESTIGATIVE PROJECT

Student Project 30: Visiting and Assessing a Nursing Home

Procedure

In this visit imagine that you are looking for a suitable nursing home for your aged parent, and you are evaluating several such institutions. You should spend at least an hour in each institution, preferably at a meal time or activity time. You will also want to obtain brochures or other literature available about each institution. During your visit, take notes if you wish and chat with those you may fall into conversation with (although you should not harass the staff). At the end of your visit, rate the nursing home on each of the following 10 scales, where 5 always indicates "optimum" or "ideal" and a rating of 1 always means "unacceptable." If you find you simply do not have the information you need for any scale, you may choose NA (not available), but try not to do that.

Rating Scales	Circle One Number
1. *Achievement fostering*: To what extent does the environment provide opportunities for and encouragement to residents to engage in goal-directed activities, or reward them for doing so?	1 2 3 4 5 NA
2. *Individualism*: To what extent are individuals encouraged to express individuality, and are treated as unique?	1 2 3 4 5 NA
3. *Dependency fostering*: To what extent are residents "coddled" in ways that discourage or prevent development of self-sufficiency or autonomy? (A rating of 5 in this case means that this was not done.)	1 2 3 4 5 NA
4. *Warmth*: Did the staff express warmth toward the residents, and did the residents express it toward each other?	1 2 3 4 5 NA
5. *Affiliation fostering*: To what extent is social interaction encouraged, or is occurring naturally in the environment?	1 2 3 4 5 NA
6. *Recognition*: To what extent does the institution recognize, respond to, and reward the activities and accomplishments of the residents?	1 2 3 4 5 NA
7. *Stimulation*: How much variety of sights, sounds, and activities is there?	1 2 3 4 5 NA
8. *Physical attractiveness*: How aesthetically appealing is the physical setting?	1 2 3 4 5 NA
9. *Cue richness*: How clear and varied are the cues for orientation, such as signs, distinctive colors, odors, textures, sounds, and clutter?	1 2 3 4 5 NA
10. *Health care adequacy*: Is the institution equipped and well-staffed to provide physical exams, physical therapy, and nursing care?	1 2 3 4 5 NA

Analysis and Report

In preparing your report, think about how confident you feel that you could make a decision about each individual nursing home based on your brief visit. What additional information would you need or like to have to do a better job of evaluating this or any other nursing home? Are there other items you would add to the checklist? Do some of the items seem more important than others? Why? If you really were making such a choice for your parent, would you use a checklist like this, or do you think you would use some other process?

Consider, also, whether your own attitudes and biases about nursing home care have been altered or strengthened by this visit. Were you impressed or depressed, if either? By what?

CHAPTER 18 ANSWER KEY

Practice Test #1 Theories of Social and Personality Development
1. T   2. F   3. T   4. F   5. T   6. T

Practice Test #2 Individual Differences
1.   successful aging
2.   individuals' responses to the health crisis of old age
3.   cognitive challenges
4.   Cognitive adventurousness
5.   give support as well as receive it
6.   Volunteerism
7.   Life satisfaction
8.   religious coping

Practice Test #3 Social Relationships
1. d   2. c   3. b   4. a   5. b   6. c   7. d

Practice Test #4 Career Issues in Late Life
1. F   2. T   3. F   4. T   5. T   6. T   7. F   8. T   9. T   10. T

Comprehensive Practice Test
Multiple Choice Questions
1. c   2. b   3. d   4. c   5. d   6. b   7. c   8. a   9. d   10. a
11. a   12. a   13. b   14. c   15. a

True-False Questions
1. T   2. F   3. T   4. F   5. T   6. T   7. F   8. T

Essay Questions

1. ▪ Achieve Identity rather than Role Confusion
   ▪ Achieve Intimacy rather than Isolation
   ▪ Achieve Generativity rather than Stagnation

2. ▪ Good physical health: Factors such as diet, exercise, avoidance of tobacco, etc. predict health and physical functioning across the lifespan.
   ▪ Retaining cognitive abilities: The degree to which elders maintain cognitive abilities seems to be linked to education—those who are best educated show the least cognitive decline. Additionally, the complexity of cognitive challenges older adults are willing to take on also influences their cognitive functioning.
   ▪ Social engagement: Social connectedness and participation in productive activities are clearly important to successful aging, but social support does not mean dependence on other. Helping other contributes to one's own health and sense of well-being.
   ▪ Productivity: Contributing to a social network, such as volunteering, may be one important way of remaining productive. Some older adults remain productive by venturing into new pursuits, such as learning new hobby.
   ▪ Life satisfaction: A sense of personal well-being is an important component of successful aging. Factors include a sense of control, the individual's perception of her or his situation, and social comparisons.

3. ▪ Higher life satisfaction
   ▪ Better health
   ▪ Lower rates of institutionalization

Puzzle It Out

Across
2. Reminiscence
7. Volunteerism
8. Institutional
9. Adventurousness
10. Compensatory
11. Activity

Down
1. Assisted
3. Skilled
4. Independent
5. Disengagement
6. Amenity

POLICY QUESTION V

HOW SHOULD STEM CELL RESEARCH
BE FUNDED AND REGULATED?

Learning Objective: *Summarize the issues about how stem cell research should be funded and regulated (pp. 512-513).*

1.   What are stem cells, and why are they important to researchers and policymakers?

2.   Distinguish among the following types of stem cells:

Type	Source	Potential Use
Totipotent		
Pluripotent		
Multipotent		

3.   List the reasons why stem cell research is controversial.

4.   What are the obstacles to using stem cells to cure diseases?

5.   Summarize the policies about stem cell research of the United States and other industrialized nations?

	United States	*Other Industrialized Nations*
Emphasis		
Regulation		
Priority		

6.   Which approach do you think is best?   Finding the answers to these questions may help you decide.

   a.   How do organizations for (e.g., the American Medical Association) and against (e.g., U.S. Conference of Catholic Bishops) embryonic stem cell research explain and support their positions?

   b.   What do the Democratic Party and Republican Party platforms say about the issue? (go to http://www.democrats.org/pdfs/2004platform.pdf and http://www.gopconvention.com/platform/2004platform.pdf to find out.)

   c.   How do scientists grow stem cells in the laboratory?

   d.   What are the top five diseases that scientists currently believe are most likely to be helped through stem cell research?

   e.   Other than the treatment of diseases, what implications might there be for stem cell research?

CHAPTER 19

DEATH, DYING, AND BEREAVEMENT

BEFORE YOU READ . . . CHAPTER SUMMARY

For most people, death happens in late adulthood. However, many younger individuals contract fatal diseases or may die in accidents. Thus, like most developmental events, the timing and mode of a particular individual's death affect its meaning and its effects on others.

The Experience of Death

- Medical personnel distinguish between clinical death, brain death, and social death.
- In the industrialized world, death most often occurs in hospitals. For the terminally ill, hospice workers and facilities provide an alternative form of care.

The Meaning of Death across the Lifespan

- By age six or seven, most children understand that death is permanent. Teens sometimes have distorted ideas about death, especially their own mortality.
- Many young adults see themselves as invulnerable to death. For middle-aged adults, the death of a loved one, often a parent, signals a change in social roles.
- Among the middle-aged, fear of death is common. Older adults fear death less, especially those who are very religious.
- Preparation for death may include practical activities such as writing a will. Many dying adults also prepare by sharing life experiences with younger family members. Some dying adults exhibit dramatic changes in cognitive and personality functioning just prior to death, a phenomenon often called terminal drop.

The Process of Dying

- Kübler-Ross's five stages of dying (denial, anger, bargaining, depression, and acceptance) have been widely studied. Research suggests that not all dying individuals go through these stages.
- Critics of Kübler-Ross suggest that her stages may be culture-specific and that the process of adjusting to impending death does not occur in stages.
- Attitudes appear to affect a terminally ill individual's longevity. Those who have a "fighting spirit" survive longer than do peers who are resigned to the inevitability of death.

Theoretical Perspectives on Grieving

- Psychoanalytic theory emphasizes the traumatic nature of grief and the defense mechanisms that often accompany the experience.
- Attachment theories suggest that grieving involves a series of stages across which the bereaved adjust to life without the deceased.
- Alternative approaches emphasize the individual nature of grieving, claiming that the experience is poorly explained by general theories.

The Experience of Grieving

- Funerals and other rituals redefine the roles of the bereaved, bring families together, and give meaning to the lives of both the deceased and the bereaved.
- Grief responses depend on the age and mode of death of the deceased, as well as characteristics of the bereaved.
- Losing a spouse appears to bring about the most intense grief response. The health of widows and widowers declines in the first year following spousal loss. The effects appear to be greater among widowers than widows.

AS YOU READ . . . LEARNING OBJECTIVES

After completing Chapter 19, you should be able to answer the following questions:

19.1   What are the characteristics of clinical death, brain death, and social death?
19.2   How do hospice and hospital care differ with respect to their effects on terminally ill patients?
19.3   What are the characteristics of children's and adolescents' ideas about death?
19.4   How do young, middle-aged, and older adults think about death?
19.5   What factors are related to fear of death in adults?
19.6   How do adults prepare for death?
19.7   How did Kübler -Ross explain the process of death?
19.8   What are some other views of the process of dying?
19.9   How do people vary in the ways they adapt to impending death?
19.10 How does Freud's psychoanalytic theory view grief?
19.11 What are the theories of Bowlby and Sanders regarding grief?
19.12 What theories of grief have been proposed by critics of psychoanalytic and attachment theories?
19.13 How do funerals and ceremonies help survivors cope with grief?
19.14 What factors influence the grieving process?
19.15 How does grief affect the physical and mental health of widows and widowers?

AS YOU READ . . . TERM IDENTIFICATION

Brain death (p. 542)	Hospice care (p. 542)	Social death (p. 542)
Clinical death (p. 542)	Palliative care (p. 543)	Thanatology (p. 553)
Grieving (p. 559)	Pathological grief (p. 564)	Unique invulnerability (p. 546)

AS YOU READ . . . GUIDED STUDY QUESTIONS

THE EXPERIENCE OF DEATH

Death Itself (p. 542)

19.1 What are the characteristics of clinical death, brain death, and social death?

1. Define the following terms:
   a. clinical death (p. 542)

   b. brain death (p. 542)

   c. social death (p. 542)

Where Death Occurs (pp. 542-544)

19.2 How do hospice and hospital care differ with respect to their effects on terminally ill patients?

2. Define the following terms:
   a. hospice care (p. 542)

   b. palliative care (p. 543)

3. List and describe the five aspects of the philosophy of the hospice care movement.
   -

   -

   -

   -

   -

4.   List and describe the three general types of hospice care.

Type	Description

AFTER YOU READ . . . PRACTICE TEST #1
THE EXPERIENCE OF DEATH

Match the letter of the term in the right column with its description in the left column.

_____ 1. A form of care for the terminally ill that focuses on relieving patients' pain rather than curing their diseases.

_____ 2. A period during which vital signs are absent but resuscitation is still possible.

_____ 3. Hospice program where a small number of patients in the last stages of a terminal disease are cared for in a homelike setting.

_____ 4. The point at which family members and medical personnel treat the deceased person as a corpse.

_____ 5. Hospice program in which one family caregiver provides constant care for the dying person with the support and assistance of specially trained staff who visit regularly.

a. Brain death
b. Clinical death
c. Home-based
d. Hospital-based
e. Palliative care
f. Social death
g. Special hospice center

THE MEANING OF DEATH ACROSS THE LIFESPAN

Children's and Adolescents' Understanding of Death (pp. 545-546)

19.3   What are the characteristics of children's and adolescents' ideas about death?

5.   Compare the understanding of death for each of the following age groups:

Preschool-Aged Children	School-Aged Children

6.   How do unrealistic beliefs about personal death contribute to adolescent suicide?

The Meaning of Death for Adults (pp. 546-548)

19.4   How do young, middle-aged, and older adults think about death?

7.   Define unique invulnerability (p. 546).

8.   Give examples of how unique invulnerability influences young adults.

9.   Explain how the deaths of relatively young celebrities provide insight into young adults' ideas about death.

10.   How does death change the roles and relationships within a family?

11.   Give examples of how the prospect of death shapes one's view of time.

12.   What is the most pervasive meaning of death for adults of all ages?

13.   How does the potential loss that is feared or dreaded the most change with age?

Age Group	Greatest Fear or Dread
Young Adults	
Older Adults	

Fear of Death (pp. 548-549)

10.5   What factors are related to fear of death in adults?

14.   Give examples to explain why middle-aged adults are the most fearful of death.

15.   The elderly think and talk more about death than do other age groups. How does this help them overcome their fear and anxiety of death?

16.   How do religious beliefs affect a person's fear of death?

17.   How are feelings about death linked to one's sense of personal worth?

Preparation for Death (pp. 549-551)

19.6   How do adults prepare for death?

18.   Describe how people prepare for death at each of the following levels:

Level	Description
Practical Level	

Level	Description
Reminiscence	
Unconscious Changes	

19.   Describe the psychological changes associated with terminal drop.

No Easy Answers: Saying Goodbye (p. 550)

20.   Why is it important for dying persons to say good-bye to family and friends?

AFTER YOU READ . . . PRACTICE TEST #2
THE MEANING OF DEATH ACROSS THE LIFESPAN

Fill in the blanks with the best answers.

1. Preschool children typically believe that _____;

    that _____.

2. By the time they start school, most children seem to understand both the _____

    and the _____ of death.

3. Unrealistic beliefs about _____ appear to contribute to adolescents' suicide.

4. Young adults have a sense of _____, a belief that bad things, including death,
    happen to others but not to themselves.

5. In middle and late adulthood, a death changes the _____ and _____

    of everyone else in a family.

6. At an individual level in middle and late adulthood, most people exhibit a shift in thinking about

    time, thinking less about "_____" and being more aware of

    "_____."

7. Although you might think that those closest to death would fear it the most, research suggests that

    _____ are most fearful of death.

8. Religious beliefs may moderate fears of death because religious people tend to view death as

    _____.

9. Adults who have successfully completed the _____,

    who have adequately fulfilled the _____, and who

    have _____ are able to face death with greater equanimity.

10. According to most people, in addition to purchasing life insurance and making a will, such

    preparations should include directives regarding end-of-life care, often called a _____.

THE PROCESS OF DYING

Kübler-Ross's Stages of Dying (p. 551-552)

19.7   How did Kübler-Ross explain the process of death?

21.   List the five stages of grief proposed by Kübler-Ross, and give examples of each. Complete the following table:

Stage	Example

Criticisms and Alternative Views (pp. 552-554)

19.8   What are some other views of the process of dying?

22.   Summarize the methodological problems of Kübler-Ross's research.

23.   Give examples of how Kübler-Ross's research may not incorporate culture-specific behaviors.

24.   Describe cultural differences about death.

Culture	Description
Western Societies	
Collectivist Cultures	
Native American Culture	
Mexican Culture	

25.   Of the five stages of Kübler-Ross's model, which one seems to be common among Western patients?

26.   Define thanatology (p. 553).

27.   List the themes involved in the dying process that were suggested by Edwin Shneidman.
■

■

■

■

■

■

■

28.   List the four tasks for the dying person suggested by Charles Corr.
■

■

■

■

Responses to Impending Death (pp. 554-556)

19.9   How do people vary in the ways they adapt to impending death?

29.   List and describe the five types of responses to impending death, according to Steven Greer.

Type	Description

30.   What were the findings of Greer's research about the relationship between the patient's survival rate and the five groups of responses to impending death?

31.   List two cautions that relate to Greer's findings.
   ■

   ■

32.   How does social support relate to an individual's response to imminent death?

AFTER YOU READ . . . PRACTICE TEST #3
THE PROCESS OF DYING

Indicate whether each of the following statements is true or false.

_____
1.
Kübler-Ross's model predicts that most people who are confronted with a terminal diagnosis react with some form of denial.

_____
2.
The anger a dying person expresses seems to be a response not only to the diagnosis itself but also to the sense of loss of control and helplessness that many patients feel in impersonal medial settings.

_____
3.
Cross-cultural studies suggest that cultures vary very little in what they believe to be a "good death."

_____
4.
Of the five stages of Kübler-Ross's model, only anger seems to be common among Western patients.

_____
5.
According to Charles Corr, coping with dying is like coping with any other problem or dilemma: You need to take care of certain specific tasks.

_____
6.
According to Steven Greer's research results, psychological responses contribute to disease progress.

_____
7.
Terminally ill patients with positive and supportive relationships describe lower levels of pain and less depression during their final months of illness.

THEORETICAL PERSPECTIVES ON GRIEVING

Freud's Psychoanalytic Theory (p. 556)

19.10 How does Freud's psychoanalytic theory view grief?

33. Explain why Freud believed that defense mechanisms were only temporary devices for dealing with negative emotions.

34. Give examples of how each of the following defense mechanisms could be used in grief therapy.

Defense Mechanism	Example
Sublimation	
Identification	

Bowlby's Attachment Theory (pp. 556-558)

19.11 What are the theories of Bowlby and Sanders regarding grief?

35.   According to John Bowlby, how is attachment to the loved one related to the experience of grief?

36.   List and describe Bowlby's and Sanders's stages of grief by completing the following table:

Stage	Bowlby's Label	Sanders's Label	Description
1			
2			
3			
4			

Alternative Perspective (pp. 558-559)

19.12 What theories of grief have been proposed by critics of psychoanalytic and attachment theories?

37.   List two reasons that revisionist views of grieving give a rather different picture from that of either Freud or of the attachment theorists.

■

■

38.   Describe a compromise model that predicts the likely trajectory of the key themes in the grieving process.

39.   List two ways in which Camille Wortman and Roxane Silver dispute the traditional view of grieving expressed in Freud's and Bowlby's theories.

■

■

40.   Describe the following patterns of grieving by completing the following table:

Pattern	Description
Normal	
Chronic	
Delayed	
Absent	

41.   Summarize the results of Wortman's and Silver's research.

42.   What is the dual-process model?

43.   Explain how the loss of a loved one can also lead to growth.

AFTER YOU READ . . . PRACTICE TEST #4
THEORETICAL PERSPECTIVES ON GRIEVING

Indicate whether each of the following statements is true or false.

_____ From the psychoanalytic perspective, the death of a loved one is an emotional trauma.
1.

_____ Psychoanalytically based grief therapy for children often emphasizes the use of
2. regression and displacement to cope with grief.

_____ According to Bowlby, the stronger the attachment between a mourner and a lost loved
3. one, the deeper and more prolonged the grief response.

_____ According to Catherine Sanders, the first stage of grief is characterized by depression
4. and despair

_____ A compromise model suggests that each of the key themes in the grieving process
5. may have a likely trajectory.

_____ According to Wortman and Silver, high levels of distress are neither an inevitable nor
6. a necessary aspect of the grieving process.

_____ The dual-process model proposes that bereaved individuals alternate confrontation
7. and restoration.

THE EXPERIENCE OF GRIEVING

Psychosocial Functions of Death Rituals (p. 560)

19.13 How do funerals influence the grieving process?

44.   Define grieving (p. 559).

45.   Give examples of how each of the following psychological functions that funerals, wakes, and other death rituals serve in helping family members cope with grief:

Function	Example
Specific set of roles to play	
Bring family members together	
Understand the meaning of death itself	
Transcendent meaning to death itself	

The Process of Grieving (pp. 560-562)

19.14 What factors influence the grieving process?

46.   How does each of the following age groups express their feelings of grief?

Age Group	Expression of Grief
Children	
Adolescents	

47.   Give examples of how the mode of death impacts the grief process.

Mode of Death	Example of Impact
Death of a spouse after a period of illness	
Death that has an intrinsic meaning	
Sudden and violent death	

Death in a natural disaster	
Death in a "politically motivated" mass murder	
Death by suicide	

Widowhood (pp. 562-566)

19.15 How does grief affect the physical and mental health of widows and widowers?

48.   Distinguish among the following terms:

Widowhood	*Widow*	*Widower*

49.   Describe the long-term and short-term effects on the immune system of the experience of widowhood.

50.   What is the relationship between widowhood and the incidence of depression?.

51.   Define pathological grief (p. 564).

52.   Explain why some psychologists believe pathological grief should be thought of as a separate disorder from depression.

53.   Give examples to explain why the death of a spouse appears to be a more negative experience for men than for women.

54.   How can support groups help a person manage their grief?

55.   What are some suggestions for preventing long-term problems following the death of a spouse?

Research Report: Ethnicity and the Widowhood Effect (p. 563)

56.   What is the widowhood effect?

57.   Describe Brian Eckersley's findings about the widowhood effect in the following ethnic groups in the U.S:

Ethnic Group	Description
White Widows and Widowers	
African American Widows and Widowers	
African American Widows of White Men & White Widowers of African American Women	
White Widows of African American Men & African American Widowers of White Women	
Hispanic Widows and Widowers	

The Real World: When an Infant Dies (p. 564)

58.   How might the grief of parents be different when an older child dies than when an infant dies?

59.   List the guidelines that can be useful to family members or friends in supporting parents who have lost an infant.

AFTER YOU READ . . . PRACTICE TEST #5
THE EXPERIENCE OF GRIEVING

Indicate whether each of the following statements is true or false.

_____ 1. In virtually every culture, the immediate response to a death is some kind of funeral ritual.

_____ 2. Funerals, wakes, and other death rituals help family members and friends manage their grief by giving them a specific set of roles to play.

_____ 3. Death rituals typically weaken family ties.

_____ 4. Teenagers may be more likely than adults to experience grief responses to the deaths of celebrities or to idealize peers' suicides.

_____ 5. In general, family and close friends of someone who commits suicide experience feelings of rejection and anger.

_____ 6. The experience of widowhood appears to have both immediate and longer-term effects on the immune system.

_____ 7. Older adults who enter widowhood with a history of depression are less likely to experience depression after the death of their spouse.

_____ 8. Many aspects of grief are culturally determined.

_____ 9. Depression and suicidal thought are more common among widows than in widowers.

_____ 10. In the long run, illness and depression among bereaved workers who return to their jobs too soon may be more costly to employers than providing additional time off.

AFTER YOU READ . . . CRITICAL REFLECTION EXERCISES

Death of a Loved One

Utilizing information from the text, provide complete answers to the following questions:

1. What do you think would be the best way to describe a grandparent's death to a four- year-old? Why would you describe it this way?

2. How does our society appear to approach the reality of death? Do you agree with this approach? Why or why not?

3. Why is mourning an important part of the grieving process? Briefly discuss at least three reasons that it is important.

Imminent Death

Imagine that you have just discovered that you have four months to live. Consider how you would address each of the following issues knowing that the four months will be pain free and you will not be debilitated.

1. Describe what you think your initial reactions might be. Why do you think you would react this way?

2. What are the five things you would do with your remaining time? Why did you pick each of these?

3. Using Erikson's theory of human development as a model, write a eulogy of your life. What would you most like people to remember about you and the life that you have lived?

AFTER YOU READ . . . COMPREHENSIVE PRACTICE TEST
MULTIPLE-CHOICE QUESTIONS

1. **Which of the following accurately describes clinical death?**
   a. The person can still breathe, but she is in a vegetative state.
   b. There is no evident brain functioning.
   c. The heart can still beat.
   d. There is no activity in the brain.

2. **In comparing hospital care to hospice care, _____.**
   a. no major differences in length of survival, or reports of pain were found
   b. it was discovered that hospital care was rated as significantly more satisfying by the dying patients
   c. hospital care was associated with increased length of survival of chronic patients
   d. significant differences in perceptions of quality of care were found

3. *When will a child most likely first be able to understand the permanence of death?*
   a. age 2
   b. age 4
   c. age 6
   d. age 10

4. **The belief that bad things, including death, only happen to others is called _____.**
   a. unique invulnerability
   b. a flashback
   c. denial
   d. sublimation

5. **Older adults _____**
   a. look forward to death
   b. fear death significantly
   c. fear the process of dying more than death itself
   d. do not contemplate death

6. **Which of the following is one of the ways a person prepares for death at a practical level?**
   a. inventing a personal fable
   b. becoming a nicer person
   c. reminiscences
   d. making out a will

7. **Which stage, according to Kübler-Ross, is a form of defense in which the patient tries to make "deals" with doctors, nurses, family, or God?**
   a. denial
   b. bargaining
   c. depression
   d. acceptance

8.   **What is the study of dying called?**
        a.   bereavement
        b.   euthanasia
        c.   thanatology
        d.   life transition analysis

9.   **Which of the following individuals fit Greer's label of stoic acceptance in response to a diagnosis of terminal cancer?**
        a.   A person who is devoid of hope.
        b.   A person who denies the diagnosis.
        c.   A person who responds with anxiety.
        d.   A person who ignores the diagnosis.

10.   **A defense mechanism in which children are encouraged to express their feelings through art is called _____.**
        a.   identification
        b.   sublimation
        c.   denial
        d.   creativity

11.   **Which of the following is the correct order of Bowlby's stages of grief?**
        a.   numbness, yearning, disorganization and despair, reorganization
        b.   yearning, awareness, healing/renewal, numbness
        c.   shock, awareness disorganization and despair, yearning
        d.   healing/renewal, reorganization, conservation/withdrawal, shock

12.   **Revisionist theories of grieving suggest that _____.**
        a.   grieving occurs in a series of distinct stages
        b.   grieving and mourning are actually the same thing
        c.   grieving displays significant gender-differences
        d.   there may be common themes in grieving, but there are no set patterns

13.   **Which of the following is NOT a psychological function of death rituals?**
        a.   bringing family members together
        b.   helping the survivors understand the meaning of death itself
        c.   showing others how much the survivors loved the person who died
        d.   giving some transcendent meaning to death

14.   **Which of the following mode of death would be most likely to cause intense grief responses?**
        a.   a soldier who died heroically in the line of duty
        b.   a spouse whose death brought an end to his long-term suffering
        c.   an elderly person who died of natural causes
        d.   a person who died a sudden and violent death

15.   **Symptoms of depression brought on by death of a loved one are called _____.**
        a.   philosophical grief
        b.   psychosomatic grief
        c.   psychological grief
        d.   pathological grief

TRUE-FALSE QUESTIONS

Indicate whether each of the following statements is true or false.

_____ 1. Brain death occurs when the deceased person is treated like a corpse by others.

_____ 2. The most pervasive meaning of death for adults of all ages is loss.

_____ 3. Feelings about death are linked to one's sense of personal worth or competence.

_____ 4. According to Kubler-Ross, in order to reach the anger stage of grief, the dying person must grieve for all that will be lost with death.

_____ 5. According to Greer's research, persons with a fighting spirit act overwhelmed by the diagnosis and see themselves as dying or gravely ill and as devoid of hope.

_____ 6. Grieving is the emotional response to a death, and it may take months or years to complete.

_____ 7. Although the behavioral aspects of adolescents' grief responses vary little from those of adults, teens may be more likely to experience prolonged grief than children or adults.

_____ 8. According to Wortman and Silver, the normal pattern of grief is one in which the person feels no notable level of distress either immediately or at any later time.

ESSAY QUESTIONS

1. Discuss the pros and cons of hospice care for someone with a terminal illness.

2. According to Piaget, children in the preoperational stage are egocentric, which may limit their ability to reason. Give examples of how egocentrism may be related to children's lack of understanding of death.

3. Give examples of how unique invulnerability may influence teenagers' understanding of death.

WHEN YOU HAVE FINISHED . . . PUZZLE IT OUT

Across

2. Stage two in Kubler Ross's model
6. Care for the dying that emphasizes individual and family control of the process
10. Defense mechanism used to help children express their feelings through art
12. The scientific study of death and dying
14. Stage three in Kubler Ross's model

Down

1. Aspect of death when resuscitation is no longer possible
2. Stage five in Kubler Ross's model
3. Aspect of death that refers to the period during which vital signs are absent, but resuscitation is still possible
4. Stage four in Kubler Ross's model
5. Aspect of death when the person is treated like a corpse by others
7. Care that emphasizes controlling pain and maximizing comfort
8. Defense mechanism used to help children manage grief by watching popular films depicting grief
9. Stage one in Kubler Ross's model
11. Grief with symptoms of depression brought on by death of a loved one
13. The emotional response to a death

Created by Puzzlemaker at DiscoverySchool.com

CHAPTER 19 ANSWER KEY

Practice Test #1 The Experience of Death
1. e   2. b   3. g   4. f   5. c

Practice Test #2 The meaning of Death Across the Lifespan
1. death can be reversed; dead people can still feel or breathe; can avoid death
2. permanence; universality
3. personal death
4. unique invulnerability
5. roles; relationships
6. time since birth; time till death
7. middle-aged adults
8. a transition from one form of life to another, from physical life to some kind of immortality
9. major tasks of adult life; demands of the roles they occupied; developed inwardly
10. living will

Practice Test #3 The Process of Dying
1. T   2. T   3. F   4. F   5. T   6. T   7. T

Practice Test #4 Theoretical Perspectives on Grieving
1. T   2. F   3. T   4. F   5. T   6. T   7. T

Practice Test #5 The Experience of Grieving
1. T   2. T   3. F   4. T   5. T   6. T   7. F   8. T   9. F   10. T

Comprehensive Practice Test
Multiple Choice Questions
1. b   2. a   3. c   4. a   5. c   6. d   7. b   8. c   9. d   10. b
11. a   12. d   13. c   14. d   15. d

True-False Questions
1. F   2. T   3. T   4. F   5. F   6. T   7. T   8. F

Essay Questions
1. ▪ Pro: Provides preparation for death; includes the family in the patient's care; control over care is in the hands of the patient and the family; medical care is palliative rather than curative; economic costs are reduced; includes grief support for caregivers.
   ▪ Con: No effort to prolong life; possible sense of burden on caregivers; some care may be too complex to be handled; hospital staff may be better able to provide pain relief.

2. ▪ Answers will vary, but should include an understanding of egocentrism and that children believe death can be reversed, that dead people can still feel or breathe, and that some people can avoid death.

3. ▪ Answers will vary, but should include an understanding of unique invulnerability (a belief that bad things, including death, happen to others but not to themselves).

Puzzle It Out

Across

2. Anger
6. Hospice
10. Sublimation
12. Thanatology
14. Bargaining

Down

1. Brain
2. Acceptance
3. Clinical
4. Depression
5. Social
7. Palliative
8. Identification
9. Denial
11. Pathological
13. Grieving

POLICY QUESTION VI

DO PEOPLE HAVE A RIGHT TO DIE?

Learning Objective: Discuss the pros and cons of the issues involved in euthanasia (pp. 542-543).

1. Define the following terms:
    a. euthanasia, or mercy killing

    b. passive euthanasia

    c. active euthanasia, or assisted suicide

    d. living will

2. Why are living wills not always followed? What legislation has been passed to ensure compliance with living wills?

3. Describe the assisted suicide law in the Netherlands.

4. List three arguments against assisted suicide, and give examples of each.

5. List reasons that most oncologist oppose assisted suicide.

6. Why is there a waiting period between a request for assisted suicide and the fulfillment of the request?

7. What arguments do proponents of assisted suicide legislation present?

8.   What are the relevant policies addressing living wills and assisted suicide in your state? Student research could include answering the following questions:

    a.   Find out from a local medical society whether hospitals and physicians in your area generally honor living wills. Does your state require medical personnel to ask all hospitalized people whether they have a living will?

    b.   The medical society should also be able to tell you whether your state allows family members to authorize health professionals to terminate aspects of care such as tube feeding in cases where a terminally ill or seriously injured individual can't speak for himself.

    c.   Has anyone in your state ever been prosecuted for helping a dying person hasten death? If so, what were the circumstances and outcome of the case(s)?

    d.   Are there efforts underway in your state to legalize assisted suicide? If so, what do opinion polls suggest about voter support for such laws?

NOTES

NOTES

NOTES

NOTES

NOTES

NOTES

NOTES

NOTES

NOTES

NOTES

NOTES